Over 425 Small HOME PLANS

Contents

Small Home Plans is published by HDA, Inc. (Home Design Alternatives), 944 Anglum Road, St. Louis, MO 63042. All rights reserved. Reproduction in whole or part without written permission of the publisher is prohibited. Printed in the U.S.A. © 2007.

COVER HOME - The house shown on the front cover is Plan #596-032D-0234 and is featured on page 272. Photo courtesy of Drummond Designs; Quebec, Canada.

MAXIMIZE
space in your smaller home

Space is a key factor when searching for your new home. And while this home plan book showcases smaller homes, you will be amazed at the amount of space that can be created to make these homes spacious retreats for you and your family. Most every home, no matter what its size, has storage space that goes unnoticed. By using creative, simple solutions for organization, space will no longer be a source of stress.

When searching for furniture to outfit your new, smaller home, look for furniture that serves more than one purpose. When space may be tight, function serves a better purpose than style, however, there are an abundance of selections where both are achieved seamlessly. Look for coffee tables with built-in drawers to unclutter magazines and papers, benches and ottomans with hinged tops for blankets and pillows, and entertainment centers with storage for all your movies and music. Sleeper sofas are also perfect for smaller homes that may not have a room designated for guests.

Many of our plans come equipped with built-in shelving, which is ideal for space concerns. These lovely spaces are a great way to showcase books, collectibles and media equipment without the need for another piece of bulky furniture.

To maximize space in your closets, plan storage that reaches all the way to the ceiling. Store seasonal items or luggage at the very top. There are many closet organizers available that are inexpensive and easy to install. You can also save closet space by adding hooks to the door for belts and ties.

Under-the-bed storage boxes are amazing space-savers for the bedroom. These boxes can organize pretty much anything and slide under the bed so they are completely out of sight.

In the kitchen, cabinet space is easy to manipulate to increase your storage possibilities. Instead of using a corner cabinet that wastes space, install a lazy Susan carousel. Also, pullout shelves or baskets are a great way to use up the space in a deep cabinet. Consider hanging pot racks for a stylish way to store big pots and pans.

And even in a small bathroom, space can be created. A decorative cabinet that fits over your toilet is ideal for storing towels, washcloths, or anything you need within reach.

No matter what the size of your new home, there will always be a way to maximize the space you have. Unique storage ideas and organizing tips are a hot topic for families today. Organizing your home from the very start is an easy way to live stress-free in your dream home.

small home plans

Small homes pack big style, as seen in our beautiful cover home. We invite you to step inside our stunning collection of best-selling small home plans to find your dream home. These plans, from the nation's leading designers and architects, showcase amazing craftsmanship that proves smaller homes do not have to skimp on beauty and function. Whether you are just starting out, have growing children, are an empty-nester or are looking for a perfect vacation getaway, you will find just what you need within the following pages. This collection is filled with plans that offer uncomplicated, stylish living. Turn the page, start the journey and discover the home of your dreams.

Special features

1,400 total square feet of living area

- Master bedroom is secluded for privacy
- Large utility room has additional cabinet space
- Covered porch provides an outdoor seating area
- Roof dormers add great curb appeal
- Living room and master bedroom feature vaulted ceilings
- Oversized two-car garage has storage space
- 3 bedrooms, 2 baths, 2-car garage
- Basement foundation, drawings also include crawl space foundation

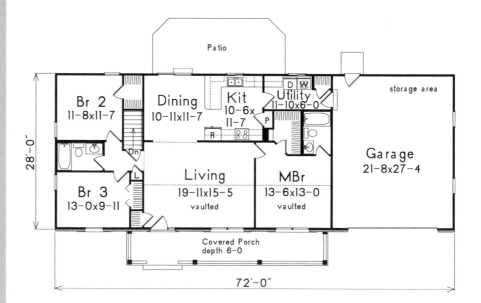

Patio

Br 2
11-8x11-7

Dining
10-11x11-7

Kit
10-6x
11-7

Utility
11-10x6-0

storage area

28'-0"

Dn

Br 3
13-0x9-11

Living
19-11x15-5
vaulted

MBr
13-6x13-0
vaulted

Garage
21-8x27-4

Covered Porch
depth 6-0

72'-0"

Paint-By-Number Wall Murals

Solar System
#75902

Photo colors may vary from kit colors

Create a unique room with *⌀WALL ART*.

You will be the envy of friends when you decorate with a Paint-By-Number Wall Mural.

Choose from over 100 custom designs for all ages and transform your room into a paradise.

You don't have to be an artist to paint a Wall Art mural. The whole family can participate in this fun and easy weekend project.

Your Wall Art kit includes everything but the wall!

Wall Art murals are available in a variety of sizes starting at the low price of $49.97.

ORDER TODAY!

It's As Easy As 1 - 2 - 3!

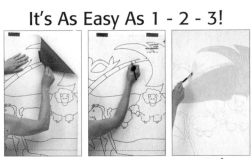

1. Tape   2. Trace   3. Paint

To order or request a catalog, call toll free

1-877-WALLMURAL (925-5687)

24 hours a day, 7 days a week, or buy online at

www.wallartdesigns.com

Deep Blue Sea
#75002

Route 66
#76305

Bug Collection
#75001

Special features

1,992 total square feet of living area

- Interesting angled walls add drama to many of the living areas including the family room, master bedroom and breakfast area
- Covered porch includes a spa and an outdoor kitchen with sink, refrigerator and cooktop
- Enter the majestic master bath to find a dramatic corner oversized tub
- 4 bedrooms, 3 baths, 2-car side entry garage
- Basement, crawl space or slab foundation, please specify when ordering

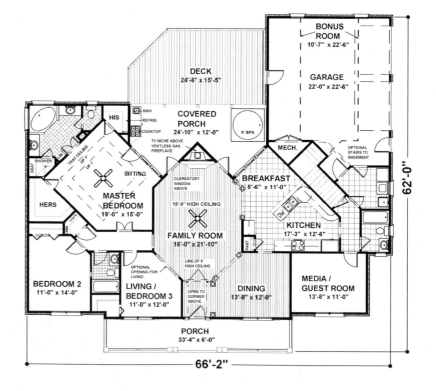

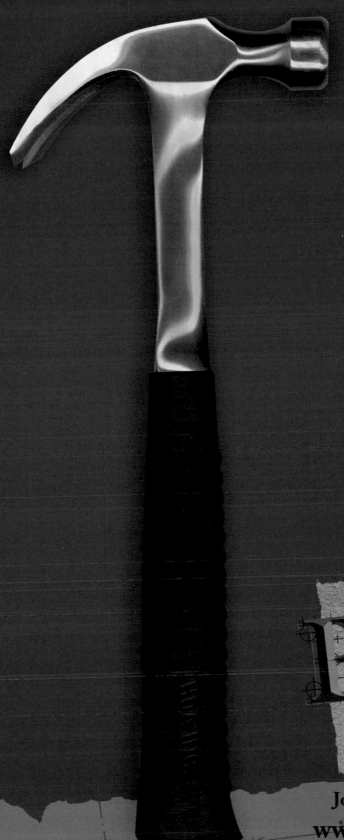

Special features

1,360 total square feet of living area

- Kitchen/dining room features an island workspace and plenty of dining area
- Master bedroom has a large walk-in closet and private bath
- Laundry room is adjacent to the kitchen for easy access
- Convenient workshop in garage
- Large closets in secondary bedrooms maintain organization
- 3 bedrooms, 2 baths, 2-car side entry garage
- Basement foundation, drawings also include crawl space and slab foundations

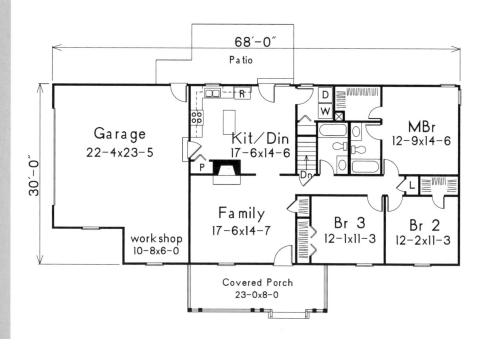

Special features

2,029 total square feet of living area

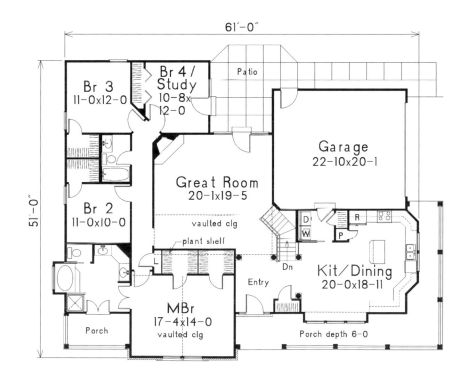

- Stonework, gables, roof dormer and double porches create a country flavor
- Kitchen enjoys extravagant cabinetry and counterspace in a bay, island snack bar, built-in pantry and cheery dining area with multiple tall windows
- Angled stair descends from large entry with wood columns and is open to a vaulted great room with corner fireplace
- Master bedroom boasts two walk-in closets, a private bath with double-door entry and a secluded porch
- 4 bedrooms, 2 baths, 2-car side entry garage
- Basement foundation, drawings also include crawl space and slab foundations

Special features

1,475 total square feet of living area

- Family room features a high ceiling and prominent corner fireplace
- Kitchen with island counter and garden window makes a convenient connection between the family and dining rooms
- Hallway leads to three bedrooms all with large walk-in closets
- Covered breezeway joins the main house and garage
- Full-width covered porch entry lends a country touch
- 3 bedrooms, 2 baths, 2-car detached side entry garage
- Slab foundation, drawings also include crawl space foundation

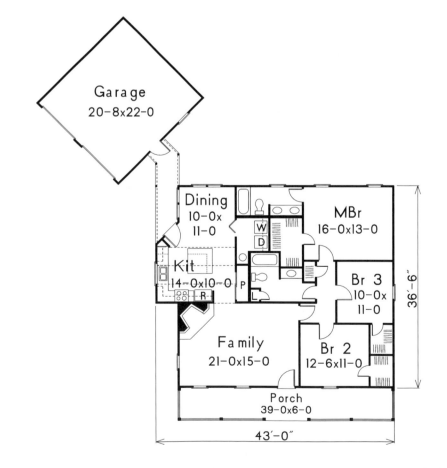

Garage
20-8x22-0

Dining
10-0x11-0

MBr
16-0x13-0

W
D

Kit
14-0x10-0

Br 3
10-0x11-0

36'-6"

Family
21-0x15-0

Br 2
12-6x11-0

Porch
39-0x6-0

43'-0"

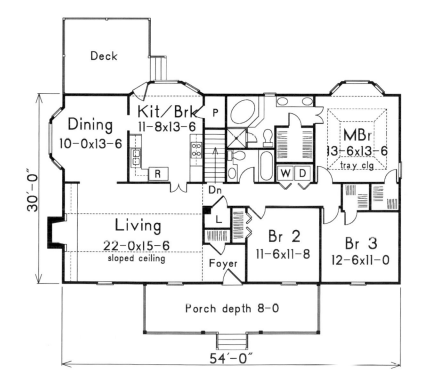

Special features

1,668 total square feet of living area

- Large bay windows grace the breakfast area, master bedroom and dining room
- Extensive walk-in closets and storage spaces are located throughout the home
- Handy covered entry porch
- Large living room has a fireplace, built-in bookshelves and a sloped ceiling
- 3 bedrooms, 2 baths, 2-car drive under garage
- Basement foundation

Special features

1,761 total square feet of living area

- Exterior window dressing, roof dormers and planter boxes provide visual warmth and charm
- Great room boasts a vaulted ceiling, fireplace and opens to a pass-through kitchen
- The vaulted master bedroom includes a luxury bath and walk-in closet
- Home features eight separate closets with an abundance of storage
- 4 bedrooms, 2 baths, 2-car side entry garage
- Basement foundation

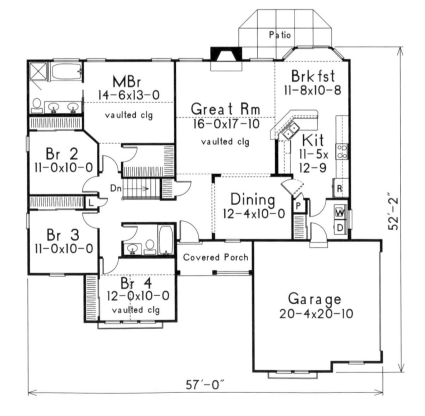

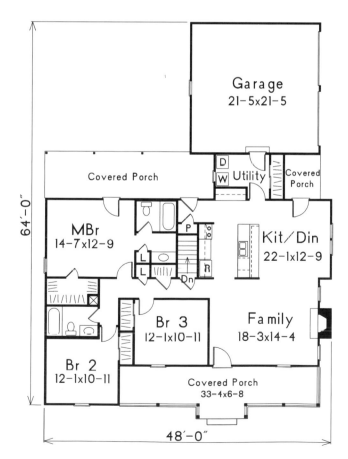

Special features

1,501 total square feet of living area

- Spacious kitchen with dining area is open to the outdoors
- Convenient utility room is adjacent to the garage
- Master bedroom features a private bath, dressing area and access to the large covered porch
- Large family room creates openness
- 3 bedrooms, 2 baths, 2-car side entry garage
- Basement foundation, drawings also include crawl space and slab foundations

Special features

1,546 total square feet of living area

- Spacious, open rooms create a casual atmosphere
- Master bedroom is secluded for privacy
- Dining room features a large bay window
- Kitchen and dinette combine for added space and include access to the outdoors
- Large laundry room includes a convenient sink
- 3 bedrooms, 2 baths, 2-car garage
- Basement foundation

Special features

1,721 total square feet of living area

- Roof dormers add great curb appeal
- Vaulted dining and great rooms are immersed in light from the atrium window wall
- Breakfast room opens onto the covered porch
- Functionally designed kitchen
- 3 bedrooms, 2 baths, 3-car garage
- Walk-out basement foundation, drawings also include crawl space and slab foundations
- 1,604 square feet on the first floor and 117 square feet on the lower level atrium

Special features

2,107 total square feet of living area

- Master bedroom is separate from other bedrooms for privacy
- Spacious breakfast room and kitchen include center island with eating space
- Centralized great room has fireplace and easy access to any area in the home
- 4 bedrooms, 2 1/2 baths, 2-car garage
- Crawl space, basement, walk-out basement or slab foundation, please specify when ordering

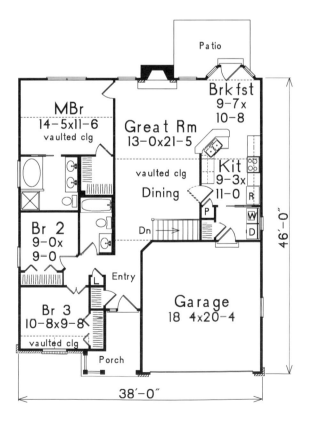

Special features

1,268 total square feet of living area

- Multiple gables, large porch and arched windows create a classy exterior
- Innovative design provides openness in the great room, kitchen and breakfast room
- Secondary bedrooms have private hall with bath
- 3 bedrooms, 2 baths, 2-car garage
- Basement foundation, drawings also include crawl space and slab foundations

Special features

1,339 total square feet of living area

- Full-length covered porch enhances front facade
- Vaulted ceiling and stone fireplace add drama to the family room
- Walk-in closets in the bedrooms provide ample storage space
- Combined kitchen/dining area adjoins the family room for the perfect entertaining space
- 2" x 6" exterior walls available, please order plan #596-058D-0072
- 3 bedrooms, 2 1/2 baths
- Crawl space foundation

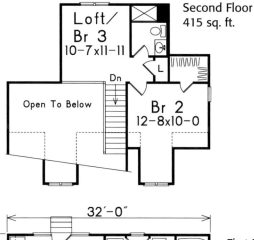

Second Floor
415 sq. ft.

Loft/
Br 3
10-7x11-11

Open To Below

Dn

Br 2
12-8x10-0

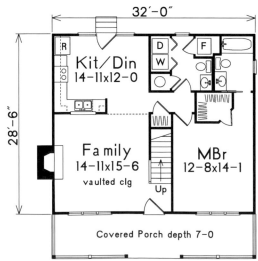

First Floor
924 sq. ft.

32'-0"

28'-6"

Kit/Din
14-11x12-0

Family
14-11x15-6
vaulted clg

Up

MBr
12-8x14-1

Covered Porch depth 7-0

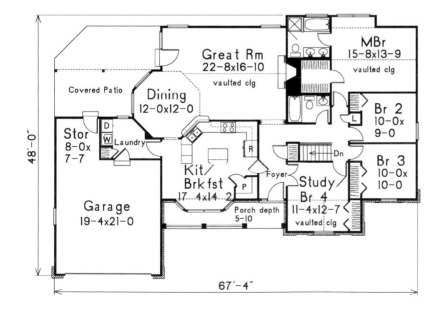

Special features

1,791 total square feet of living area

- Vaulted great room and octagon-shaped dining area enjoy a spectacular view of the covered patio
- Kitchen features a pass-through to the dining area, center island, large walk-in pantry and breakfast room with large bay window
- The master bedroom enjoys a vaulted ceiling and a sitting area
- The garage includes extra storage space
- 4 bedrooms, 2 baths, 2-car garage with storage
- Basement foundation, drawings also include crawl space and slab foundations

Special features

1,657 total square feet of living area

- Stylish pass-through between living and dining areas
- Master bedroom is secluded from the living area for privacy
- Large windows in the breakfast and dining areas create a bright and cheerful atmosphere
- 3 bedrooms, 2 1/2 baths, 2-car drive under garage
- Basement foundation

QUICK FACT - The clothes line was a backyard necessity before the advent of the clothes dryer, and even today people continue to prefer the fresh smell that only sun drying provides. To turn the poles into a landscape asset, plant climbing annuals at the base.

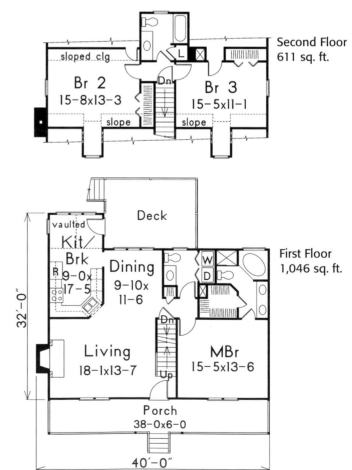

Second Floor
611 sq. ft.

Br 2
15-8x13-3

Br 3
15-5x11-1

First Floor
1,046 sq. ft.

Special features

1,749 total square feet of living area

- A tray ceiling tops the master suite
- A breakfast bar overlooks the vaulted great room
- Additional bedrooms are located away from the master suite for privacy
- Optional bonus room above the garage has an additional 308 square feet of living area
- 3 bedrooms, 2 baths, 2-car garage
- Slab, crawl space or walk-out basement foundation, please specify when ordering

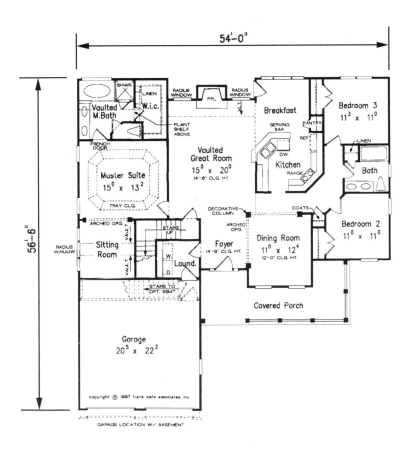

Special features

1,384 total square feet of living area

- Wrap-around country porch for peaceful evenings
- Vaulted great room enjoys a large bay window, stone fireplace, pass-through kitchen and awesome rear views through an atrium window wall
- Master bedroom features a double-door entry, walk-in closet and a fabulous bath
- Atrium opens to 611 square feet of optional living area below
- 2 bedrooms, 2 baths, 1-car side entry garage
- Walk-out basement foundation

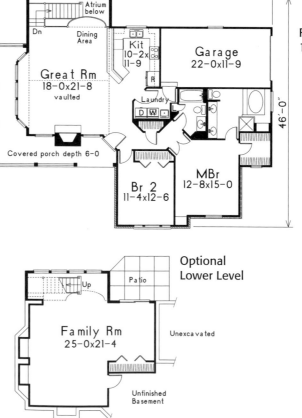

First Floor
1,384 sq. ft.

55'-8"

46'-0"

Atrium below

Dn

Dining Area

Kit
10-2x11-9

Garage
22-0x11-9

Great Rm
18-0x21-8
vaulted

Laundry

D W

R

Covered porch depth 6-0

Br 2
11-4x12-6

MBr
12-8x15-0

Optional Lower Level

Up

Patio

Family Rm
25-0x21-4

Unexcavated

Unfinished Basement

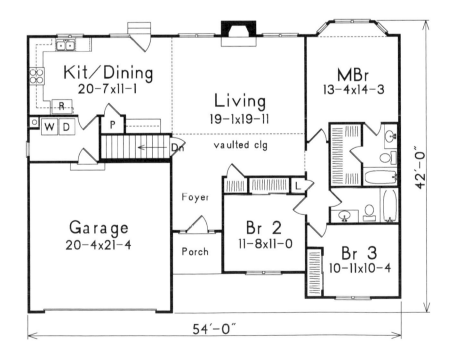

Special features

1,558 total square feet of living area

- The spacious utility room is located conveniently between the garage and kitchen/dining area
- Bedrooms are separated from the living area by a hallway
- Enormous living area with fireplace and vaulted ceiling opens to the kitchen and dining area
- Master bedroom is enhanced with a large bay window, walk-in closet and private bath
- 2" x 6" exterior walls available, please order plan #596-058D-0078
- 3 bedrooms, 2 baths, 2-car garage
- Basement foundation

Special features

1,567 total square feet of living area

- Energy efficient home with 2" x 6" exterior walls
- Living room flows into the dining room shaped by an angled pass-through into the kitchen
- Cheerful, windowed dining area
- Master bedroom is separated from other bedrooms for privacy
- Future area available on the second floor has an additional 338 square feet of living area
- 3 bedrooms, 2 baths, 2-car side entry garage
- Partial basement/crawl space foundation, drawings also include slab foundation

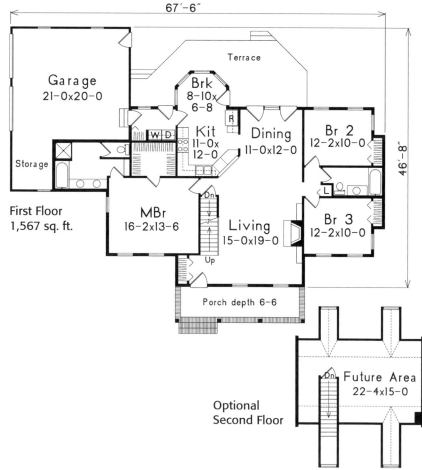

First Floor
1,567 sq. ft.

Garage
21-0x20-0

Storage

Terrace

Brk
8-10x
6-8

Kit
11-0x
12-0

W D

Dining
11-0x12-0

Br 2
12-2x10-0

MBr
16-2x13-6

Living
15-0x19-0

Br 3
12-2x10-0

Dn

Up

Porch depth 6-6

67'-6"

46'-8"

Optional
Second Floor

Future Area
22-4x15-0

Dn

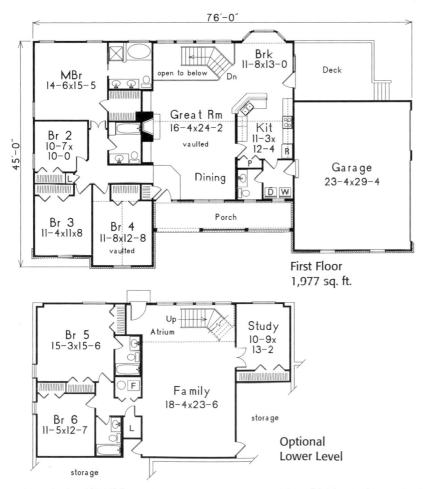

First Floor
1,977 sq. ft.

Optional
Lower Level

Special features

1,977 total square feet of living area

- Classic traditional exterior is always in style
- Spacious great room boasts a vaulted ceiling, dining area, atrium with elegant staircase and feature windows
- Atrium opens to 1,416 square feet of optional living area below which consists of a family room, two bedrooms, two baths and a study
- 4 bedrooms, 2 1/2 baths, 3-car side entry garage
- Walk-out basement foundation

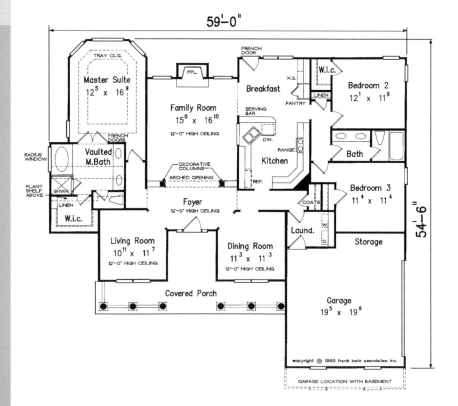

Special features

1,856 total square feet of living area

- Beautiful covered porch creates a Southern accent
- Kitchen has an organized feel with lots of cabinetry
- Large foyer has a grand entrance and leads into the family room through columns and an arched opening
- 3 bedrooms, 2 baths, 2-car side entry garage
- Walk-out basement, crawl space or slab foundation, please specify when ordering

59'-0"

54'-6"

TRAY CLG.

Master Suite
12⁵ x 16⁹

FRENCH DOOR

FPL.

W.i.c.

Breakfast

K.S.

LINEN

PANTRY

Bedroom 2
12¹ x 11⁸

Family Room
15⁰ x 16¹⁰
12'-0" HIGH CEILING

SERVING BAR

DW.

RADIUS WINDOW

Vaulted M.Bath

FRENCH DOORS

Kitchen

RANGE

Bath

PLANT SHELF ABOVE

SHWR.

LINEN

DECORATIVE COLUMNS
ARCHED OPENING

REF.

Bedroom 3
11⁴ x 11⁴

W.i.c.

Foyer
12'-0" HIGH CEILING

COATS

Living Room
10¹¹ x 11⁷
12'-0" HIGH CEILING

Dining Room
11³ x 11³
12'-0" HIGH CEILING

Laund.

W. D.

Storage

Covered Porch

Garage
19⁵ x 19⁹

copyright © 1995 frank betz associates, inc.

GARAGE LOCATION WITH BASEMENT

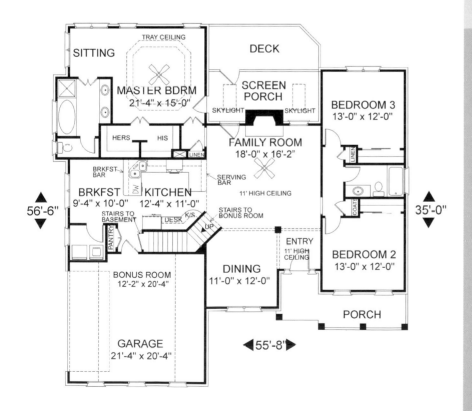

Special features

1,787 total square feet of living area

- Skylights brighten the screen porch which connects to the family room and deck outdoors
- Master bedroom features a comfortable sitting area, large private bath and direct access to the screen porch
- Kitchen has a serving bar which extends dining into the family room
- 3 bedrooms, 2 baths, 2-car side entry garage
- Basement, crawl space or slab foundation, please specify when ordering

Special features

1,882 total square feet of living area

- Wide, handsome entrance opens to the vaulted great room with fireplace
- Living and dining areas are conveniently joined but still allow privacy
- Private covered porch extends breakfast area
- Practical passageway runs through the laundry room from the garage to the kitchen
- Vaulted ceiling in the master bedroom
- 3 bedrooms, 2 baths, 2-car garage
- Basement foundation

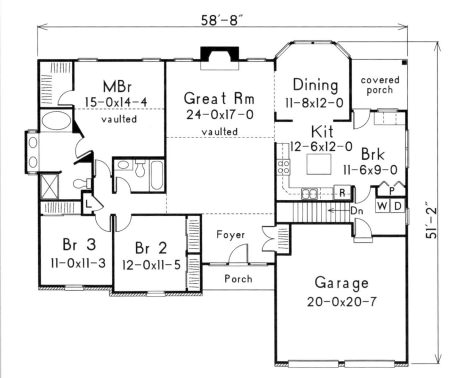

Special features

1,793 total square feet of living area

- Beautiful foyer leads into the great room that has a fireplace flanked by two sets of beautifully transomed doors
- Dramatic eat-in kitchen includes an abundance of cabinets and workspace in an exciting angled shape
- Optional bonus room above the garage has an additional 779 square feet of living area
- 3 bedrooms, 2 baths, 2-car side entry garage
- Basement, crawl space or slab foundation, please specify when ordering

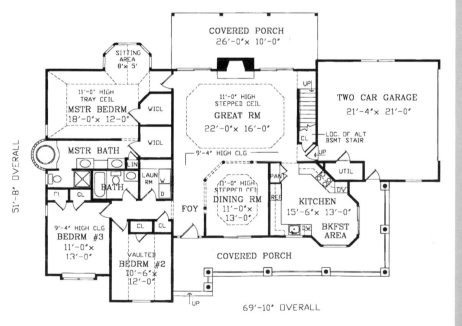

COVERED PORCH
26'-0" x 10'-0"

SITTING AREA
8' x 5'

11'-0" HIGH TRAY CEIL
MSTR BEDRM
18'-0" x 12'-0"

WICL

WICL

11'-0" HIGH STEPPED CEIL
GREAT RM
22'-0" x 16'-0"

TWO CAR GARAGE
21'-4" x 21'-0"

UP

CL

LOC. OF ALT BSMT STAIR

9'-4" HIGH CLG

MSTR BATH

LAUN RM

LIN

BATH

CL

CL

51'-8" OVERALL

PANT

REF

UP

DV

UTIL

9'-4" HIGH CLG
BEDRM #3
11'-0" x 13'-0"

CL

CL

11'-0" HIGH STEPPED CEIL
DINING RM
11'-0" x 13'-0"

FOY

KITCHEN
15'-6" x 13'-0"

DW

BKFST AREA

VAULTED
BEDRM #2
10'-6" x 12'-0"

COVERED PORCH

UP

69'-10" OVERALL

Special features

1,191 total square feet of living area

- Energy efficient home with 2" x 6" exterior walls
- Master bedroom is located near the living areas for maximum convenience
- Living room has a cathedral ceiling and stone fireplace
- 3 bedrooms, 2 baths, 2-car side entry garage
- Slab foundation, drawings also include crawl space foundation

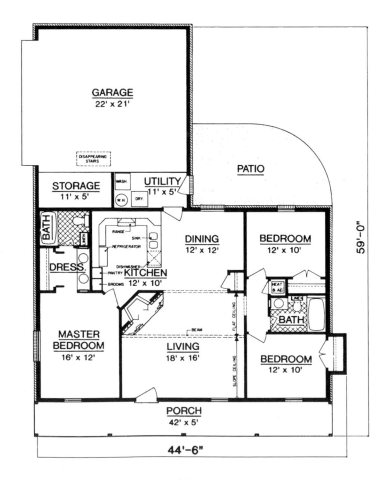

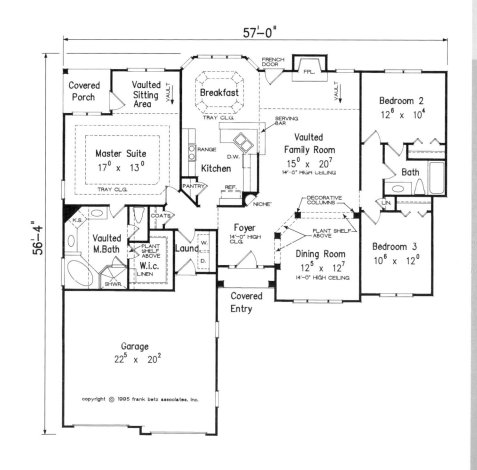

57'-0"

56'-4"

Covered Porch

Vaulted Sitting Area

VAULT

Breakfast

TRAY CLG.

FRENCH DOOR

FPL.

Bedroom 2
12⁶ x 10⁴

VAULT

SERVING BAR

Master Suite
17⁰ x 13⁰

TRAY CLG.

RANGE

Kitchen

D.W.

PANTRY

REF.

NICHE'

Vaulted Family Room
15⁰ x 20⁷
14'-0" HIGH CEILING

Bath

LIN.

K.S.

COATS

Vaulted M.Bath

PLANT SHELF ABOVE

Laund.

W.

D.

W.i.c.

LINEN

SHWR.

Foyer
14'-0" HIGH CLG.

DECORATIVE COLUMNS

PLANT SHELF ABOVE

Dining Room
12⁵ x 12⁷
14'-0" HIGH CEILING

Bedroom 3
10⁶ x 12⁰

Covered Entry

Garage
22⁵ x 20²

copyright © 1995 frank betz associates, inc.

Special features

1,779 total square feet of living area

- Well-designed floor plan has a vaulted family room with fireplace and access to the outdoors
- Decorative columns separate the dining area from the foyer
- A vaulted ceiling adds spaciousness in the master bath that also features a walk-in closet
- 3 bedrooms, 2 baths, 2-car garage
- Walk-out basement, slab or crawl space foundation, please specify when ordering

Special features

1,408 total square feet of living area

- Energy efficient home with 2" x 6" exterior walls
- A bright country kitchen boasts an abundance of counterspace and cupboards
- The front entry is sheltered by a broad veranda
- A spa tub is brightened by a box-bay window in the master bath
- 3 bedrooms, 2 baths, 2-car side entry garage
- Basement or crawl space foundation, please specify when ordering

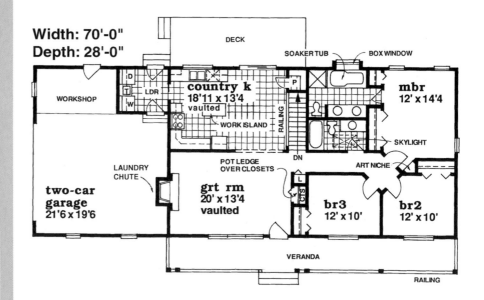

Width: 70'-0"
Depth: 28'-0"

DECK

SOAKER TUB   BOX WINDOW

WORKSHOP

D
T
W

LDR

country k
18'11 x 13'4
vaulted

WORK ISLAND

RAILING

P

mbr
12' x 14'4

SKYLIGHT

DN

POT LEDGE
OVER CLOSETS

ART NICHE

LAUNDRY
CHUTE

two-car
garage
21'6 x 19'6

grt rm
20' x 13'4
vaulted

L
CTS

br3
12' x 10'

br2
12' x 10'

VERANDA

RAILING

QUICK FACT - Many house plants thrive in the steamy and humid atmosphere of a kitchen, so use their lush foliage to enhance a country scheme or liven up a windowsill.

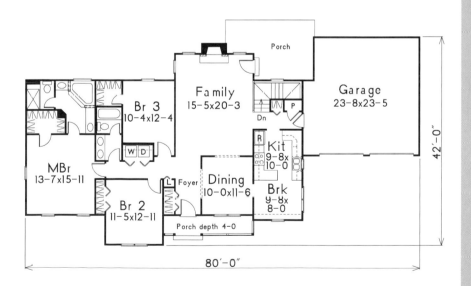

Special features

1,708 total square feet of living area

- Massive family room is enhanced with several windows, a fireplace and access to the porch
- Deluxe master bath is accented by a step-up corner tub flanked by double vanities
- Closets throughout maintain organized living
- Bedrooms are isolated from living areas
- 3 bedrooms, 2 baths, 2-car garage
- Basement foundation, drawings also include crawl space foundation

Special features

2,126 total square feet of living area

- Kitchen overlooks the vaulted family room with a handy serving bar
- Two-story foyer creates an airy feeling
- Second floor includes an optional bonus room with an additional 251 square feet of living area
- 4 bedrooms, 3 baths, 2-car side entry garage
- Walk-out basement, crawl space or slab foundation, please specify when ordering

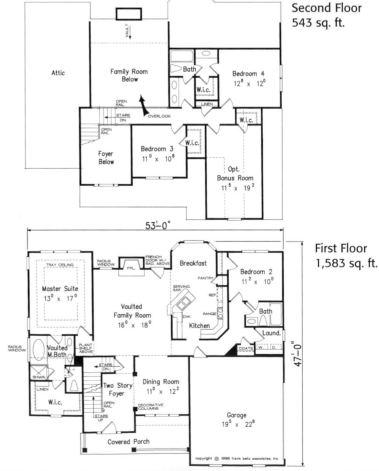

Second Floor
543 sq. ft.

First Floor
1,583 sq. ft.

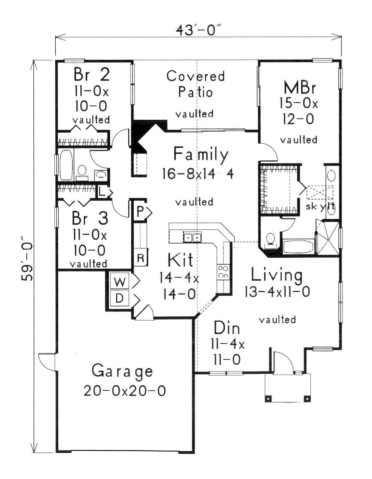

43'-0"

Br 2
11-0x
10-0
vaulted

Covered
Patio
vaulted

MBr
15-0x
12-0
vaulted

Family
16-8x14-4
vaulted

sk ylt

Br 3
11-0x
10-0
vaulted

P

R

Kit
14-4x
14-0

Living
13-4x11-0
vaulted

W
D

Din
11-4x
11-0

Garage
20-0x20-0

59'-0"

Special features

1,550 total square feet of living area

- Alcove in the family room can be used as a cozy corner fireplace or as a media center
- Master bedroom features a large walk-in closet, skylight and separate tub and shower
- Convenient laundry closet
- Kitchen with pantry and breakfast bar connects to the family room
- Family room and master bedroom access the covered patio
- 3 bedrooms, 2 baths, 2-car garage
- Slab foundation

Special features

1,945 total square feet of living area

- Master suite is separate from other bedrooms for privacy
- Vaulted breakfast room is directly off the great room
- Kitchen includes a built-in desk area
- Elegant dining room has an arched window
- 4 bedrooms, 2 baths, 2-car side entry garage
- Walk-out basement, crawl space or slab foundation, please specify when ordering

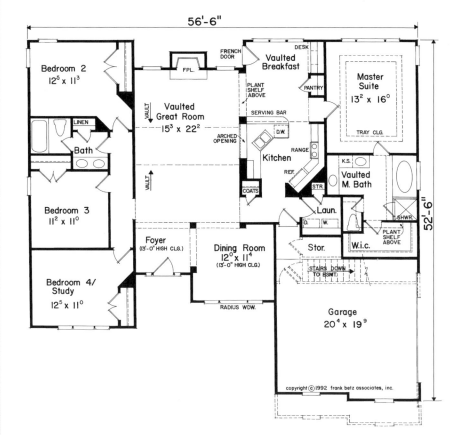

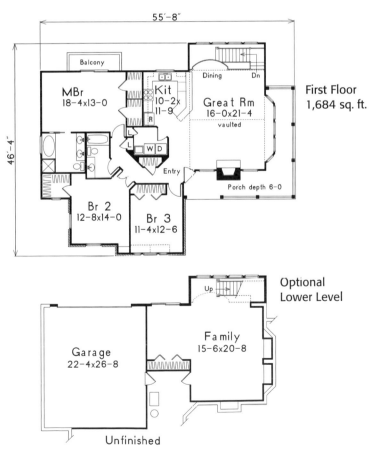

55'-8"

Balcony

MBr
18-4x13-0

Kit
10-2x
11-9

Dining

Dn

Great Rm
16-0x21-4
vaulted

**First Floor
1,684 sq. ft.**

46'-4"

W D

Entry

Br 2
12-8x14-0

Br 3
11-4x12-6

Porch depth 6-0

Up

**Optional
Lower Level**

Garage
22-4x26-8

Family
15-6x20-8

Unfinished

Special features

1,684 total square feet of living area

- Delightful wrap-around porch is anchored by a full masonry fireplace
- The vaulted great room includes a large bay window, fireplace, dining balcony and atrium window wall
- Double walk-in closets, large luxury bath and sliding doors to an exterior balcony are a few fantastic features of the master bedroom
- Atrium opens to 611 square feet of optional living area on the lower level
- 3 bedrooms, 2 baths, 2-car drive under garage
- Walk-out basement foundation

Special features

1,915 total square feet of living area

- Large breakfast area overlooks the vaulted great room
- Master suite has a cheerful sitting room and private bath
- Plan features a unique in-law suite with private bath and walk-in closet
- 4 bedrooms, 3 baths, 2-car garage
- Walk-out basement, slab or crawl space foundation, please specify when ordering

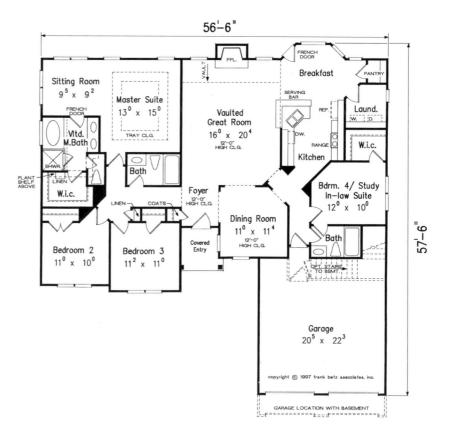

56'-6"

57'-6"

Sitting Room
9⁵ x 9²

Master Suite
13⁰ x 15⁰
TRAY CLG.

FPL.

FRENCH DOOR

Breakfast

PANTRY

VAULT

SERVING BAR

Vaulted Great Room
16⁰ x 20⁴
12'-0" HIGH CLG.

REF.

Laund.
W.   D.

DW.

RANGE

W.i.c.

Kitchen

FRENCH DOOR

Vltd. M.Bath

SHWR.

PLANT SHELF ABOVE

LINEN

W.i.c.

Bath

Foyer
12'-0" HIGH CLG.

Bdrm. 4/ Study In-law Suite
12' x 10⁰

LINEN   COATS

Dining Room
11⁰ x 11⁴
12'-0" HIGH CLG.

Bath

Bedroom 2
11⁰ x 10⁰

Bedroom 3
11² x 11⁰

Covered Entry

OPT. STAIRS TO BSMT.

Garage
20⁵ x 22³

copyright © 1997 frank betz associates, inc.

GARAGE LOCATION WITH BASEMENT

Special features

1,220 total square feet of living area

- A vaulted ceiling adds luxury to the living room and master bedroom
- Spacious living room is accented with a large fireplace and hearth
- Gracious dining area is adjacent to the convenient wrap-around kitchen
- Washer and dryer are handy to the bedrooms
- Covered porch entry adds appeal
- Rear deck adjoins dining area
- 3 bedrooms, 2 baths, 2-car drive under garage
- Basement foundation

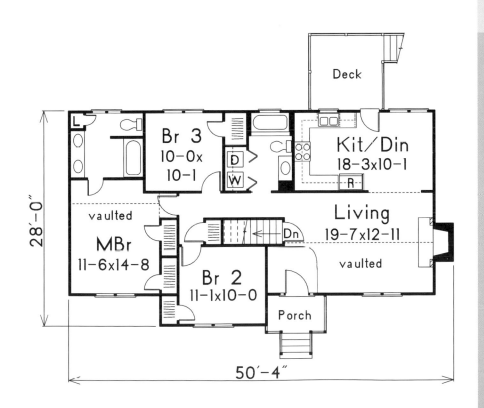

Deck

Br 3
10-0x
10-1

Kit/Din
18-3x10-1

D
W
R

vaulted

28'-0"

MBr
11-6x14-8

Living
19-7x12-11

Dn

Br 2
11-1x10-0

vaulted

Porch

50'-4"

Special features

1,380 total square feet of living area

- Built-in bookshelves complement the fireplace in the great room
- An abundance of storage space is near the laundry room and kitchen
- Covered porch has a view of the backyard
- 3 bedrooms, 2 baths, optional 2-car side entry garage
- Basement, crawl space or slab foundation, please specify when ordering

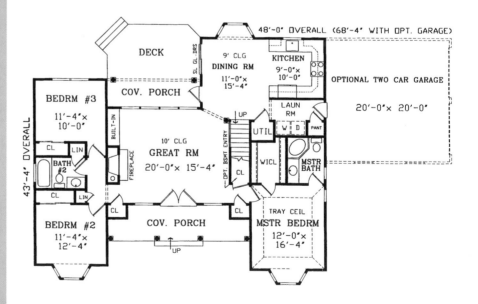

Special features

1,480 total square feet of living area

- Energy efficient home with 2" x 6" exterior walls
- Cathedral ceilings in the family and dining rooms
- Master bedroom has a walk-in closet and access to bath
- 2 bedrooms, 2 baths
- Basement foundation

Second Floor
456 sq. ft.

9'-0" X 12'-0"
2,70 X 3,60

10'-0" X 13'-0"
3,00 X 3,90

14'-8" X 12'-0"
1,10 X 3,60

14'-0" X 22'-8"
4,20 X 6,80

14'-8" X 12'-0"
4,40 X 3,60

First Floor
1,024 sq. ft.

40'-0"
12,0 m

◀ 32'-0" ▶
9,6 m

Special features

1,524 total square feet of living area

- Delightful balcony overlooks two-story entry illuminated by an oval window
- Roomy first floor master bedroom offers quiet privacy
- All bedrooms feature one or more walk-in closets
- 3 bedrooms, 2 1/2 baths, 2-car garage
- Basement foundation, drawings also include crawl space and slab foundations

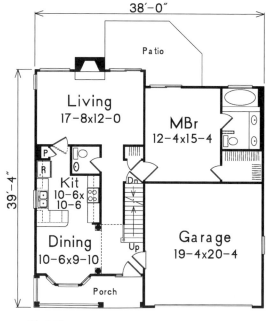

First Floor
951 sq. ft.

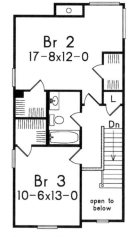

Second Floor
573 sq. ft.

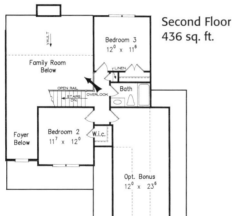

Second Floor
436 sq. ft.

Bedroom 3
12⁰ x 11⁶

Family Room Below

LINEN

OPEN RAIL
STAIRS DN.
OVERLOOK

Bath

Foyer Below

Bedroom 2
11⁷ x 12⁰

W.i.c.

Opt. Bonus
12⁰ x 23⁶

VAULT

Special features

1,818 total square feet of living area

- Spacious breakfast area extends into the family room and kitchen
- Master suite has a tray ceiling and vaulted bath with walk-in closet
- Optional bonus room above the garage has an additional 298 square feet of living area
- 3 bedrooms, 2 1/2 baths, 2-car garage
- Walk-out basement, slab or crawl space foundation, please specify when ordering

52'-4"

FPL
FRENCH DOOR

TRAY CEILING
Master Suite
13⁰ x 16⁰

Vaulted Family Room
18² x 15⁸

Breakfast

SERVING BAR
DW.

RADIUS WINDOW
Vltd. M.Bath
CLG. HT.
COATS

SHWR
PLANT SHELF ABOVE
Pwdr.

LINEN

W.i.c.

FRENCH DOOR

OPEN RAIL
STAIRS UP   STAIRS DN.

Kitchen

PANTRY

REF.

RANGE

Laund.
W. D.

Two Story Foyer

Dining Room
11⁷ x 12⁰

DECORATIVE COLUMNS

Garage
20⁰ x 21⁰

Covered Porch

45'-10"

copyright © 1997 frank betz associates, inc.

First Floor
1,382 sq. ft.

Special features

1,140 total square feet of living area

- Open and spacious living and dining areas for family gatherings
- Well-organized kitchen has an abundance of cabinetry and a built-in pantry
- Roomy master bath features a double-bowl vanity
- 3 bedrooms, 2 baths, 2-car drive under garage
- Basement foundation

QUICK FACT - A single shelf or a collection of corner shelves are surprisingly appealing offering an opportunity to show off collectibles in an exciting new way. Plus, they also work well in more compact homes with smaller rooms.

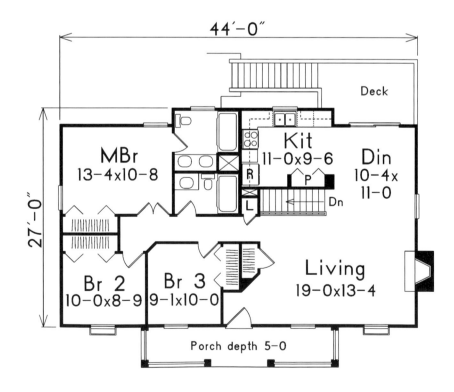

44'-0"

27'-0"

Deck

MBr
13-4x10-8

Kit
11-0x9-6

Din
10-4x 11-0

R

P

L

Dn

Br 2
10-0x8-9

Br 3
9-1x10-0

Living
19-0x13-4

Porch depth 5-0

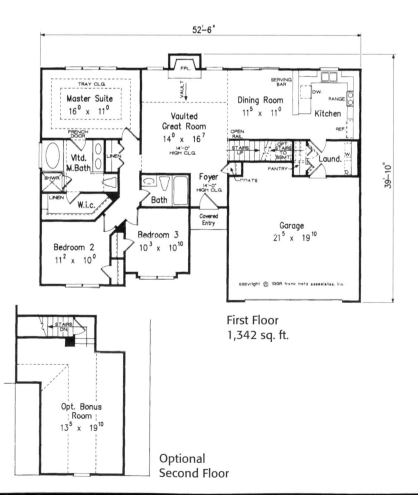

52'-6"

TRAY CLG.

Master Suite
16⁰ x 11⁰

FPL.

VAULT

Dining Room
11⁵ x 11⁰

SERVING BAR

DW. RANGE

Kitchen

REF.

Vaulted
Great Room
14⁰ x 16⁷
14'-0"
HIGH CLG.

FRENCH DOOR

OPEN RAIL

STAIRS UP

OPT. STAIRS TO BSMT.

Laund. W.

Vltd.
M.Bath

LINEN

SHWR

LINEN

W.i.c.

Bath

Foyer
14'-0"
HIGH CLG.

COATS

PANTRY

D.

Covered
Entry

Bedroom 2
11² x 10⁰

Bedroom 3
10³ x 10¹⁰

Garage
21⁵ x 19¹⁰

copyright ® 1998 frank betz associates, inc.

39'-10"

First Floor
1,342 sq. ft.

STAIRS DN.

Opt. Bonus
Room
13⁵ x 19¹⁰

Optional
Second Floor

Special features

1,342 total square feet of living area

- 9' ceilings throughout the home
- Master suite has a tray ceiling and wall of windows that overlooks the backyard
- Dining room includes a serving bar connecting it to the kitchen and sliding glass doors that lead outdoors
- Optional second floor has an additional 350 square feet of living area
- 3 bedrooms, 2 baths, 2-car garage
- Slab, walk-out basement or crawl space foundation, please specify when ordering

Special features

1,428 total square feet of living area

- Large vaulted family room opens to the dining area and kitchen with breakfast bar
- First floor master bedroom offers a large bath, walk-in closet and nearby laundry facilities
- A spacious loft/bedroom #3 overlooking the family room and an additional bedroom and bath complement the second floor
- 2" x 6" exterior walls available, please order plan #596-058D-0080
- 3 bedrooms, 2 baths
- Basement foundation

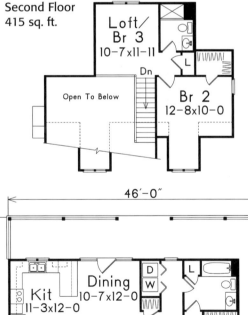

Second Floor
415 sq. ft.

Loft/
Br 3
10-7x11-11

Open To Below

Dn

L

Br 2
12-8x10-0

46'-0"

42'-6"

Kit
11-3x12-0

Dining
10-7x12-0

D
W

L

R

Dn

Family
14-11x15-6

Up

MBr
12-8x14-0

First Floor
1,013 sq. ft.

Covered Porch
depth 7-0

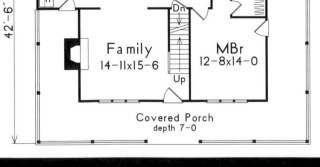

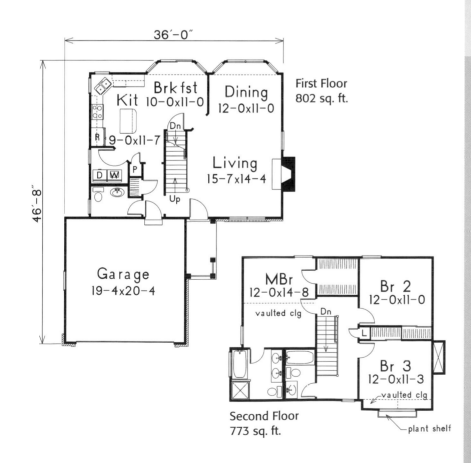

36'-0"

Kit
9-0x11-7

Brkfst
10-0x11-0

Dining
12-0x11-0

First Floor
802 sq. ft.

Dn

Living
15-7x14-4

Up

D W P

46'-8"

Garage
19-4x20-4

MBr
12-0x14-8
vaulted clg

Dn

Br 2
12-0x11-0

L

Br 3
12-0x11-3
vaulted clg

plant shelf

Second Floor
773 sq. ft.

Special features

1,575 total square feet of living area

- Inviting porch leads to spacious living and dining rooms
- Kitchen with corner windows features an island snack bar, attractive breakfast room bay, convenient laundry area and built-in pantry
- A luxury bath and walk-in closet adorn the master bedroom suite
- 3 bedrooms, 2 1/2 baths, 2-car garage
- Basement foundation, drawings also include crawl space and slab foundations

Special features

1,600 total square feet of living area

- Energy efficient home with 2" x 6" exterior walls
- Impressive sunken living room features a massive stone fireplace and 16' vaulted ceiling
- The dining room is conveniently located next to the kitchen and divided for privacy
- Special amenities include a sewing room, glass shelves in the kitchen, a grand master bath and a large utility area
- Sunken master bedroom features a distinctive sitting room
- 3 bedrooms, 2 baths, 2-car side entry garage
- Slab foundation, drawings also include crawl space and basement foundations

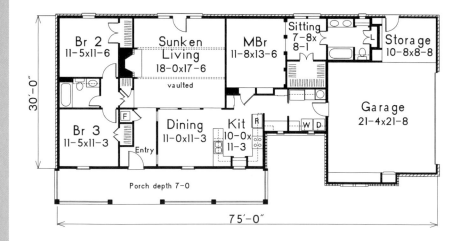

Special features

864 total square feet of living area

- L-shaped kitchen with convenient pantry is adjacent to the dining area
- Easy access to laundry area, linen closet and storage closet
- Both bedrooms include ample closet space
- 2 bedrooms, 1 bath
- Crawl space foundation, drawings also include basement and slab foundations

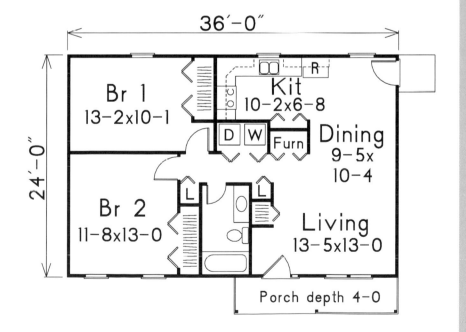

QUICK FACT - Brown, beige and tan colors represent spring, youth, prosperity, family, harmony, nutrition, strength, growth and vitality.

Special features

2,073 total square feet of living area

- Family room provides an ideal gathering area with a fireplace, large windows and vaulted ceiling
- Private first floor master bedroom enjoys a vaulted ceiling and luxury bath
- Kitchen features an angled bar connecting it to the breakfast area
- 4 bedrooms, 2 1/2 baths, 2-car side entry garage
- Basement foundation

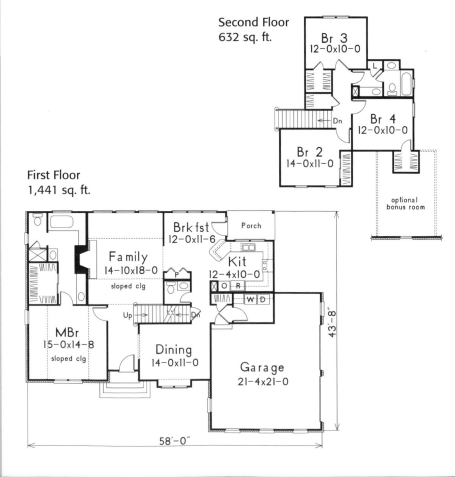

Second Floor
632 sq. ft.

Br 3
12-0x10-0

Br 4
12-0x10-0

Br 2
14-0x11-0

optional bonus room

First Floor
1,441 sq. ft.

Brkfst
12-0x11-6

Porch

Family
14-10x18-0
sloped clg

Kit
12-4x10-0

MBr
15-0x14-8
sloped clg

Dining
14-0x11-0

Garage
21-4x21-0

43'-8"

58'-0"

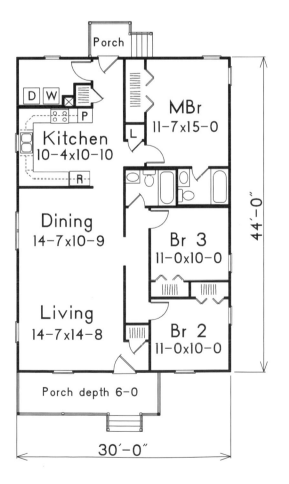

Porch

D W ☒ ☐ P

MBr
11-7x15-0

Kitchen
10-4x10-10

L

R

Dining
14-7x10-9

Br 3
11-0x10-0

Living
14-7x14-8

Br 2
11-0x10-0

44'-0"

Porch depth 6-0

30'-0"

Special features

1,320 total square feet of living area

- Functional U-shaped kitchen features a pantry
- Large living and dining areas join to create an open atmosphere
- Secluded master bedroom includes a private full bath
- Covered front porch opens into a large living area with convenient coat closet
- Utility/laundry room is located near the kitchen
- 3 bedrooms, 2 baths
- Crawl space foundation

QUICK FACT - Clutter can really detract from an open floor plan. When planning your living area, make a list of all of the items that will need to be stored. Everything from media equipment to children's toy bins should be considered. Also, don't forget to list books and collectibles. Often times when rooms are designed there is not enough storage for all of the everyday living items, and rooms pile up with unwanted clutter. Designing a room initially with these needs in mind will not compromise the overall beauty of the space once all of your belongings are in place.

Special features

1,608 total square feet of living area

- The lovely front porch leads into the formal dining room that is ideal for entertaining guests
- The kitchen, dining and family rooms combine at the rear of the house for a casual living area complete with a fireplace and access to the backyard
- The laundry room is conveniently located on the second floor along with all of the bedrooms
- 3 bedrooms, 2 1/2 baths, 2-car garage
- Basement foundation

First Floor
802 sq. ft.

Width: 43'-0"
Depth: 43'-6"

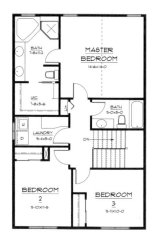

Second Floor
806 sq. ft.

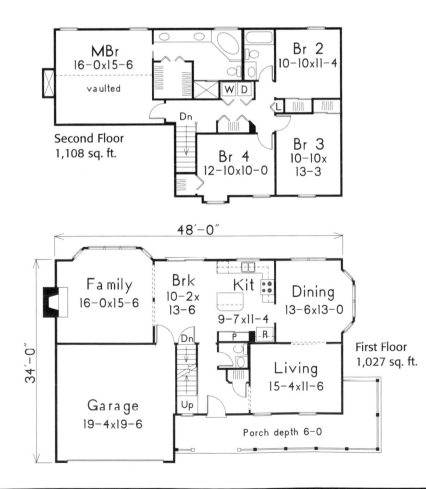

MBr
16-0x15-6

vaulted

Br 2
10-10x11-4

W D

Dn

L

Second Floor
1,108 sq. ft.

Br 4
12-10x10-0

Br 3
10-10x
13-3

48'-0"

Family
16-0x15-6

Brk
10-2x
13-6

Kit
9-7x11-4

Dining
13-6x13-0

34'-0"

Dn

P   R

Up

Living
15-4x11-6

First Floor
1,027 sq. ft.

Garage
19-4x19-6

Porch depth 6-0

Special features

2,135 total square feet of living area

- Family room features extra space, an impressive fireplace and full wall of windows that joins the breakfast room creating a spacious entertainment area
- Washer and dryer are conveniently located on the second floor near the bedrooms
- The kitchen features an island counter and pantry
- 4 bedrooms, 2 1/2 baths, 2-car garage
- Basement foundation

Special features

1,674 total square feet of living area

- Vaulted great room, dining area and kitchen all enjoy a central fireplace and log bin
- Convenient laundry/mud room is located between the garage and the rest of the home with handy stairs to the basement
- Easily expandable screened porch and adjacent patio access the dining area
- Master bedroom features a full bath with tub, separate shower and walk-in closet
- 3 bedrooms, 2 baths, 2-car garage
- Basement foundation, drawings also include crawl space and slab foundations

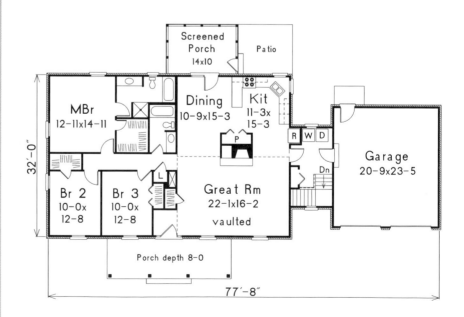

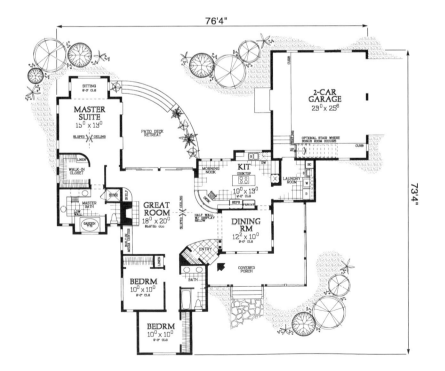

76'4"

73'4"

SITTING
8'-0" CLG

MASTER
SUITE
15'0 x 19'0
SLOPED CEILING

WALK-IN
CLOSET

LINEN

MASTER
BATH

PATIO DECK
RETREAT

2-CAR
GARAGE
23'0 x 25'6

OPTIONAL STAIRS WHERE
BONUS ROOM OCCURS

MORNING
NOOK

KIT
10'0 x 19'0

COOKTOP

LAUNDRY
ROOM

GREAT
ROOM
18'0 x 20'0

DINING
RM
12'2 x 10'0

ENTRY

BEDRM
10'0 x 10'0

BATH

LINEN

COVERED
PORCH

BEDRM
10'0 x 10'0

Special features

1,937 total square feet of living area

- Energy efficient home with 2" x 6" exterior walls
- Upscale great room offers a sloped ceiling, fireplace with extended hearth and built-in shelves for an entertainment center
- Gourmet kitchen includes a cooktop island counter and a quaint morning room
- Master suite features a sloped ceiling, cozy sitting room, walk-in closet and a private bath with whirlpool tub
- 3 bedrooms, 2 baths, 2-car side entry garage
- Crawl space foundation

Special features

1,597 total square feet of living area

- Spacious family room includes a fireplace and coat closet
- Open kitchen and dining room provide a breakfast bar and access to the outdoors
- Convenient laundry area is located near the kitchen
- Secluded master bedroom enjoys a walk-in closet and private bath
- 4 bedrooms, 2 1/2 baths, 2-car detached garage
- Basement foundation

Br 3
14-0x10-0

Br 4
12-0x12-4

Dn

Second Floor
615 sq. ft.

Br 2
14-0x10-10

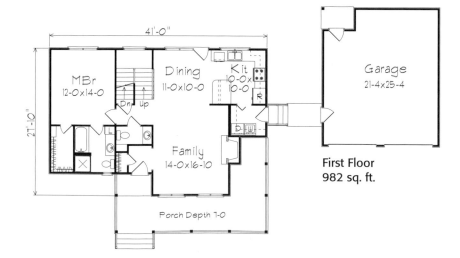

41'-0"

MBr
12-0x14-0

Dining
11-0x10-0

Kit
10-0x
10-0

Garage
21-4x25-4

27'-10"

Dn   Up

Family
14-0x16-10

First Floor
982 sq. ft.

Porch Depth 7-0

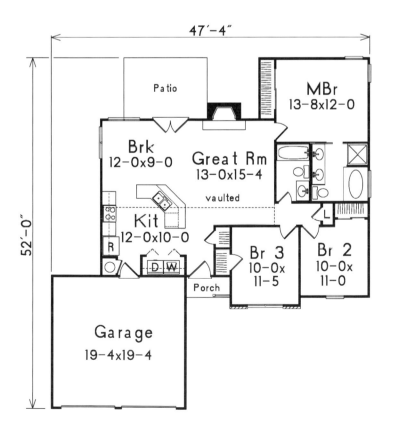

Special features

1,170 total square feet of living area

- Master bedroom enjoys privacy at the rear of this home
- Kitchen has an angled bar that overlooks the great room and breakfast area
- Living areas combine to create a greater sense of spaciousness
- Great room has a cozy fireplace
- 3 bedrooms, 2 baths, 2-car garage
- Slab foundation

QUICK FACT - As well as serving as decorative features and essential dressing aids, mirrors also play a less obvious role in a room scheme. They are invaluable for reflecting light, and can increase the illusion of space in a small room.

Special features

1,882 total square feet of living area

- Handsome brick facade
- Spacious great room and dining area combination is brightened by unique corner windows and patio access
- Well-designed kitchen incorporates a breakfast bar peninsula, sweeping casement window above sink and a walk-in pantry island
- Master bedroom features a large walk-in closet and private bath with bay window
- 4 bedrooms, 2 baths, 2-car side entry garage
- Basement foundation

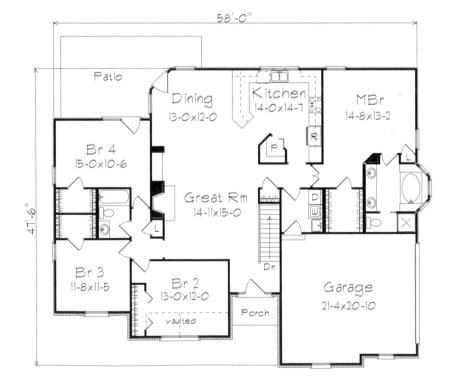

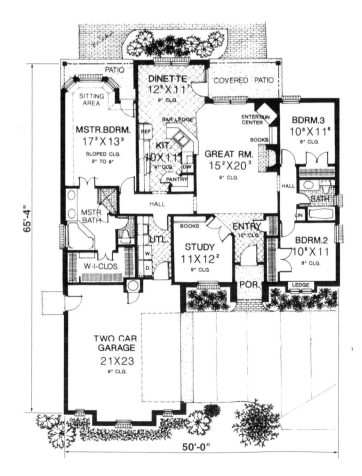

Special features

1,760 total square feet of living area

- Stone and brick exterior has old-world charm
- Master bedroom includes a sitting area and is situated away from other bedrooms for privacy
- Kitchen and dinette access the outdoors
- Great room includes fireplace, built-in bookshelves and an entertainment center
- 3 bedrooms, 2 baths, 2-car side entry garage
- Slab foundation

Special features

1,393 total square feet of living area

- L-shaped kitchen features a walk-in pantry, island cooktop and is convenient to the laundry room and dining area
- Master bedroom features a large walk-in closet and private bath with separate tub and shower
- Convenient storage/coat closet in hall
- View to the patio from the dining area
- 3 bedrooms, 2 baths, 2-car detached garage
- Crawl space foundation, drawings also include slab foundation

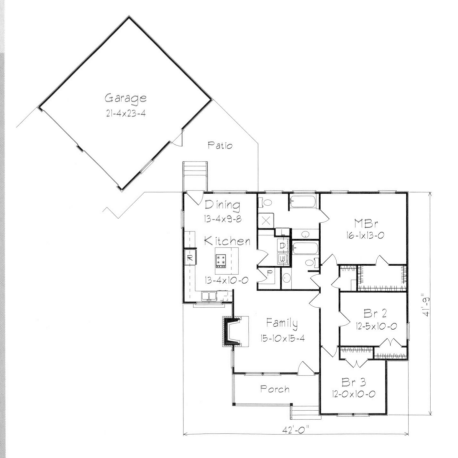

Garage
21-4x23-4

Patio

Dining
13-4x9-8

Kitchen
13-4x10-0

MBr
16-1x13-0

Family
15-10x15-4

Br 2
12-5x10-0

Br 3
12-0x10-0

Porch

42'-0"

41'-9"

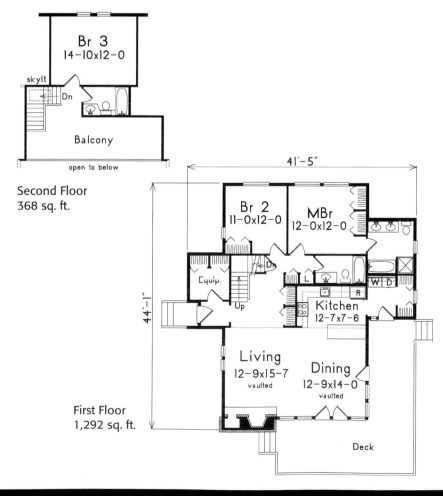

Br 3
14-10x12-0

skylt

Dn

Balcony

open to below

Second Floor
368 sq. ft.

41'-5"

Br 2
11-0x12-0

MBr
12-0x12-0

44'-1"

Equip.

Dn

Up

Kitchen
12-7x7-6

L

W D

R

Living
12-9x15-7
vaulted

Dining
12-9x14-0
vaulted

First Floor
1,292 sq. ft.

Deck

Special features

1,660 total square feet of living area

- Energy efficient home with 2" x 6" exterior walls
- Convenient gear and equipment room
- Spacious living and dining rooms look even larger with the openness of the foyer and kitchen
- Large wrap-around deck is a great plus for outdoor living
- Broad balcony overlooks living and dining rooms
- 3 bedrooms, 3 baths
- Partial basement/crawl space foundation, drawings also include slab foundation

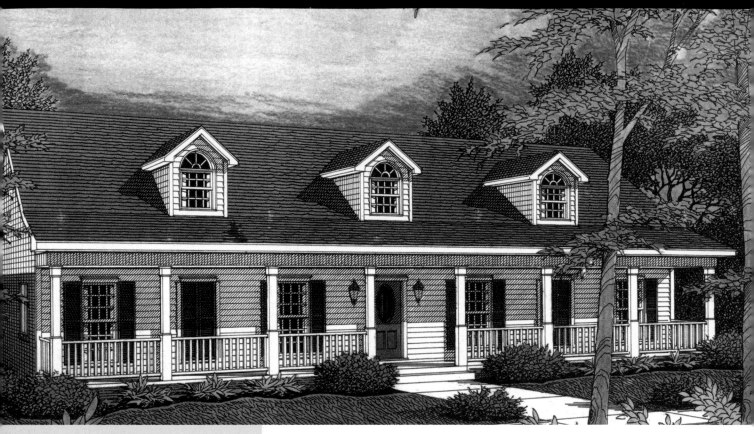

Special features

2,156 total square feet of living area

- Secluded master bedroom has a spa-style bath with a corner whirlpool tub, large shower, double sinks and a walk-in closet
- Kitchen overlooks rear patio
- Plenty of windows add an open, airy feel to the great room
- 4 bedrooms, 3 baths, 2-car side entry garage
- Basement, crawl space or slab foundation, please specify when ordering

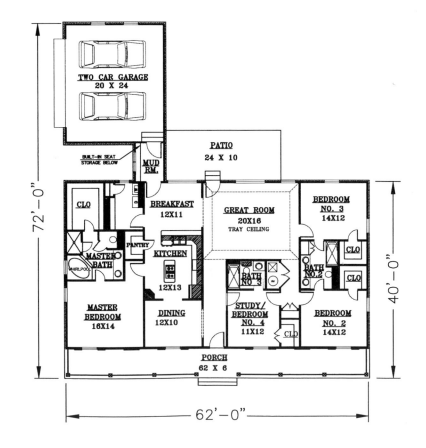

TWO CAR GARAGE
20 X 24

BUILT-IN SEAT
STORAGE BELOW

MUD RM.

PATIO
24 X 10

72' - 0"

CLO

BREAKFAST
12X11

GREAT ROOM
20X16
TRAY CEILING

BEDROOM
NO. 3
14X12

PANTRY

MASTER BATH

KITCHEN
12X13

WHIRLPOOL

BATH
NO. 3

BATH
NO. 2

CLO

CLO

40' - 0"

MASTER BEDROOM
16X14

DINING
12X10

STUDY/
BEDROOM
NO. 4
11X12

BEDROOM
NO. 2
14X12

CLO

PORCH
62 X 6

62' - 0"

First Floor 796 sq. ft.

28'-0"

28'-0"

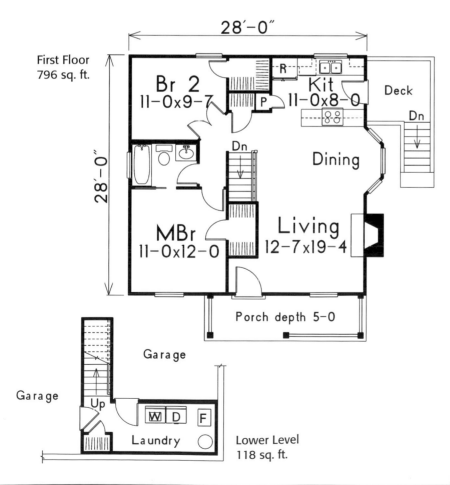

Br 2
11-0x9-7

R

Kit
11-0x8-0

Deck

P

Dn

Dn

Dining

MBr
11-0x12-0

Living
12-7x19-4

Porch depth 5-0

Garage

Garage

Up

W D F

Laundry

Lower Level 118 sq. ft.

Special features

914 total square feet of living area

- Large porch for leisure evenings
- Dining area with bay window, open stair and pass-through kitchen create openness
- Basement includes generous garage space, storage area, finished laundry and mechanical room
- 2 bedrooms, 1 bath, 2-car drive under garage
- Basement foundation

QUICK FACT - Engineered wood siding is a lot easier and less costly to install than real wood siding. It's lighter in weight and includes advancements making it easier to install. Engineered wood can be bought pre-primed, ready to paint or pre-finished in a number of options which reduces field and labor costs.

Special features

1,859 total square feet of living area

- Fireplace highlights the vaulted great room
- Master bedroom includes a large closet and private bath
- Kitchen adjoins breakfast room providing easy access to the outdoors
- 3 bedrooms, 2 1/2 baths, 2-car garage
- Basement foundation

QUICK FACT - Before dipping a brush in paint, dip it into water (for water based paints) or paint thinner (for oil-based paints) and spin out the excess. This wets the bristles in the ferrule (the metal base) and prevents paint from building up in there, which makes cleanup easier and extends the life of the brush.

Second Floor
789 sq. ft.

First Floor
1,070 sq. ft.

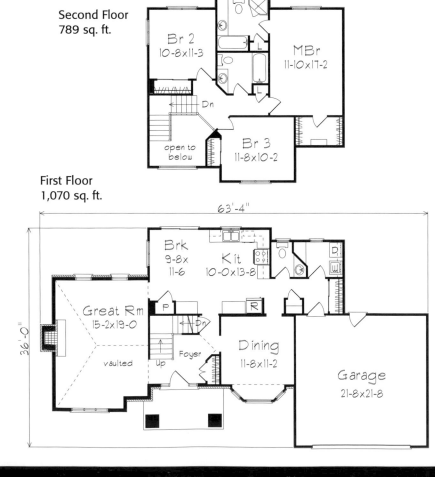

Special features

2,001 total square feet of living area

- Energy efficient home with 2" x 6" exterior walls
- Large wrap-around counter in kitchen is accessible from the dining area
- A double-door entry keeps the den secluded from other living areas making it an ideal home office
- Decorative columns adorn the entry leading into the great room
- 3 bedrooms, 2 baths, 3-car garage
- Crawl space foundation

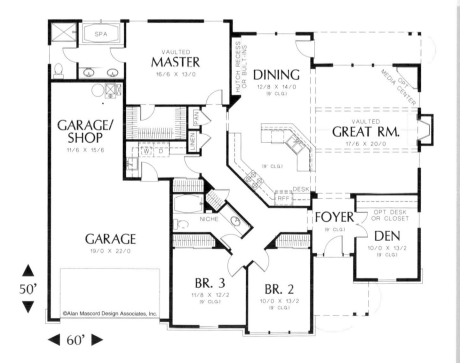

GARAGE/SHOP
11/6 X 15/6

VAULTED MASTER
16/6 X 13/0

SPA

HUTCH RECESS OR BUILT-INS

DINING
12/8 X 14/0
(9' CLG.)

OPT MEDIA CENTER

VAULTED GREAT RM.
17/6 X 20/0

(9' CLG.)

PAN

LINEN

W D

DESK

REF

GARAGE
19/0 X 22/0

NICHE

FOYER
(9' CLG.)

OPT DESK OR CLOSET

DEN
10/0 X 13/2
(9' CLG.)

BR. 3
11/8 X 12/2
(9' CLG.)

BR. 2
10/0 X 13/2
(9' CLG.)

50'

60'

©Alan Mascord Design Associates, Inc.

Special features

2,069 total square feet of living area

- 9' ceilings throughout this home
- Kitchen has many amenities including a snack bar
- Large front and rear porches offer outdoor living spaces
- 3 bedrooms, 2 1/2 baths, 2-car garage
- Slab or crawl space foundation, please specify when ordering

QUICK FACT - A telescopic extension pole when painting high ceilings is an invaluable tool. Trying to balance yourself and a paint tray is a problem that gets eliminated when using this highly functional tool.

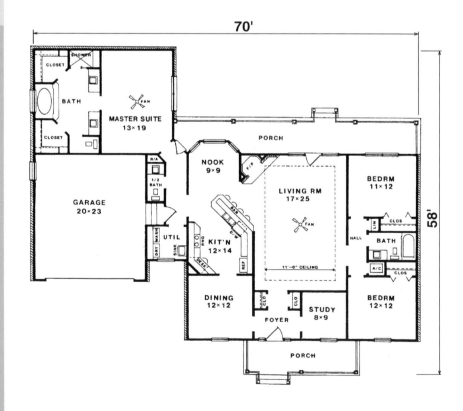

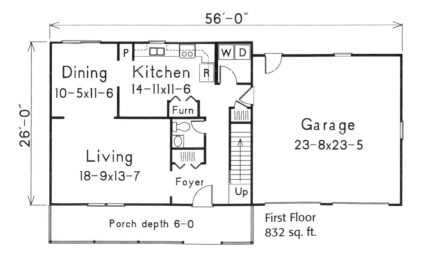

Second Floor
832 sq. ft.

MBr
12-11x12-11

Br 2
11-8x12-2

Br 3
11-3x12-2

Dn

56'-0"

26'-0"

P

Dining
10-5x11-6

Kitchen
14-11x11-6

R

W D

Furn

Living
18-9x13-7

Foyer

Up

Garage
23-8x23-5

Porch depth 6-0

First Floor
832 sq. ft.

Special features

1,664 total square feet of living area

- L-shaped country kitchen includes pantry and cozy breakfast area
- Bedrooms are located on the second floor for privacy
- Master bedroom includes a walk-in closet, dressing area and bath
- 2" x 6" exterior walls available, please order plan #596-001D-0121
- 3 bedrooms, 2 1/2 baths, 2-car garage
- Crawl space foundation, drawings also include basement and slab foundations

Special features

1,787 total square feet of living area

- Large great room with fireplace and vaulted ceiling features three large skylights and windows galore
- Cooking is sure to be a pleasure in this L-shaped well-appointed kitchen which includes a bayed breakfast area with access to the rear deck
- Every bedroom offers a spacious walk-in closet with a convenient laundry room just steps away
- 415 square feet of optional living area available on the lower level
- 3 bedrooms, 2 baths, 2-car drive under garage
- Walk-out basement foundation

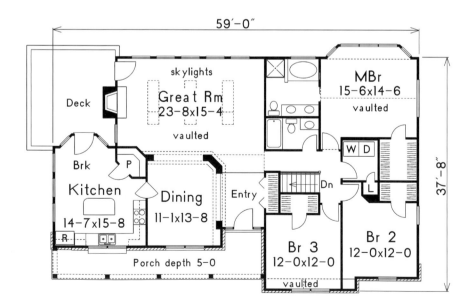

Special features

1,288 total square feet of living area

- Kitchen, dining area and great room join to create an open living space
- Master bedroom includes a private bath
- Secondary bedrooms enjoy ample closet space
- Hall bath features a convenient laundry closet
- Dining room accesses the outdoors
- 3 bedrooms, 2 baths
- Crawl space foundation, drawings also include basement and slab foundations

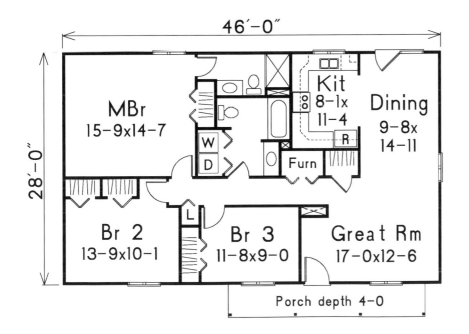

46'-0"

28'-0"

MBr
15-9x14-7

Kit
8-1x
11-4

Dining
9-8x
14-11

W
D

Furn

Br 2
13-9x10-1

Br 3
11-8x9-0

Great Rm
17-0x12-6

Porch depth 4-0

Special features

1,161 total square feet of living area

- Brickwork and feature window add elegance to this home for a narrow lot
- Living room enjoys a vaulted ceiling, fireplace and opens to the kitchen
- U-shaped kitchen offers a breakfast area with bay window, snack bar and built-in pantry
- 3 bedrooms, 2 baths
- Basement foundation

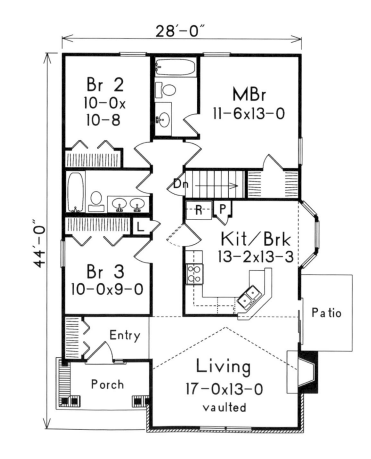

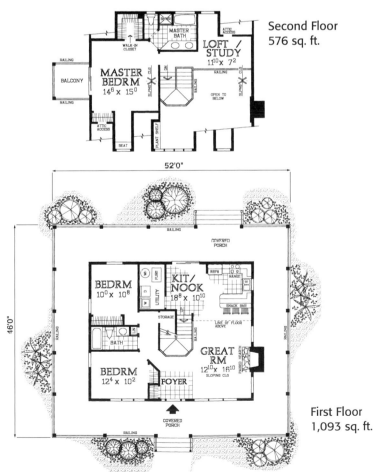

Second Floor
576 sq. ft.

First Floor
1,093 sq. ft.

Special features

1,669 total square feet of living area

- Energy efficient home with 2" x 6" exterior walls
- Windows add exciting visual elements to the exterior as well as plenty of natural light to the interior
- Two-story great room has a raised hearth
- Second floor loft/study would easily make a terrific home office
- 3 bedrooms, 2 baths
- Crawl space foundation

Special features

1,642 total square feet of living area

- Built-in cabinet in dining room adds a custom feel
- Secondary bedrooms share an oversized bath
- Master bedroom includes a private bath with dressing table
- 3 bedrooms, 2 baths, 2-car garage
- Crawl space foundation

QUICK FACT - When making a bed, the top sheet or flat sheet always goes the "wrong" side up. This way when you fold back the top of the sheet the decorative or printed side will be seen.

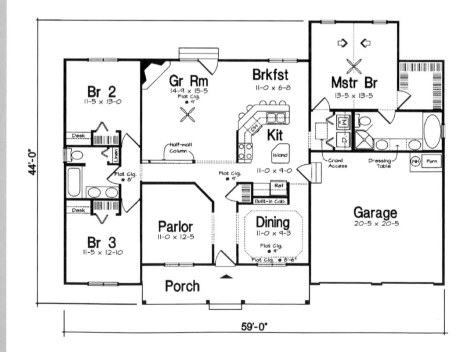

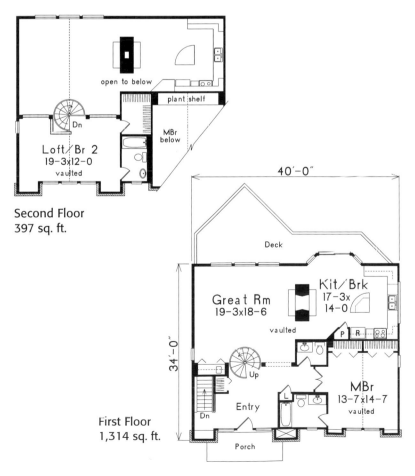

Second Floor
397 sq. ft.

Loft/Br 2
19-3x12-0
vaulted

open to below

plant shelf

MBr below

Dn

40'-0"

34'-0"

Deck

Great Rm
19-3x18-6
vaulted

Kit/Brk
17-3x
14-0

Up

MBr
13-7x14-7
vaulted

Entry

Dn

Porch

First Floor
1,314 sq. ft.

Special features

1,711 total square feet of living area

- Entry leads to a vaulted great room with exposed beams, two-story window wall, fireplace, wet bar and balcony
- Bayed breakfast room shares the fireplace and joins a sun-drenched kitchen and deck
- Vaulted first floor master bedroom features a double-door entry, two closets and bookshelves
- Spiral stairs and a balcony dramatize the loft that doubles as a spacious second bedroom
- 2 bedrooms, 2 1/2 baths
- Basement foundation

Special features

1,000 total square feet of living area

- Bath includes convenient closeted laundry area
- Master bedroom includes double closets and private access to the bath
- The foyer features a handy coat closet
- L-shaped kitchen provides easy access outdoors
- 3 bedrooms, 1 bath
- Crawl space foundation, drawings also include basement and slab foundations

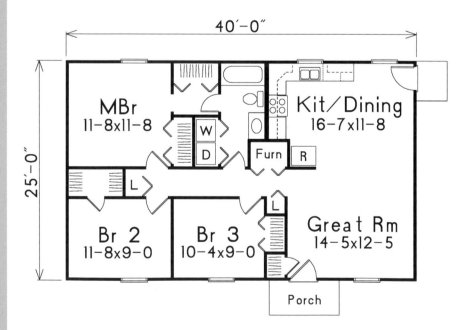

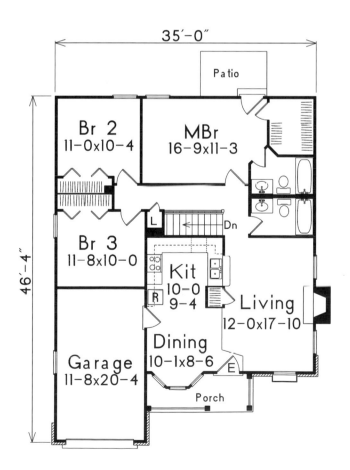

35'-0"

46'-4"

Patio

Br 2
11-0x10-4

MBr
16-9x11-3

Br 3
11-8x10-0

L

Dn

Kit
10-0
9-4

Living
12-0x17-10

Garage
11-8x20-4

Dining
10-1x8-6

E

Porch

Special features

1,169 total square feet of living area

- Front facade features a distinctive country appeal
- Living room enjoys a wood-burning fireplace and pass-through to kitchen
- A stylish U-shaped kitchen offers an abundance of cabinet and counterspace with view to living room
- A large walk-in closet, access to rear patio and private bath are many features of the master bedroom
- 3 bedrooms, 2 baths, 1-car garage
- Basement foundation

Special features

1,640 total square feet of living area

- An open great room and dining area is topped by a stepped ceiling treatment that reaches a 9' height
- The functional kitchen enjoys a walk-in pantry, angles and a delightful snack bar
- Warmth and charm radiate through the combined living areas from the corner fireplace; while a covered porch offers outdoor enjoyment
- 3 bedrooms, 2 baths, 2-car garage
- Basement foundation

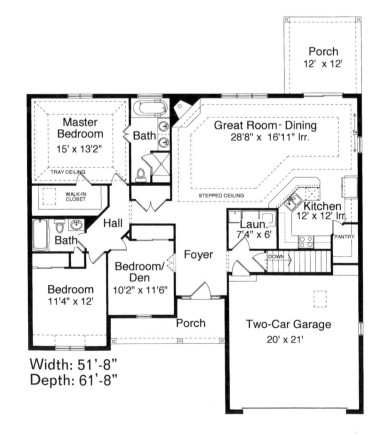

Width: 51'-8"
Depth: 61'-8"

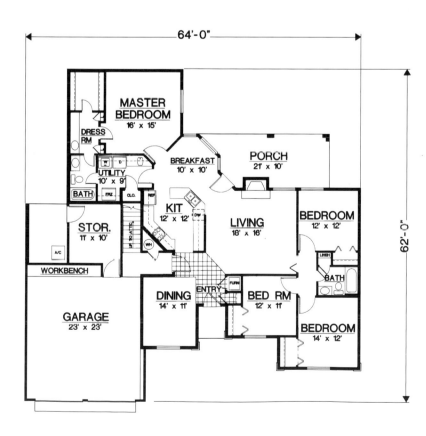

64'-0"

62'-0"

MASTER BEDROOM
16' x 15'

DRESS RM

BATH

UTILITY
10' x 9'

BREAKFAST
10' x 10'

PORCH
21' x 10'

KIT
12' x 12'

LIVING
18' x 16'

BEDROOM
12' x 12'

BATH

STOR.
11' x 10'

A/C

WORKBENCH

GARAGE
23' x 23'

DINING
14' x 11'

ENTRY

BED RM
12' x 11'

BEDROOM
14' x 12'

Special features

1,828 total square feet of living area

- Energy efficient home with 2" x 6" exterior walls
- Master bath features a giant walk-in closet and built-in linen storage with convenient access to utility room
- Kitchen has a unique design that is elegant and practical
- 4 bedrooms, 2 baths, 2-car garage
- Slab foundation, drawings also include crawl space and basement foundations

Special features

2,125 total square feet of living area

- A cozy porch leads to the vaulted great room with fireplace through the entry which has a walk-in closet and bath
- Large and well-arranged kitchen offers spectacular views from its cantilevered sink cabinetry through a two-story atrium window wall
- Master bedroom boasts a sitting room, large walk-in closet and bath with garden tub overhanging a brightly lit atrium
- 1,047 square feet of optional living area on the lower level featuring a study and family room with walk-in bar and full bath below the kitchen
- 3 bedrooms, 2 1/2 baths, 2-car side entry garage
- Walk-out basement foundation

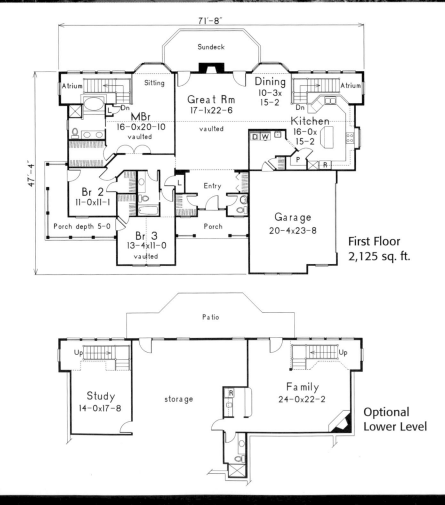

First Floor
2,125 sq. ft.

Optional
Lower Level

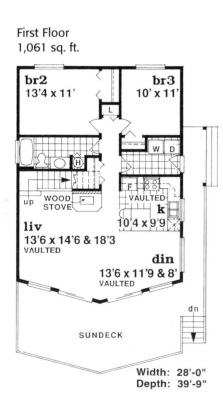

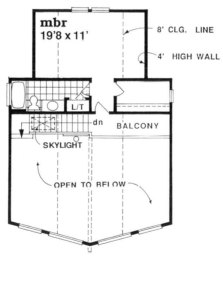

First Floor
1,061 sq. ft.

br2
13'4 x 11'

br3
10' x 11'

W D

WOOD STOVE

up

liv
13'6 x 14'6 & 18'3
VAULTED

VAULTED

k
10'4 x 9'9

din
13'6 x 11'9 & 8'
VAULTED

dn

SUNDECK

Width: 28'-0"
Depth: 39'-9"

Second Floor
482 sq. ft.

mbr
19'8 x 11'

8' CLG. LINE

4' HIGH WALL

L/T

dn

BALCONY

SKYLIGHT

OPEN TO BELOW

Special features

1,543 total square feet of living area

- Energy efficient home with 2" x 6" exterior walls
- Enormous sundeck makes this a popular vacation style
- A woodstove warms the vaulted living and dining rooms
- A vaulted kitchen has a prep island and breakfast bar
- Second floor vaulted master bedroom has a private bath and walk-in closet
- 3 bedrooms, 2 baths
- Crawl space foundation

Special features

1,491 total square feet of living area

- Two-story family room has a vaulted ceiling
- The well-organized kitchen has a serving bar that overlooks the family and dining rooms
- First floor master suite has a tray ceiling, walk-in closet and master bath
- 3 bedrooms, 2 1/2 baths, 2-car drive under garage
- Walk-out basement foundation

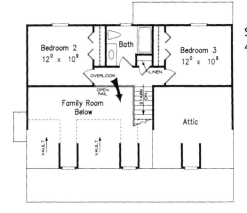

Second Floor
430 sq. ft.

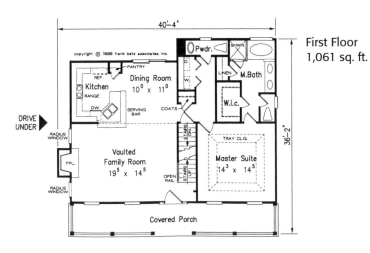

First Floor
1,061 sq. ft.

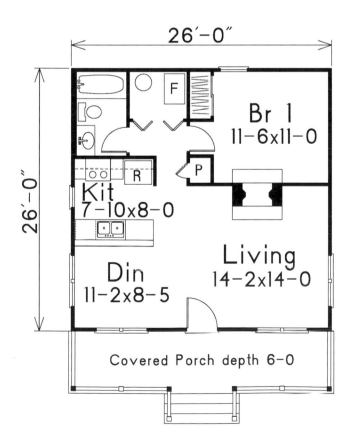

26'-0"

26'-0"

Br 1
11-6x11-0

Kit
7-10x8-0

R
P
F

Din
11-2x8-5

Living
14-2x14-0

Covered Porch depth 6-0

Special features

676 total square feet of living area

- See-through fireplace between bedroom and living area adds character
- Combined dining and living areas create an open feeling
- Full-length front covered porch is perfect for enjoying the outdoors
- Additional storage is available in the utility room
- 2" x 6" exterior walls available, please order plan #596-058D-0074
- 1 bedroom, 1 bath
- Crawl space foundation

Special features

1,452 total square feet of living area

- Large living room features a cozy corner fireplace, bayed dining area and access from the entry with guest closet
- Forward master bedroom enjoys having its own bath and linen closet
- Three additional bedrooms share a bath with a double-bowl vanity
- 4 bedrooms, 2 baths
- Basement foundation

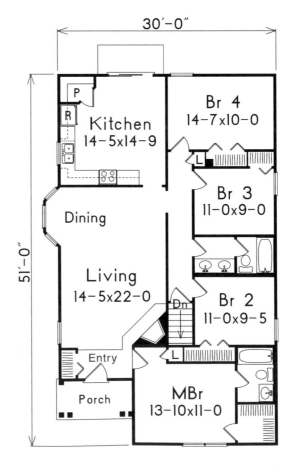

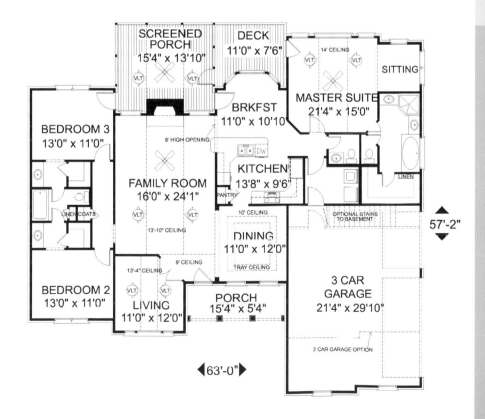

Special features

1,992 total square feet of living area

- Bayed breakfast room overlooks the outdoor deck and connects to the screened porch
- Private formal living room in the front of the home could easily be converted to a home office or study
- A compact, yet efficient kitchen is conveniently situated between the breakfast and dining rooms
- 3 bedrooms, 2 1/2 baths, 3-car side entry garage
- Basement, crawl space or slab foundation, please specify when ordering

Special features

1,985 total square feet of living area

- Charming design for a narrow lot
- Dramatic sunken great room features a vaulted ceiling, large double-hung windows and transomed patio doors
- Grand master bedroom includes a double-door entry, large closet, elegant bath and patio access
- 4 bedrooms, 3 1/2 baths, 2-car garage
- Basement foundation

QUICK FACT - For a stylish and long lasting flower arrangement, pick flowers from your garden in the early morning or late evening. Place them in water immediately, or the stems will form an air-lock that prevents them from drinking.

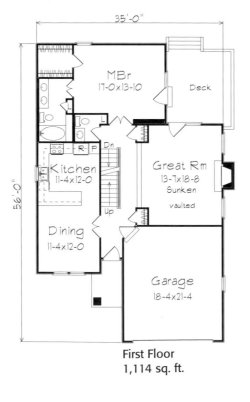

First Floor
1,114 sq. ft.

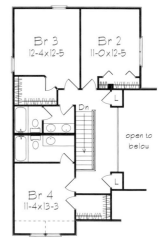

Second Floor
871 sq. ft.

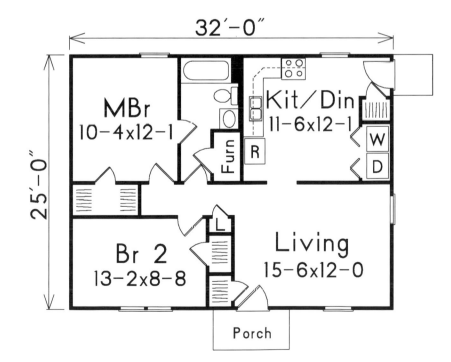

32'-0"

25'-0"

MBr
10-4x12-1

Kit/Din
11-6x12-1

Furn

R

W

D

Br 2
13-2x8-8

Living
15-6x12-0

L

Porch

Special features

800 total square feet of living area

- Master bedroom has a walk-in closet and private access to the bath
- Large living room features a handy coat closet
- Kitchen includes side entrance, closet and convenient laundry area
- 2 bedrooms, 1 bath
- Crawl space foundation, drawings also include basement foundation

Special features

1,143 total square feet of living area

- Enormous stone fireplace in the family room adds warmth and character
- Spacious kitchen with breakfast bar overlooks the family room
- Separate dining area is great for entertaining
- Vaulted family room and kitchen create an open atmosphere
- 2" x 6" exterior walls available, please order plan #596-058D-0075
- 2 bedrooms, 1 bath
- Crawl space foundation

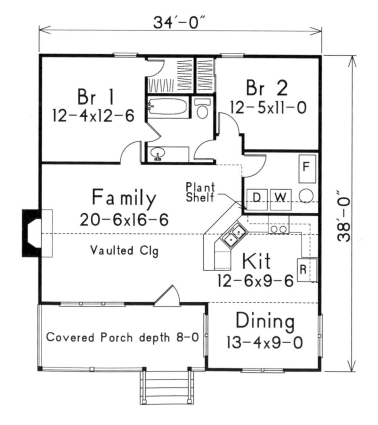

34'-0"

Br 1
12-4x12-6

Br 2
12-5x11-0

F

Family
20-6x16-6

Plant Shelf

D W

Vaulted Clg

Kit
12-6x9-6

R

38'-0"

Covered Porch depth 8-0

Dining
13-4x9-0

Special features

1,092 total square feet of living area

- A box window and inviting porch with dormers create a charming facade
- Eat-in kitchen offers a pass-through breakfast bar, corner window wall to patio, pantry and convenient laundry room with half bath
- Master bedroom features a double-door entry and walk-in closet
- 3 bedrooms, 1 1/2 baths, 1-car garage
- Basement foundation

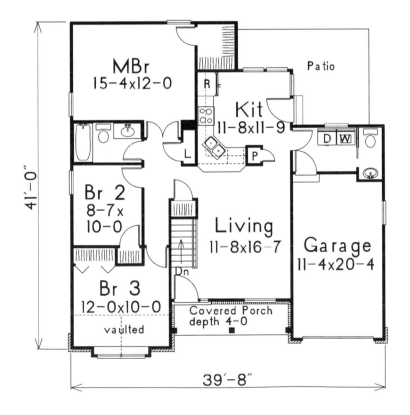

Special features

1,863 total square feet of living area

- Luxurious master bedroom has a private bath, double walk-in closets and two sets of double French doors leading onto the balcony
- The kitchen is open to the dining area and includes a center island large enough for eating
- Bedrooms on the second floor both enjoy a private bath and lots of closet space
- 4 bedrooms, 3 baths
- Crawl space or pier foundation, please specify when ordering

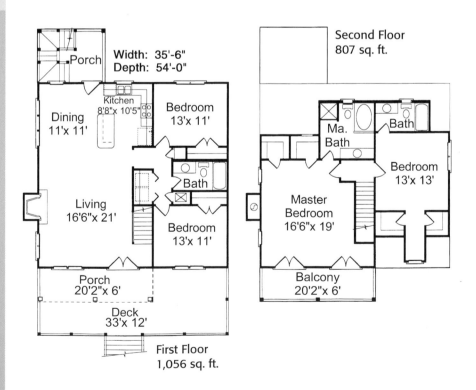

Porch

Width: 35'-6"
Depth: 54'-0"

Second Floor
807 sq. ft.

Dining
11'x 11'

Kitchen
8'8"x 10'5"

Bedroom
13'x 11'

Ma. Bath

Bath

Bath

Living
16'6"x 21'

Bedroom
13'x 13'

Bedroom
13'x 11'

Master Bedroom
16'6"x 19'

Porch
20'2"x 6'

Balcony
20'2"x 6'

Deck
33'x 12'

First Floor
1,056 sq. ft.

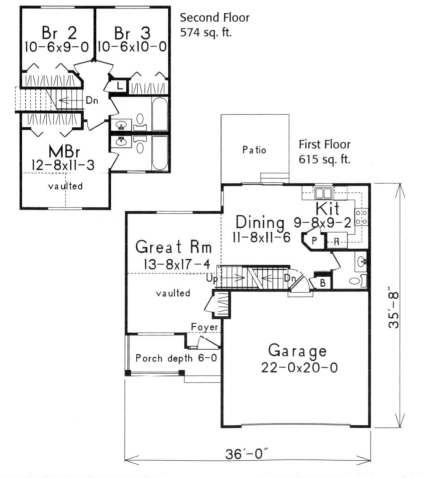

Second Floor
574 sq. ft.

Br 2
10-6x9-0

Br 3
10-6x10-0

Dn

L

MBr
12-8x11-3

vaulted

First Floor
615 sq. ft.

Patio

Great Rm
13-8x17-4

vaulted

Dining
11-8x11-6

Kit
9-8x9-2

P

R

Up

Dn

B

Foyer

Porch depth 6-0

Garage
22-0x20-0

35'-8"

36'-0"

Special features

1,189 total square feet of living area

- All bedrooms are located on the second floor
- Dining room and kitchen both have views of the patio
- Convenient half bath is located near the kitchen
- Master bedroom has a private bath
- 3 bedrooms, 2 1/2 baths, 2-car garage
- Basement foundation

Special features

2,061 total square feet of living area

- Charming stone facade entry
- Centrally located great room
- Private study in the front of the home is ideal as a home office
- Varied ceiling heights throughout this home
- 3 bedrooms, 2 1/2 baths, 2-car garage
- Crawl space or slab foundation, please specify when ordering

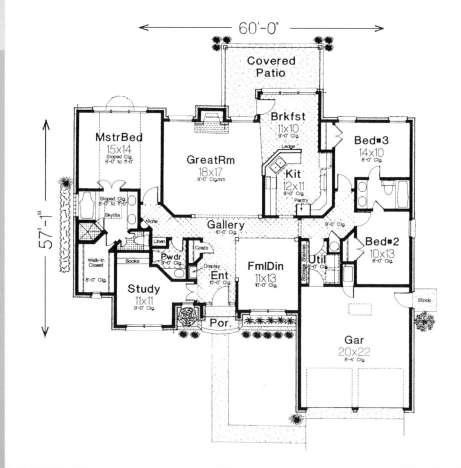

Special features

1,538 total square feet of living area

- Dining and great rooms are highlighted in this design
- Master suite has many amenities
- Kitchen and laundry room are accessible from any room in the house
- 3 bedrooms, 2 baths, 2-car garage
- Walk-out basement, basement, crawl space or slab foundation, please specify when ordering

QUICK FACT - An all brick home has many advantages. While easy to maintain, it offers beauty and a variety of colors perfect for creative design choices while building.

Special features

1,923 total square feet of living area

- The foyer opens into a spacious living room with fireplace and splendid view of the covered porch
- Kitchen has a walk-in pantry adjacent to the laundry area and breakfast room
- All bedrooms feature walk-in closets
- Secluded master bedroom includes unique angled bath with spacious walk-in closet
- 3 bedrooms, 2 baths, 2-car garage
- Slab foundation

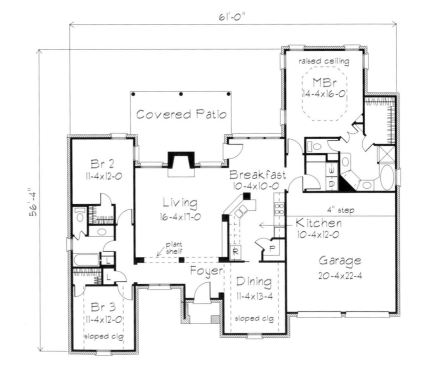

Special features

2,076 total square feet of living area

- Vaulted great room has a fireplace flanked by windows and skylights that welcome the sun
- Kitchen leads to the vaulted breakfast room and rear deck
- Study located off the foyer provides a great location for a home office
- Large bay windows grace the master bedroom and bath
- 3 bedrooms, 2 baths, 2-car garage
- Basement foundation

Special features

1,978 total square feet of living area

- Elegant arched openings are located throughout the interior
- Vaulted living room off foyer is quiet and intimate
- Master suite features a cheerful sitting room and a private bath
- 3 bedrooms, 2 1/2 baths, 2-car garage
- Walk-out basement, slab or crawl space foundation, please specify when ordering

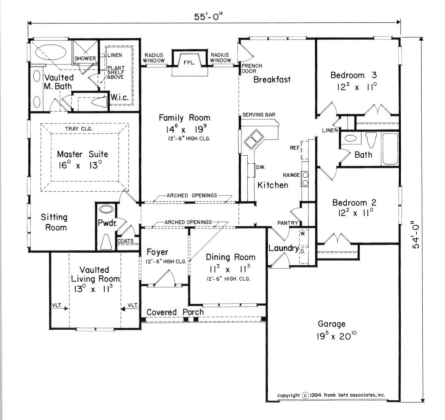

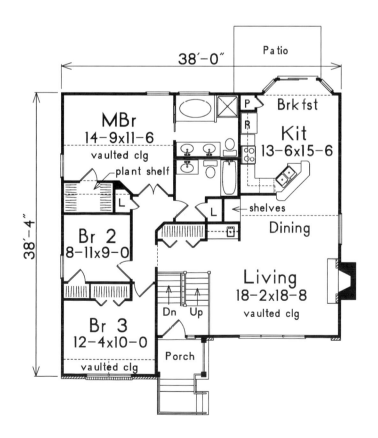

Special features

1,340 total square feet of living area

- Grand-sized vaulted living and dining rooms offer fireplace, wet bar and breakfast counter open to a spacious kitchen
- Vaulted master bedroom features a double-door entry, walk-in closet and an elegant bath
- Basement includes a huge two-car garage and space for a bedroom/bath expansion
- 3 bedrooms, 2 baths, 2-car drive under garage with storage area
- Basement foundation

Special features

840 total square feet of living area

- Energy efficient home with 2" x 6" exterior walls
- Prominent gazebo located in the rear of the home for superb outdoor living
- Enormous bath has a corner oversized tub
- Lots of windows create a cheerful and sunny atmosphere throughout this home
- 1 bedroom, 1 bath
- Walk-out basement foundation

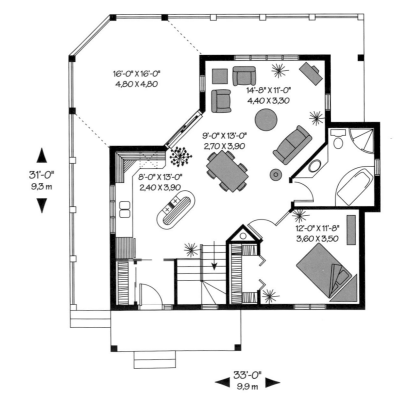

16'-0" X 16'-0"
4,80 X 4,80

14'-8" X 11'-0"
4,40 X 3,30

9'-0" X 13'-0"
2,70 X 3,90

8'-0" X 13'-0"
2,40 X 3,90

12'-0" X 11'-8"
3,60 X 3,50

31'-0"
9,3 m

33'-0"
9,9 m

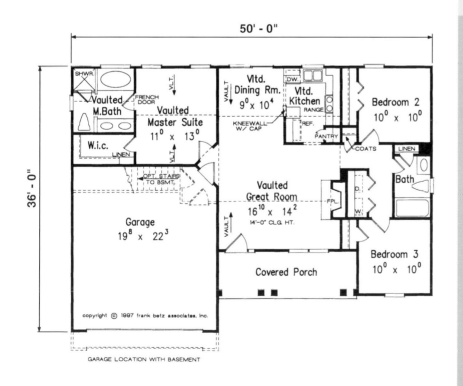

50' - 0"

36' - 0"

SHWR.

Vaulted M.Bath

FRENCH DOOR

VLT.

Vaulted Master Suite
11⁰ x 13⁰

W.i.c.

LINEN

VLT.

Vltd. Dining Rm.
9⁰ x 10⁴

DW.

Vltd. Kitchen
RANGE

REF.

KNEEWALL W/ CAP

PANTRY

COATS

LINEN

Bedroom 2
10⁰ x 10⁰

Bath

OPT. STAIRS TO BSMT.

VAULT

Vaulted Great Room
16¹⁰ x 14²
14'-0" CLG. HT.

FPL.

D.

W.

Garage
19⁸ x 22³

Covered Porch

Bedroom 3
10⁰ x 10⁰

copyright © 1997 frank betz associates, Inc.

GARAGE LOCATION WITH BASEMENT

Special features

1,080 total square feet of living area

- Secondary bedrooms are separate from the vaulted master suite allowing privacy
- Compact kitchen is well organized
- The laundry closet is conveniently located next to the secondary bedrooms
- 3 bedrooms, 2 baths, 2-car garage
- Walk-out basement or crawl space foundation, please specify when ordering

Special features

1,830 total square feet of living area

- Inviting covered verandas in the front and rear of the home
- Great room has a fireplace and cathedral ceiling
- Handy service porch allows easy access
- Master bedroom has a vaulted ceiling and private bath
- 3 bedrooms, 2 baths, 3-car side entry garage
- Basement, crawl space or slab foundation, please specify when ordering

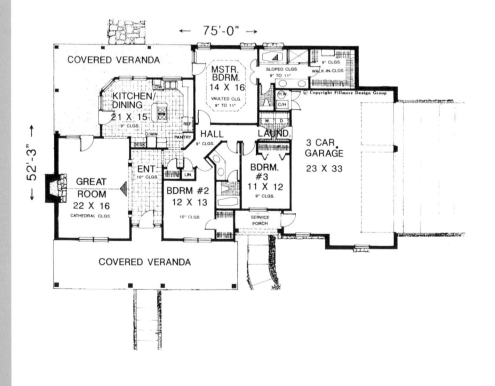

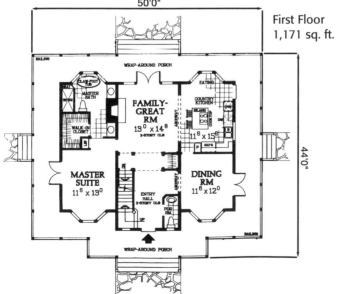

Second Floor
600 sq. ft.

50'0"

First Floor
1,171 sq. ft.

44'0"

Special features

1,771 total square feet of living area

- Energy efficient home with 2" x 6" exterior walls
- Efficient country kitchen shares space with a bayed eating area
- Two-story family/great room is warmed by a fireplace in winter and open to outdoor country comfort in the summer with double French doors
- First floor master suite offers a bay window and access to the porch through French doors
- 3 bedrooms, 2 1/2 baths, optional 2-car detached garage
- Basement foundation

Special features

2,177 total square feet of living area

- Master bedroom features a sitting area and double-door entry to an elegant master bath
- Secondary bedrooms are spacious with walk-in closets and a shared bath
- Breakfast room with full windows opens to the rear porch
- Exterior window treatments create a unique style
- Kitchen features an island cooktop, eating bar and wet bar that is accessible to the living room
- 3 bedrooms, 2 baths, 2-car garage
- Slab foundation, drawings also include basement and crawl space foundations

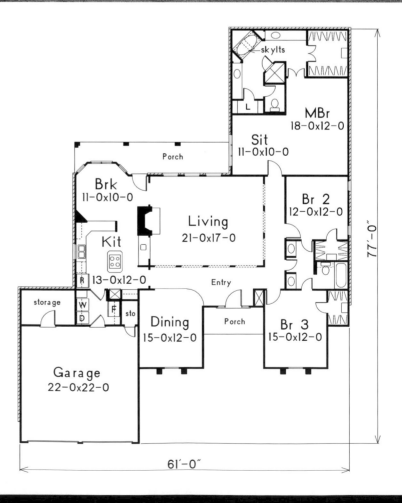

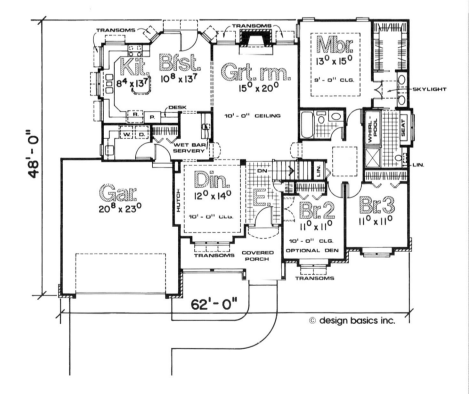

© design basics inc.

48'-0"

62'-0"

TRANSOMS

TRANSOMS

Kit.
8⁴ x 13⁷

Bfst.
10⁸ x 13⁷

Grt. rm.
15⁰ x 20⁰

Mbr.
13⁰ x 15⁰
9'-0" CLG.

SKYLIGHT

10'-0" CEILING

DESK

R. P.

W. D.

WET BAR
SERVERY

WHIRL-POOL

SEAT

LIN.

Gar.
20⁸ x 23⁰

Din.
12⁰ x 14⁰
10'-0" CLG.

HUTCH

DN

E.

LIN.

Br. 2
11⁰ x 11⁰
10'-0" CLG.

Br. 3
11⁰ x 11⁰

TRANSOMS

COVERED
PORCH

OPTIONAL DEN

TRANSOMS

Special features

1,850 total square feet of living area

- Oversized rooms throughout
- Great room spotlights fireplace with sunny windows on both sides
- Master bedroom has a private skylighted bath
- Interesting wet bar between the kitchen and dining area is an added bonus when entertaining
- 3 bedrooms, 2 baths, 2-car garage
- Basement foundation

Special features

1,593 total square feet of living area

- The rear porch is a pleasant surprise and perfect for enjoying the outdoors
- Great room is filled with extras such as a corner fireplace, sloping ceiling and view to the outdoors
- A large island with seating separates the kitchen from the dining area
- 3 bedrooms, 2 baths, 2-car garage
- Basement foundation

QUICK FACT - In the winter, opening drapes and curtains on sunny days takes advantage of the sun's heating power. Then, close all drapes, blinds or shades at night in the winter to make use of their insulating properties.

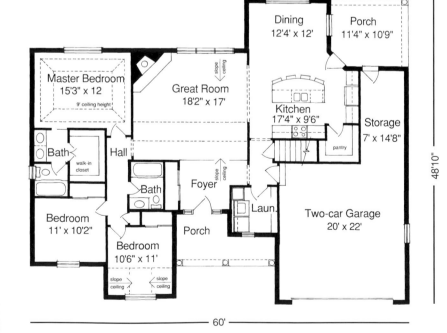

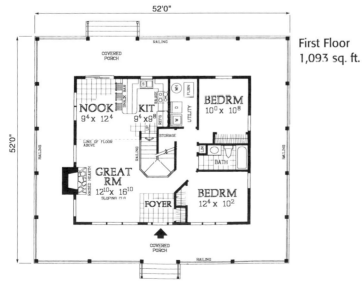

Second Floor
580 sq. ft.

First Floor
1,093 sq. ft.

Special features

1,673 total square feet of living area

- Energy efficient home with 2" x 6" exterior walls
- Great room flows into the breakfast nook with outdoor access and beyond to an efficient kitchen
- Master bedroom on the second floor has access to a loft/study, private balcony and bath
- Covered porch surrounds the entire home for outdoor living area
- 3 bedrooms, 2 baths
- Crawl space foundation

Special features

1,154 total square feet of living area

- U-shaped kitchen features a large breakfast bar and handy laundry area
- Private second floor bedrooms share a half bath
- Large living/dining area opens to deck
- 3 bedrooms, 1 1/2 baths
- Crawl space foundation, drawings also include slab foundation

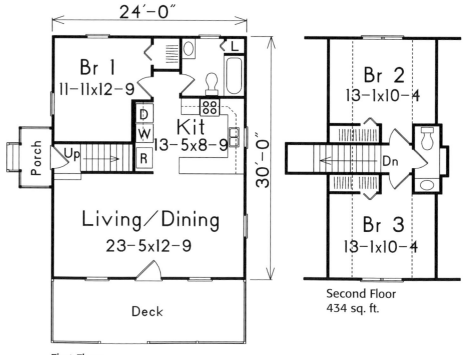

24'-0"

30'-0"

Br 1
11-11x12-9

Kit
13-5x8-9

Porch

Up

D
W
R

Living/Dining
23-5x12-9

Deck

First Floor
720 sq. ft.

Br 2
13-1x10-4

Dn

Br 3
13-1x10-4

Second Floor
434 sq. ft.

Second Floor
715 sq. ft.

BEDROOM
11'4"x10'3"
9' CLG

BEDROOM
11'4"x10'3"
9' CLG

DN

BATH
10'5"x5'10"

OPEN TO
BELOW

BEDROOM
11'2"x9'3"
9' CLG

First Floor
1,354 sq. ft.

COVERED PORCH

MASTER
BEDROOM
13'6"x15'1"
9' CLG

OFFICE
9'2"x8'2"
9' CLG

CLOSET

LIVING
ROOM
14'9"x12'7"
8' CLG

KITCHEN
9'0"x12'5"

CLOSET

MSTR
BATH

LDRY

1/2
BATH

PANTRY

2-CAR
GARAGE

ENTRY
OPEN TO
ABOVE

DINING
11'5"x12'5"
8' CLG

FOYER

Width: 48'0"
Depth: 54'-6"

Special features

2,069 total square feet of living area

- Stucco siding, a tile roof and arched windows create a magnificent facade
- Double doors lead to the two-story foyer and back to the living room that features French doors accessing a trellis-covered porch
- A butler's pantry bridges the kitchen and formal dining room for easy serving
- 4 bedrooms, 2 1/2 baths, 2-car garage
- Crawl space foundation

Special features

1,676 total square feet of living area

- The living area skylights and large breakfast room with bay window provide plenty of sunlight
- The master bedroom has a walk-in closet and both the secondary bedrooms have large closets
- Vaulted ceilings, plant shelving and a fireplace provide a quality living area
- 3 bedrooms, 2 baths, 2-car garage
- Basement foundation, drawings also include crawl space and slab foundations

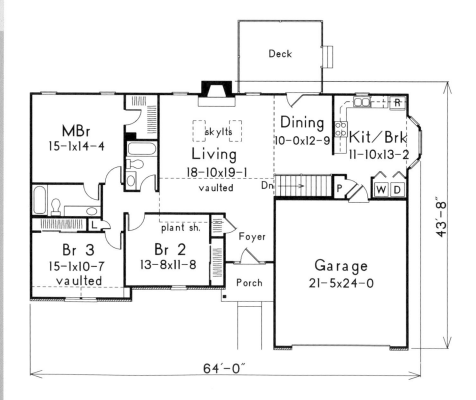

Special features

1,639 total square feet of living area

- The great room has a trayed ceiling and a welcoming fireplace
- The kitchen is well designed with plenty of counterspace and conveniently placed pantry and refrigerator
- The eating area opens onto the back covered porch through beautiful French doors
- 3 bedrooms, 2 baths, 2-car side entry garage
- Slab or crawl space foundation, please specify when ordering

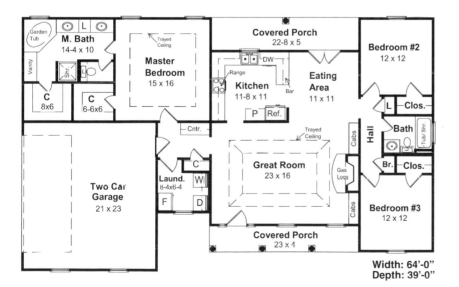

Width: 64'-0"
Depth: 39'-0"

Special features

2,126 total square feet of living area

- Elegant bay windows in the master bedroom welcome the sun
- Double vanities in the master bath are separated by a large whirlpool tub
- Secondary bedrooms each include a walk-in closet
- Nook has access to the outdoors onto the rear porch
- 3 bedrooms, 2 baths, 2-car side entry garage
- Slab foundation

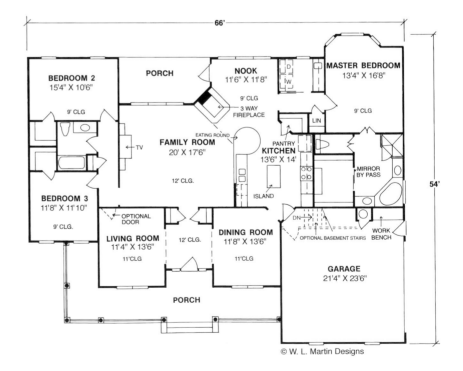

© W. L. Martin Designs

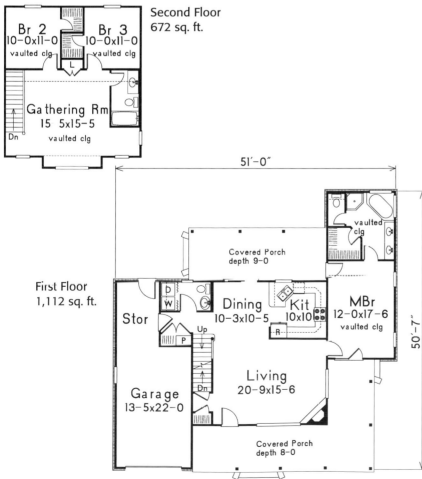

Second Floor
672 sq. ft.

Br 2
10-0x11-0
vaulted clg

Br 3
10-0x11-0
vaulted clg

L

Gathering Rm
15 5x15-5
vaulted clg

Dn

First Floor
1,112 sq. ft.

51'-0"

50'-7"

Covered Porch
depth 9-0

vaulted clg

D W

Stor

Dining
10-3x10-5

Kit
10x10

MBr
12-0x17-6
vaulted clg

Up

P

R

Garage
13-5x22-0

Dn

Living
20-9x15-6

Covered Porch
depth 8-0

Special features

1,784 total square feet of living area

- Spacious living area with corner fireplace offers a cheerful atmosphere with large windows
- The large second floor gathering room is great for a children's play area
- Secluded master bedroom has separate porch entrances and a large master bath with walk-in closet
- 3 bedrooms, 2 1/2 baths, 1-car garage
- Basement foundation, drawings also include crawl space foundation

Special features

1,477 total square feet of living area

- Oversized porch provides protection from the elements
- Innovative kitchen employs step-saving design
- Kitchen has a snack bar which opens to the breakfast room with bay window
- 2" x 6" exterior walls available, please order plan #596-058D-0081
- 3 bedrooms, 2 baths, 2-car side entry garage with storage area
- Basement foundation

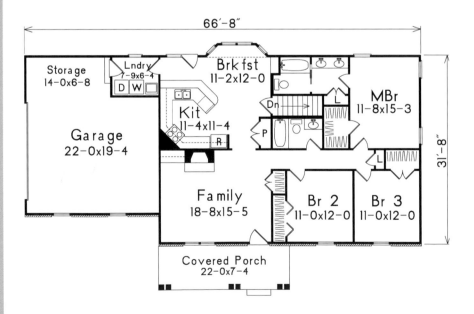

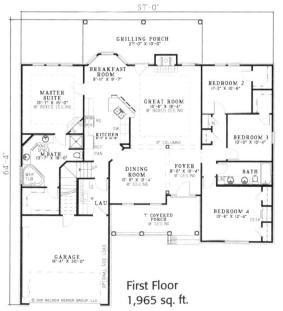

Optional
Second Floor

BONUS ROOM
11'-6" X 20'-0"

4" WALL   8" LINE   4" WALL

GRILLING PORCH
27'-0" X 10'-0"

57'-0"

BREAKFAST
ROOM
9'-11" X 9'-7"

MASTER
SUITE
13'-7" X 15'-0"
10' BOXED CEILING

GREAT ROOM
15'-6" X 19'-4"
10' BOXED CEILING

BEDROOM 2
11'-2" X 10'-6"

KNEE
SPACE
M.BATH
13'-7" X 16'-0"

KITCHEN
9'-11" X 14'-8"

64'-4"

WHP
TUB

8' COLUMNS

BEDROOM 3
10'-0" X 10'-4"

DINING
ROOM
12' 0" X 12'-0"
10' CEILING

FOYER
8'-0" X 10'-4"
10' CEILING

BATH

LAU

7' COVERED
PORCH
10' CEILING

BEDROOM 4
13'-6" X 12'-4"

GARAGE
19'-4" X 20'-0"

OPTIONAL SIDE-LOAD

First Floor
1,965 sq. ft.

© 2001 Nelson Design Group, LLC.

Special features

1,965 total square feet of living area

- Master bedroom has a cozy fireplace and luxurious bath featuring a whirlpool tub, double vanity and large walk-in closet
- Breakfast room has sunny bay windows
- Great room with fireplace has access to a rear grilling porch
- Optional second floor has an additional 251 square feet of living area
- 4 bedrooms, 2 baths, 2-car garage
- Slab or crawl space foundation, please specify when ordering

Special features

1,812 total square feet of living area

- A corner fireplace in the vaulted family room sets the stage for a cozy atmosphere
- The spacious kitchen includes a work island with seating for quick meals
- The master bedroom boasts a coffered ceiling and deluxe bath with whirlpool tub and walk-in closet
- Optional second floor has an additional 323 square feet of living area
- 3 bedrooms, 2 baths, 2-car side entry garage
- Slab foundation

Optional Second Floor

DN.

"FUTURE" STOR.

"FUTURE" REC. ROOM 12 x 18

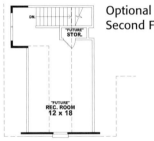

First Floor 1,812 sq. ft.

CLOSET 9 x 7

"VAULTED" MASTER BATH 10 x 10

TUB

SHWR.

PORCH 11 x 5

F.P

BEDROOM #3 12 x 11

"COFFERED" MASTER BEDROOM 14 x 16

BRKFST. AREA 11 x 11

"VAULTED" FAMILY ROOM 15 x 20

UTILITY 6 x 6

HALL

L.

CLOS.

BATH #2

HALL

STORAGE

UP

P.

C.

CLOS.

KITCHEN 11 x 13

49'

DOUBLE GARAGE 20 x 20

DINING ROOM 12 x 12

FOYER

BEDROOM #2 12 x 11

© Sullivan & Assoc.

PORCH 32 x 5

61'

Second Floor
872 sq. ft.

Bedroom
11'x 9'4"

Bath

Master
Bath

Bedroom
11'x 9'2"

WIC

Master
Bedroom
19'x 13'4"

Balcony
14'x 8'

Special features

1,779 total square feet of living area

- Sunny living room has walls covered with windows and is attached to a sunroom with a double-door entry
- Master bedroom has a private bath and double-door access onto a balcony
- Kitchen has an open feel with a center island and overlooks the dining area
- 3 bedrooms, 2 1/2 baths
- Pier foundation

Width: 34'-0"
Depth: 30'-0"

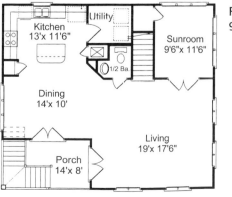

First Floor
907 sq. ft.

Kitchen
13'x 11'6"

Utility

Sunroom
9'6"x 11'6"

1/2 Ba.

Dining
14'x 10'

Living
19'x 17'6"

Porch
14'x 8'

Special features

1,084 total square feet of living area

- Delightful country porch for quiet evenings
- The living room offers a front feature window which invites the sun and includes a fireplace and dining area with private patio
- The U-shaped kitchen features lots of cabinets and a bayed breakfast room with built-in pantry
- Both bedrooms have walk-in closets and access to their own bath
- 2 bedrooms, 2 baths
- Basement foundation

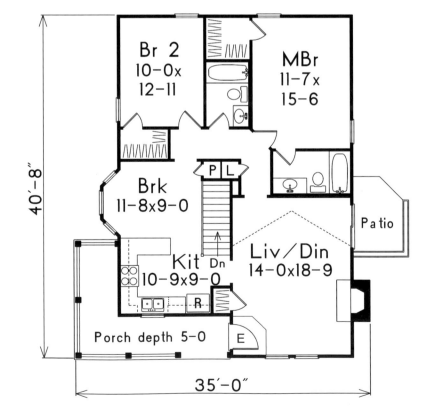

Br 2
10-0x
12-11

MBr
11-7 x
15-6

P L

Brk
11-8x9-0

Patio

Kit
10-9x9-0
Dn

Liv/Din
14-0x18-9

R

Porch depth 5-0

E

40'-8"

35'-0"

First Floor
1,845 sq. ft.

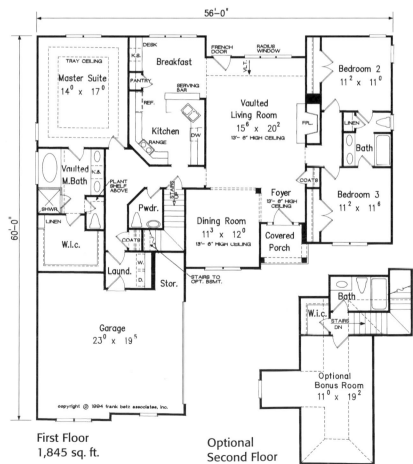

56'-0"

60'-0"

Master Suite 14⁰ x 17⁰
TRAY CEILING

DESK
K.S.
Breakfast
FRENCH DOOR
RADIUS WINDOW

PANTRY
SERVING BAR
REF.
Kitchen
RANGE
DW

Vaulted Living Room 15⁶ x 20² 13'- 8" HIGH CEILING

Bedroom 2 11² x 11⁰

LINEN
FPL.
Bath

Vaulted M.Bath
K.B.
PLANT SHELF ABOVE
Pwdr.
STAIRS UP

SHWR.
LINEN
COATS
W.i.c.

Dining Room 11³ x 12⁰ 13'- 8" HIGH CEILING

Foyer 13'- 8" HIGH CEILING

COATS

Bedroom 3 11² x 11⁶

Covered Porch

Laund.
W.
D.
Stor.
STAIRS TO OPT. BSMT.

Garage 23⁰ x 19⁵

copyright © 1994 frank betz associates, inc.

Optional Second Floor

Bath
W.i.c.
STAIRS DN

Optional Bonus Room 11⁰ x 19²

Special features

1,845 total square feet of living area

- Vaulted living room has a cozy fireplace
- Breakfast area and kitchen are lovely gathering places
- Dining room overlooks the living room
- Optional second floor with bath has an additional 354 square feet of living area
- 3 bedrooms, 2 1/2 baths, 2-car side entry garage
- Walk-out basement or crawl space foundation, please specify when ordering

Special features

1,104 total square feet of living area

- Master bedroom includes a private bath
- Convenient side entrance to the dining area/kitchen
- Laundry area is located near the kitchen
- Large living area creates a comfortable atmosphere
- 3 bedrooms, 2 baths
- Crawl space foundation, drawings also include basement and slab foundations

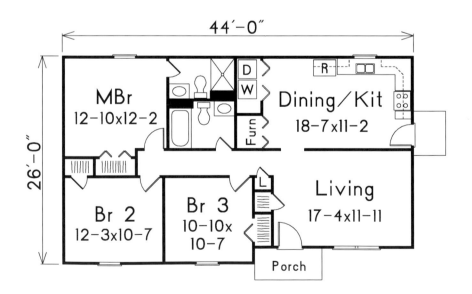

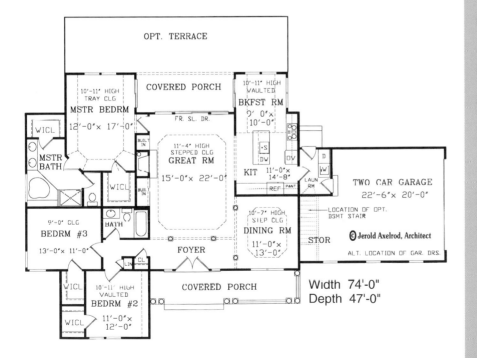

Special features

1,783 total square feet of living area

- The front to rear flow of the great room, with built-ins on one side is a furnishing delight
- Bedrooms are all quietly zoned on one side of the home
- The master bedroom is separated for privacy
- Every bedroom features a walk-in closet
- 3 bedrooms, 2 baths, 2-car side entry garage
- Basement, crawl space or slab foundation, please specify when ordering

Width 74'-0"
Depth 47'-0"

Special features

1,771 total square feet of living area

- Den has a sloped ceiling and charming window seat
- Private master bedroom has access to the outdoors
- Central kitchen allows for convenient access when entertaining
- 2 bedrooms, 2 baths, 2-car garage
- Basement, crawl space or slab foundation, please specify when ordering

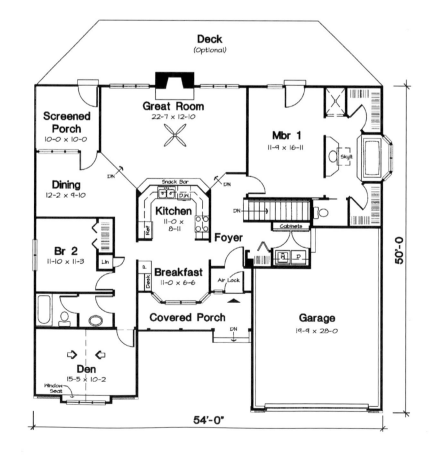

Deck
(Optional)

Great Room
22-7 x 12-10

Screened Porch
10-0 x 10-0

Mbr 1
11-9 x 16-11

Skylt

Dining
12-2 x 9-10

Snack Bar

Kitchen
11-0 x 8-11

Foyer

DN

Cabinets

Br 2
11-10 x 11-3

Lin

Desk P

Breakfast
11-0 x 6-6

Air Lock

50'-0"

Covered Porch

DN

Garage
19-9 x 28-0

Den
15-5 x 10-2

Window Seat

54'-0"

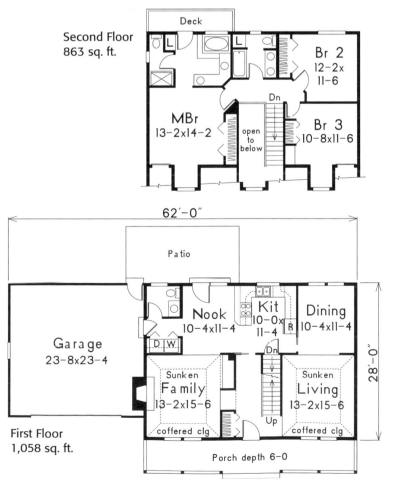

Second Floor 863 sq. ft.

Deck

L | L

Br 2
12-2x
11-6

MBr
13-2x14-2

open to below

Dn

Br 3
10-8x11-6

62'-0"

Patio

Garage
23-8x23-4

Nook
10-4x11-4

Kit
10-0x
11-4

Dining
10-4x11-4

D | W

Sunken
Family
13-2x15-6

Dn

Up

Sunken
Living
13-2x15-6

coffered clg

coffered clg

28'-0"

First Floor 1,058 sq. ft.

Porch depth 6-0

Special features

1,921 total square feet of living area

- Energy efficient home with 2" x 6" exterior walls
- Sunken family room includes a built-in entertainment center and coffered ceiling
- Sunken formal living room features a coffered ceiling
- Master bedroom dressing area has double sinks, spa tub, shower and French door to private deck
- Large front porch adds to the home's appeal
- 3 bedrooms, 2 1/2 baths, 2-car garage
- Basement foundation

Special features

1,246 total square feet of living area

- Corner living room window adds openness and light
- Out-of-the-way kitchen with dining area accesses the outdoors
- Private first floor master bedroom has a corner window
- Large walk-in closet is located in bedroom #3
- Easily built perimeter allows economical construction
- 3 bedrooms, 2 baths, 2-car garage
- Basement foundation

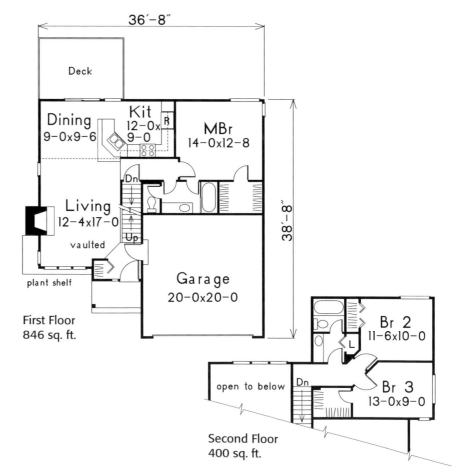

36'-8"

Deck

Dining
9-0x9-6

Kit
12-0x
9-0

R

MBr
14-0x12-8

Dn

Living
12-4x17-0

vaulted

Up

38'-8"

plant shelf

Garage
20-0x20-0

First Floor
846 sq. ft.

Br 2
11-6x10-0

L

open to below

Dn

Br 3
13-0x9-0

Second Floor
400 sq. ft.

QUICK FACT - Heat loss through windows represents a significant amount of most heating bills. Some sources estimate that heat loss through windows alone could account to 35% of heating bills. In home designs that feature multiple or large windows like this one, it is important to caulk cracks, install clear plastic film to the window trim inside the house or decorate windows for efficiency. Decorating solutions include closed shutters, shades, blinds or lined draperies. For long-range solutions, installing storm windows and doors will eliminate problem drafts.

Special features

1,680 total square feet of living area

- Highly functional lower level includes a wet hall with storage, laundry area, workshop and cozy ski lounge with an enormous fireplace
- First floor is warmed by a large fireplace in the living/dining area which features a spacious wrap-around deck
- Lots of sleeping space for guests or a large family
- 5 bedrooms, 2 1/2 baths
- Basement foundation

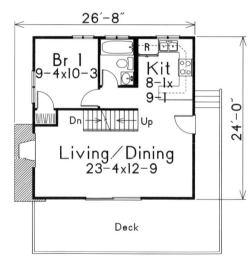

First Floor
576 sq. ft.

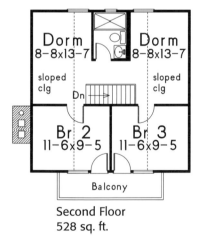

Second Floor
528 sq. ft.

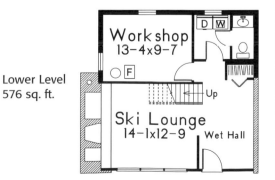

Lower Level
576 sq. ft.

Special features

1,404 total square feet of living area

- Split-foyer entrance
- Bayed living area features a unique vaulted ceiling and fireplace
- Wrap-around kitchen has corner windows for added sunlight and a bar that overlooks the dining area
- Master bath features a garden tub with separate shower
- Rear deck provides handy access to the dining room and kitchen
- 3 bedrooms, 2 baths, 2-car drive under garage
- Basement foundation, drawings also include partial crawl space foundation

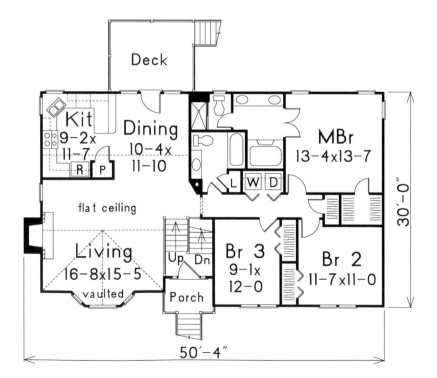

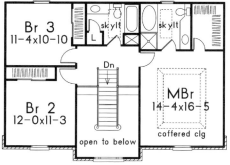

Br 3
11-4x10-10

Br 2
12-0x11-3

sky lt

sky lt

Dn

open to below

MBr
14-4x16-5
coffered clg

Second Floor
859 sq. ft.

Special features

1,996 total square feet of living area

- Dining area features an octagon-shaped coffered ceiling and built-in china cabinet
- Both the master bath and second floor bath have cheerful skylights
- Family room includes a wet bar and fireplace flanked by attractive quarter round windows
- 9' ceilings throughout the first floor with plant shelving in foyer and dining area
- 3 bedrooms, 2 1/2 baths, 2-car side entry garage
- Basement foundation, drawings also include crawl space and slab foundations

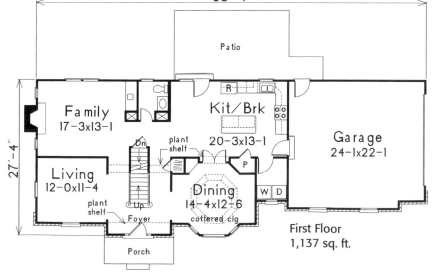

68'-4"

Patio

27'-4"

Family
17-3x13-1

Kit/Brk
20-3x13-1

Garage
24-1x22-1

Dn

plant shelf

R

P

Living
12-0x11-4

Up

plant shelf

Dining
14-4x12-6
coffered clg

W D

Foyer

Porch

First Floor
1,137 sq. ft.

Special features

1,767 total square feet of living area

- Vaulted dining room has a view onto the patio
- Master suite is vaulted with a private bath and walk-in closet
- An arched entry leads to the vaulted living room featuring tall windows and a fireplace
- 3 bedrooms, 2 1/2 baths, 2-car garage
- Basement foundation

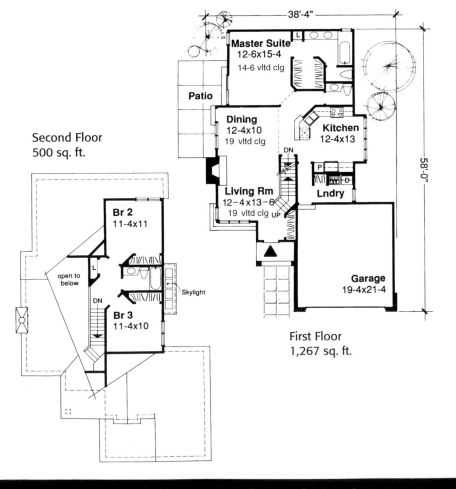

Second Floor
500 sq. ft.

38'-4"

Master Suite
12-6x15-4
14-6 vltd clg

Patio

Dining
12-4x10
19 vltd clg

Kitchen
12-4x13

DN

Living Rm
12-4x13-6
19 vltd clg UP

Lndry

58'-0"

Garage
19-4x21-4

Br 2
11-4x11

open to below

Skylight

DN

Br 3
11-4x10

First Floor
1,267 sq. ft.

Special features

1,283 total square feet of living area

- Vaulted breakfast room has sliding doors that open onto the deck
- Kitchen features a convenient corner sink and pass-through to the dining room
- Open living atmosphere in dining area and great room
- Vaulted great room features a fireplace
- 3 bedrooms, 2 baths, 2-car garage
- Basement foundation

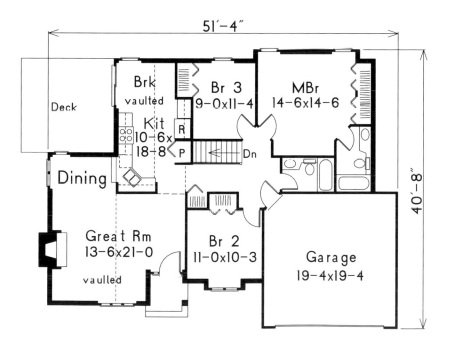

51'-4"

40'-8"

Deck

Brk
vaulted

Br 3
9-0x11-4

MBr
14-6x14-6

Kit
10-6x
18-8

R

P

Dn

Dining

Great Rm
13-6x21-0
vaulted

Br 2
11-0x10-3

Garage
19-4x19-4

Special features

2,089 total square feet of living area

- Family room features a fireplace, built-in bookshelves and triple sliders opening to the covered patio
- Kitchen overlooks the family room and features a pantry and desk
- Separated from the three secondary bedrooms, the master bedroom becomes a quiet retreat with patio access
- Master bedroom features an oversized bath with walk-in closet and corner tub
- 4 bedrooms, 3 baths, 2-car garage
- Slab foundation

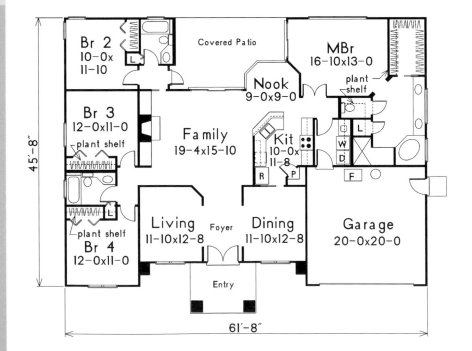

Second Floor
574 sq. ft.

First Floor
1,080 sq. ft.

Special features

1,654 total square feet of living area

- This country inspired home has plenty of quality space for family living
- A large extended counter in the kitchen creates instant dining space
- The second floor consists of a bedroom, full bath and a private loft
- 3 bedrooms, 2 baths
- Slab foundation

Special features

1,630 total square feet of living area

- Crisp facade and full windows front and back offer open viewing
- Wrap-around rear deck is accessible from the breakfast room, dining room and master bedroom
- Vaulted ceilings top the living room and master bedroom
- Sitting area and large walk-in closet complement the master bedroom
- 3 bedrooms, 2 baths, 2-car garage
- Basement foundation

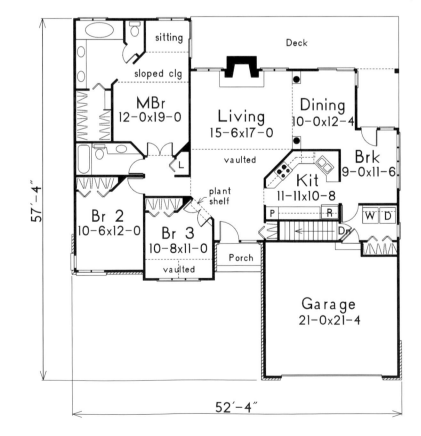

Second Floor
199 sq. ft.

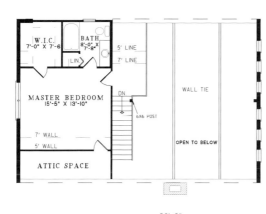

First Floor
1,392 sq. ft.

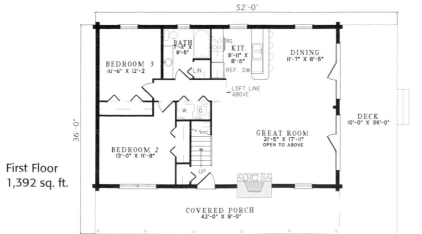

Special features

1,591 total square feet of living area

- Expansive beams span the length of the great room and dining area adding rustic appeal
- Private master bedroom has a walk-in closet and bath
- Central first floor laundry and full bath
- 3 bedrooms, 2 baths
- Crawl space foundation

QUICK FACT - Adjustable plastic coated wire shelving mounted above the washer and dryer is great for drying clothes when you have limited space. When not in use as a drying rack, the shelving can serve as extra storage space for detergent, starch and your iron.

Special features

1,606 total square feet of living area

- Kitchen has a snack bar which overlooks the dining area for convenience
- Master bedroom has lots of windows with a private bath and large walk-in closet
- Cathedral vault in the great room adds spaciousness
- 3 bedrooms, 2 baths, 2-car garage
- Slab foundation

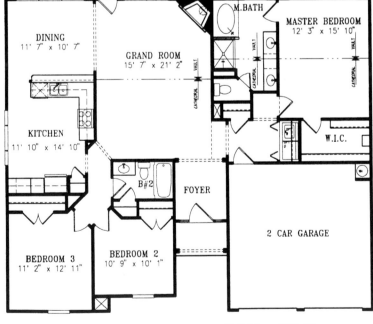

Width: 50'-0"
Depth: 42'-0"

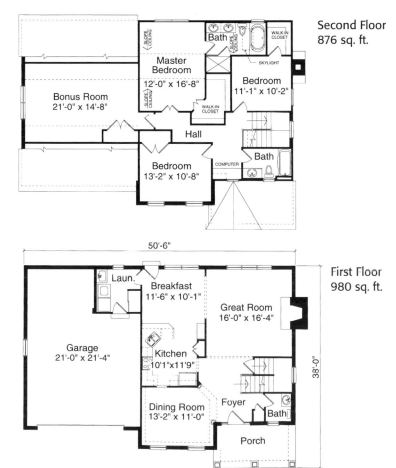

Second Floor
876 sq. ft.

First Floor
980 sq. ft.

Special features

1,856 total square feet of living area

- The roomy kitchen offers an abundance of cabinets and counterspace as well as a convenient pantry
- Master bedroom includes a sloped ceiling and a deluxe bath
- Bonus room on the second floor has an additional 325 square feet of living area
- 3 bedrooms, 2 1/2 baths, 2-car garage
- Basement foundation

Special features

1,420 total square feet of living area

- Energy efficient home with 2" x 6" exterior walls
- Living room has a 12' ceiling, corner fireplace and atrium doors leading to the covered porch
- Secluded master suite has a garden bath and walk-in closet
- 3 bedrooms, 2 baths, 2-car garage
- Slab foundation, drawings also include crawl space foundation

Second Floor
1,124 sq. ft.

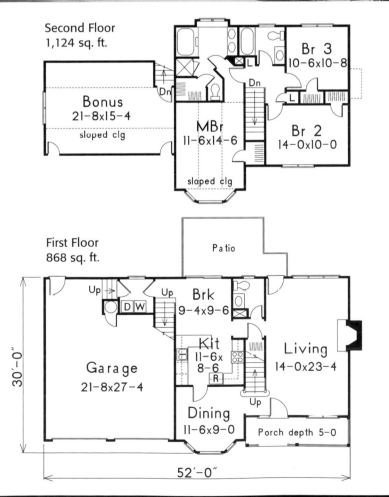

Bonus
21-8x15-4
sloped clg

Br 3
10-6x10-8

MBr
11-6x14-6

Br 2
14-0x10-0

sloped clg

First Floor
868 sq. ft.

Patio

Brk
9-4x9-6

Kit
11-6x
8-6

Living
14-0x23-4

Garage
21-8x27-4

Dining
11-6x9-0

Porch depth 5-0

30'-0"

52'-0"

Special features

1,992 total square feet of living area

- Distinct living, dining and breakfast areas
- Master bedroom boasts a full-end bay window and a cathedral ceiling
- Storage and laundry area are located adjacent to the garage
- Bonus room over the garage for future office or playroom is included in the square footage
- 3 bedrooms, 2 1/2 baths, 2-car garage
- Crawl space foundation, drawings also include basement foundation

Special features

1,533 total square feet of living area

- Multiple gables and stonework deliver a warm and inviting exterior
- The vaulted great room has a fireplace and spectacular views accomplished with a two-story atrium window wall
- A covered rear porch is easily accessed from the breakfast room or garage
- The atrium provides an ideal approach to an optional finished walk-out basement
- 3 bedrooms, 2 baths, 2-car garage
- Walk-out basement foundation

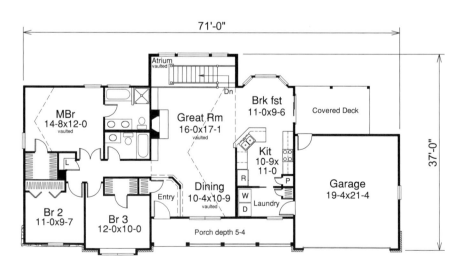

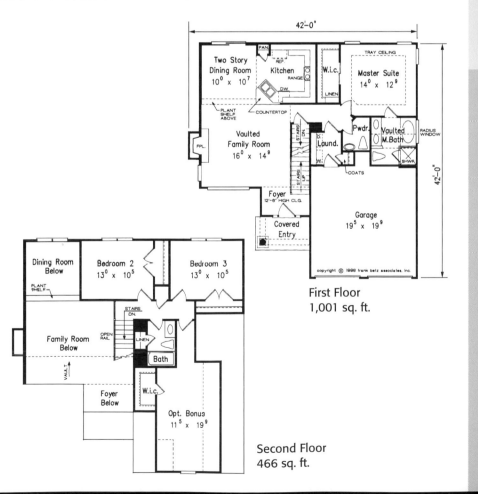

First Floor
1,001 sq. ft.

Second Floor
466 sq. ft.

Special features

1,467 total square feet of living area

- 9' ceilings throughout this home
- Two-story family and dining rooms are open and airy
- Bonus room above the garage has an additional 292 square feet of living area
- 3 bedrooms, 2 1/2 baths, 2-car garage
- Walk-out basement, slab or crawl space foundation, please specify when ordering

Special features

1,870 total square feet of living area

- Kitchen is open to the living and dining areas
- Breakfast area has a cathedral ceiling creating a sunroom effect
- Master bedroom is spacious with all the amenities
- Second floor bedrooms share a hall bath
- 3 bedrooms, 2 1/2 baths, 2-car drive under garage
- Basement foundation

Second Floor
711 sq. ft.

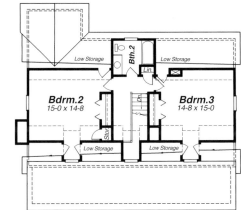

First Floor
1,159 sq. ft.

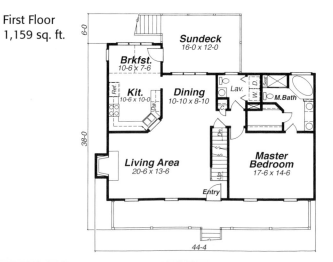

Second Floor
691 sq. ft.

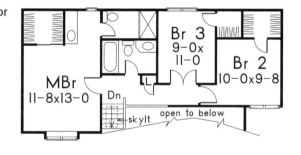

Special features

1,359 total square feet of living area

- Covered porch, stone chimney and abundant windows lend an outdoor appeal
- The spacious and bright kitchen has a pass-through to the formal dining room
- Large walk-in closets can be found in all bedrooms
- Extensive deck expands dining and entertaining areas
- 3 bedrooms, 2 1/2 baths, 2-car garage
- Basement foundation

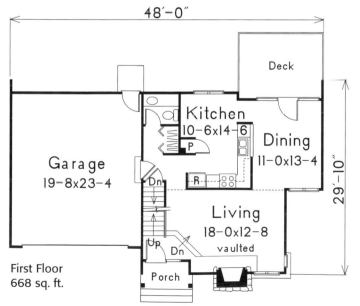

First Floor
668 sq. ft.

Special features

1,816 total square feet of living area

- This inviting home has country styling with upscale features
- The front and rear covered porches add usable outdoor living space
- The master bedroom has a raised ceiling and opens into the well-equipped bath with dual lavatories, a corner tub and walk-in closet
- The bonus room above the garage has an additional 302 square feet of living area
- 3 bedrooms, 2 baths, 2-car side entry garage
- Basement foundation

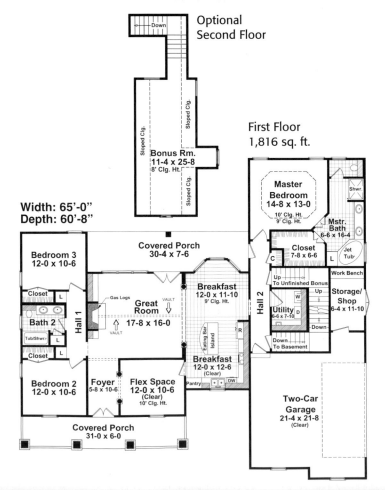

Optional Second Floor

Bonus Rm.
11-4 x 25-8
8' Clg. Ht.

Sloped Clg.

First Floor
1,816 sq. ft.

Width: 65'-0"
Depth: 60'-8"

Master Bedroom
14-8 x 13-0
10' Clg. Ht.
9' Clg. Ht.

Mstr. Bath
6-6 x 16-4

Shwr.

Jet Tub

Closet
7-8 x 6-6

Work Bench

Bedroom 3
12-0 x 10-6

Closet

Bath 2

Tub/Shwr.

Closet

Gas Logs

Great Room
17-8 x 16-0
VAULT

Hall 1

Breakfast
12-0 x 11-10
9' Clg. Ht.

Eating Bar Island

Hall 2

Up To Unfinished Bonus

Utility
6-6 x 7-10

Storage/Shop
6-4 x 11-10

Down To Basement

Covered Porch
30-4 x 7-6

Bedroom 2
12-0 x 10-6

Foyer
5-8 x 10-6

Flex Space
12-0 x 10-6
(Clear)
10' Clg. Ht.

Pantry

Breakfast
12-0 x 12-6
(Clear)

DW

Two-Car Garage
21-4 x 21-8
(Clear)

Covered Porch
31-0 x 6-0

Special features

1,442 total square feet of living area

- Energy efficient home with 2" x 6" exterior walls
- Kitchen accesses bayed area and porch which provide a cozy atmosphere
- Open living area makes relaxing a breeze
- 3 bedrooms, 2 baths
- Basement foundation

Second Floor
520 sq. ft.

First Floor
922 sq. ft.

QUICK FACT - Ceiling fans can save energy in both the summer and the winter. In the summer, fan blades should revolve in a counterclockwise direction. In winter months, set your fan at its slowest speed and reverse it in order to push warm air down.

Special features

1,177 total square feet of living area

- The vaulted master bedroom enjoys two walk-in closets, a whirlpool tub and a double vanity
- A grand fireplace flanked by windows graces the spacious family room
- Kitchen and breakfast area combine for a relaxing atmosphere and feature access onto the rear patio
- 3 bedrooms, 2 baths, 2-car side entry garage
- Slab foundation

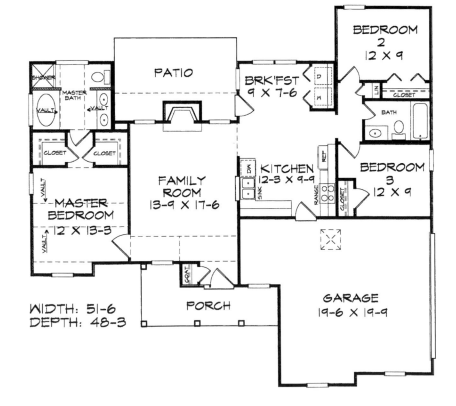

WIDTH: 51-6
DEPTH: 48-3

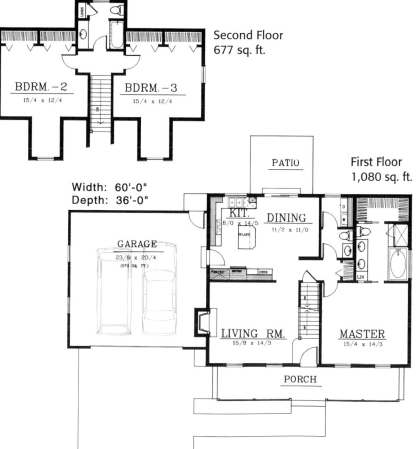

Second Floor
677 sq. ft.

BDRM.—2
15/4 x 12/4

BDRM.—3
15/4 x 12/4

Width: 60'-0"
Depth: 36'-0"

First Floor
1,080 sq. ft.

PATIO

GARAGE
23/8 x 23/4
(670 SQ. FT.)

KIT.
8/0 x 14/5

DINING
11/2 x 11/0

LIVING RM.
15/8 x 14/3

MASTER
15/4 x 14/3

PORCH

Special features

1,757 total square feet of living area

- Energy efficient home with 2" x 6" exterior walls
- First floor master bedroom has privacy as well as its own bath and walk-in closet
- Cozy living room includes fireplace for warmth
- 3 bedrooms, 2 1/2 baths, 2-car garage
- Crawl space, basement or slab foundation, please specify when ordering

Special features

1,611 total square feet of living area

- Sliding doors lead to a delightful screened porch creating a wonderful summer retreat
- Master bedroom has a lavishly appointed dressing room and large walk-in closet
- The kitchen offers an abundance of cabinets and counterspace with convenient access to the laundry room and garage
- 3 bedrooms, 2 baths, 2-car side entry garage
- Basement foundation

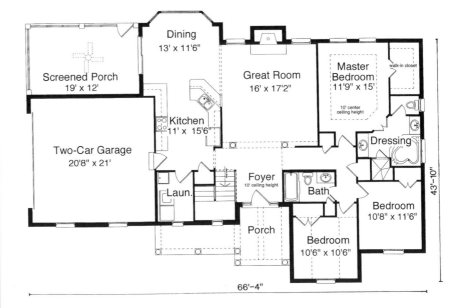

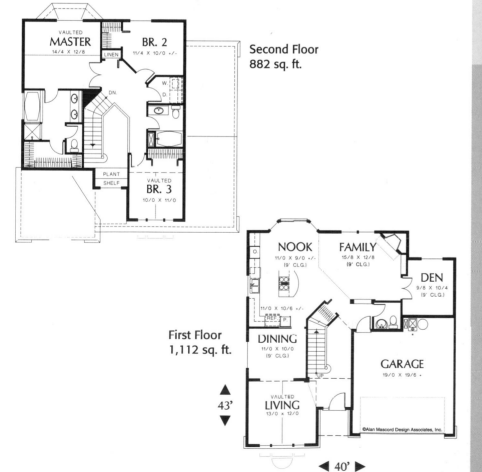

Second Floor
882 sq. ft.

VAULTED
MASTER
14/4 X 12/8

BR. 2
11/4 X 10/0 +/-

LINEN

DN.

W.
D.

PLANT
SHELF

VAULTED
BR. 3
10/0 X 11/0

First Floor
1,112 sq. ft.

NOOK
11/0 X 9/0 +/-
(9' CLG.)

FAMILY
15/8 X 12/8
(9' CLG.)

DEN
9/8 X 10/4
(9' CLG.)

11/0 X 10/6 +/-

REF. P.

DINING
11/0 X 10/0
(9' CLG.)

GARAGE
19/0 X 19/6

43'

VAULTED
LIVING
13/0 X 12/0

40'

©Alan Mascord Design Associates, Inc.

Special features

1,994 total square feet of living area

- Energy efficient home with 2" x 6" exterior walls
- Breakfast nook overlooks the kitchen and great room creating an airy feeling
- A double-door entry off the family room leads to a cozy den ideal as a home office
- Master suite has a walk-in closet and private bath
- 3 bedrooms, 2 1/2 baths, 2-car garage
- Crawl space foundation

Special features

1,310 total square feet of living area

- The combination of brick quoins, roof dormers and an elegant porch creates a classic look
- Open-space floor plan has vaulted kitchen, living and dining rooms
- The master bedroom is vaulted and enjoys privacy from other bedrooms
- A spacious laundry room is convenient to the kitchen and master bedroom with access to an oversized garage
- 3 bedrooms, 2 baths, 2-car garage
- Basement foundation, drawings also include crawl space and slab foundations

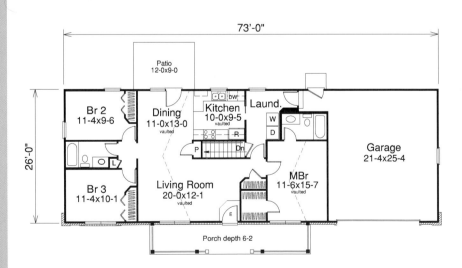

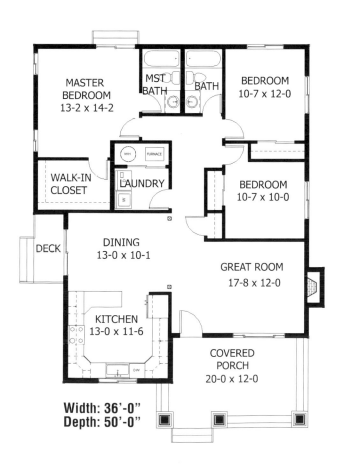

MASTER BEDROOM
13-2 x 14-2

MST BATH

BATH

BEDROOM
10-7 x 12-0

WALK-IN CLOSET

WH

FURNACE

LAUNDRY

BEDROOM
10-7 x 10-0

DECK

DINING
13-0 x 10-1

GREAT ROOM
17-8 x 12-0

KITCHEN
13-0 x 11-6

DW

COVERED PORCH
20-0 x 12-0

Width: 36'-0"
Depth: 50'-0"

Special features

1,388 total square feet of living area

- A stone-lined covered porch adds a superb outdoor living area and decorates the exterior
- The efficient kitchen offers a counter that opens to the dining room and enjoys the great room nearby
- A lovely master bedroom retreat is equipped with a private bath, walk-in closet and sliding glass doors leading to the rear yard
- 3 bedrooms, 2 baths
- Crawl space foundation

Special features

1,544 total square feet of living area

- Great room has a vaulted ceiling and fireplace
- 32' x 8' grilling porch in rear also features a supply room and a cleaning table with sink
- Kitchen features a center island
- 3 bedrooms, 2 baths
- Crawl space or slab foundation, please specify when ordering

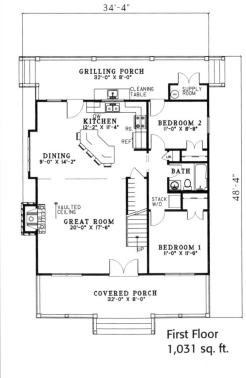

First Floor
1,031 sq. ft.

Second Floor
513 sq. ft.

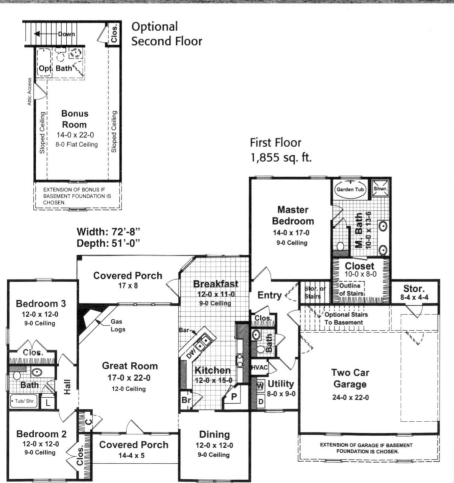

Optional Second Floor

Down | Clos.

Opt. Bath

Attic Access | Sloped Ceiling | Sloped Ceiling

Bonus Room
14-0 x 22-0
8-0 Flat Ceiling

EXTENSION OF BONUS IF BASEMENT FOUNDATION IS CHOSEN.

First Floor
1,855 sq. ft.

Garden Tub | Shwr.

Master Bedroom
14-0 x 17-0
9-0 Ceiling

M. Bath
10-0 x 13-6

Closet
10-0 x 8-0

Width: 72'-8"
Depth: 51'-0"

Covered Porch
17 x 8

Breakfast
12-0 x 11-0
9-0 Ceiling

Entry

Stor. or Stairs

Outline of Stairs

Stor.
8-4 x 4-4

Bedroom 3
12-0 x 12-0
9-0 Ceiling

Gas Logs

Clos.

Bar

Clos.

Bath

Optional Stairs To Basement

Great Room
17-0 x 22-0
12-0 Ceiling

DW

Kitchen
12-0 x 15-0

HVAC

Two Car Garage
24-0 x 22-0

Bath
Tub/ Shr.

Clos.

Hall

L

Br

P

Utility
8-0 x 9-0

W
D

Bedroom 2
12-0 x 12-0
9-0 Ceiling

Clos.

C

Covered Porch
14-4 x 5

Dining
12-0 x 12-0
9-0 Ceiling

EXTENSION OF GARAGE IF BASEMENT FOUNDATION IS CHOSEN.

Special features

1,855 total square feet of living area

- The great room boasts a 12' ceiling and corner fireplace
- Bayed breakfast area adjoins the kitchen that features a walk-in pantry
- The relaxing master bedroom includes a private bath with walk-in closet and garden tub
- Optional second floor has an additional 352 square feet of living area
- 3 bedrooms, 2 1/2 baths, 2-car side entry garage
- Basement, crawl space or slab foundation, please specify when ordering

Special features

1,833 total square feet of living area

- Large master bedroom includes a spacious bath with garden tub, separate shower and large walk-in closet
- The spacious dining area is brightened by large windows and patio access
- Detached two-car garage with walkway leading to house adds charm to this country home
- 3 bedrooms, 2 1/2 baths, 2-car detached side entry garage
- Crawl space foundation, drawings also include slab foundation

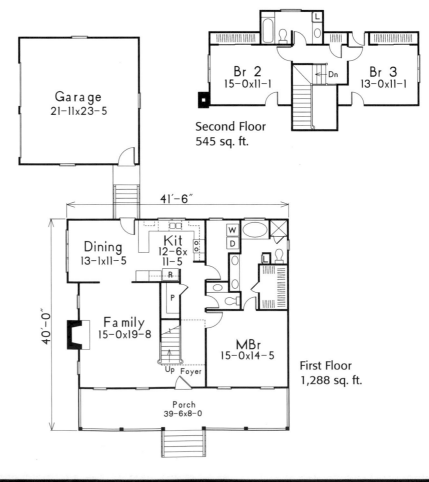

Garage
21-11x23-5

Br 2
15-0x11-1

Br 3
13-0x11-1

Second Floor
545 sq. ft.

41'-6"

Dining
13-1x11-5

Kit
12-6x
11-5

Family
15-0x19-8

MBr
15-0x14-5

Up Foyer

40'-0"

First Floor
1,288 sq. ft.

Porch
39-6x8-0

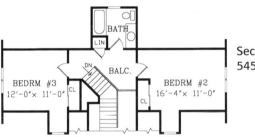

Second Floor
545 sq. ft.

BATH

LIN

DN BALC.

BEDRM #3
12'-0" x 11'-0"

CL

CL

BEDRM #2
16'-4" x 11'-0"

UP

© Jerold Axelrod, Architect

COVERED PORCH
37'-0" x 10'-0"

First Floor
1,134 sq. ft.

KITCHEN
12'-8" x
14'-6"

MUD RM

W

DW

MSTR BEDRM
12'-0" x 16'-0"

REF

CLOS W/O BSMT

CLOS OR BUILT-IN

9'-4" HIGH STEP'D CEIL

GREAT ROOM
14'/18'-0" x
26'-4"

DN DW

UP

CL

BUILT-IN FOR T.V.

WICL

MSTR BATH

9'-4" HI CEIL

VAULTED FOYER

LAV

COVERED PORCH
37'-0" x 8'-0"

UP

Width 42'-0"
Depth 45'-0"

Special features

1,679 total square feet of living area

- Wide, angled spaces in both the great room and the master bedroom create roomy appeal and year-round comfort
- Amenities in the luxurious master bedroom include a large walk-in closet, a whirlpool bath and double-vanity
- The nicely appointed kitchen offers nearby laundry facilities and porch access
- 3 bedrooms, 2 1/2 baths, 2-car drive under garage
- Basement, crawl space or slab foundation, please specify when ordering

Special features

1,591 total square feet of living area

- Energy efficient home with 2" x 6" exterior walls
- Fireplace in great room is accented by windows on both sides
- Practical kitchen is splendidly designed for organization
- Large screen porch is ideal for three-season entertaining
- 3 bedrooms, 2 baths, 3-car garage
- Basement foundation

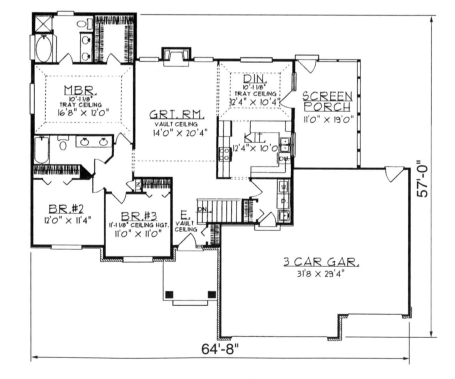

Special features

1,301 total square feet of living area

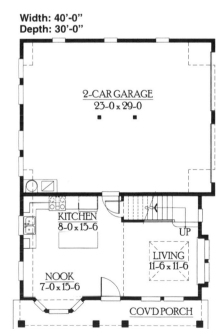

Width: 40'-0"
Depth: 30'-0"

2-CAR GARAGE
23-0 x 29-0

KITCHEN
8-0 x 15-6

UP

LIVING
11-6 x 11-6

NOOK
7-0 x 15-6

COV'D PORCH

First Floor
472 sq. ft.

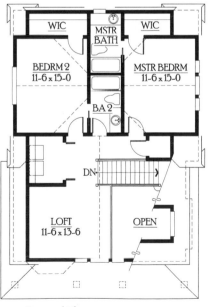

WIC

MSTR
BATH

WIC

BEDRM 2
11-6 x 15-0

MSTR BEDRM
11-6 x 15-0

BA 2

DN

LOFT
11-6 x 13-6

OPEN

Second Floor
829 sq. ft.

- Energy efficient home with 2" x 6" exterior walls
- This charming cottage features an open family center with living room, bayed nook and kitchen with island
- Both bedrooms enjoy walk-in closets for easy organization
- A loft area and laundry closet add convenience and style to the second floor
- 2 bedrooms, 2 baths, 2-car side entry garage
- Slab foundation

Special features

828 total square feet of living area

- Vaulted ceiling in living area enhances space
- Convenient laundry room
- Sloped ceiling creates unique style in bedroom #2
- Efficient storage space under the stairs
- Covered entry porch provides a cozy sitting area and plenty of shade
- 2 bedrooms, 1 bath
- Crawl space foundation

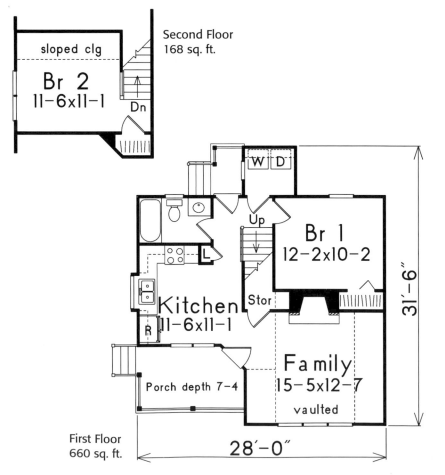

Second Floor
168 sq. ft.

sloped clg

Br 2
11-6x11-1

Dn

W D

Up

Br 1
12-2x10-2

31'-6"

Kitchen
11-6x11-1

Stor

L

R

Porch depth 7-4

Family
15-5x12-7
vaulted

First Floor
660 sq. ft.

28'-0"

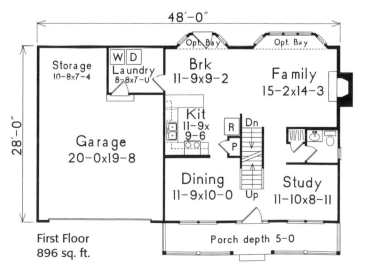

Second Floor
784 sq. ft.

Br 2
11-8x10-9

L

Dn

Br 3
11-8x10-9

MBr
11-10x15-0

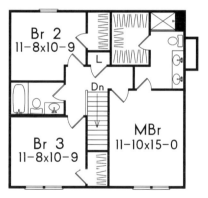

48'-0"

28'-0"

Storage
10-8x7-4

W D
Laundry
8-8x7-0

Brk
11-9x9-2

Family
15-2x14-3

Kit
11-9x
9-6

R

Dn

P

Garage
20-0x19-8

Dining
11-9x10-0

Up

Study
11-10x8-11

First Floor
896 sq. ft.

Porch depth 5-0

Special features

1,680 total square feet of living area

- Compact and efficient layout in an affordable package
- Second floor has three bedrooms all with oversized closets
- All bedrooms are located on the second floor for privacy
- 3 bedrooms, 2 1/2 baths, 2-car garage
- Basement foundation

QUICK FACT - Protect against sparks by enclosing a fireplace's opening with glass doors or a sturdy screen. Never close the flue while a fire is still smoldering. Carbon monoxide can build up.

Special features

1,285 total square feet of living area

- Energy efficient home with 2" x 6" exterior walls
- Dining and living areas both access a large wrap-around porch
- First floor bath has convenient laundry closet as well as a shower
- 2 bedrooms, 2 baths
- Basement foundation

QUICK FACT - Draperies are getting longer and longer. One of the best ways to add height to any room is to place window treatments just below the ceiling line. Use this designer trick in any room that could use a little lift.

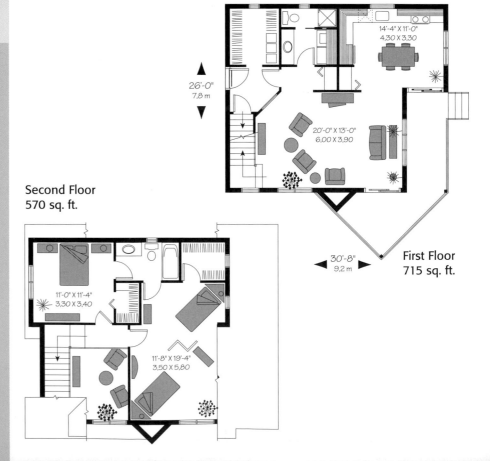

Second Floor
570 sq. ft.

14'-4" X 11'-0"
4,30 X 3,30

26'-0"
7,8 m

20'-0" X 13'-0"
6,00 X 3,90

30'-8"
9,2 m

First Floor
715 sq. ft.

11'-0" X 11'-4"
3,30 X 3,40

11'-8" X 19'-4"
3,50 X 5,80

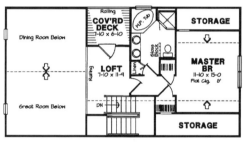

Second Floor
500 sq. ft.

First Floor
1,062 sq. ft.

Optional
Lower Level

Special features

1,562 total square feet of living area

- Energy efficient home with 2" x 6" exterior walls
- Access the large deck from two sets of French doors which fill the home with sunlight
- Kitchen with breakfast bar allows for additional dining space
- Unique second floor loft is open to the first floor and has a private covered deck
- Optional lower level has an additional 678 square feet of living area
- 3 bedrooms, 2 baths
- Walk-out basement foundation

Special features

1,677 total square feet of living area

- Master suite has a secluded feel with a private and remote location from other bedrooms
- Great room is complete with fireplace and beautiful windows
- Optional second floor has an additional 350 square feet of living area
- 3 bedrooms, 2 baths, 2-car side entry garage
- Slab foundation

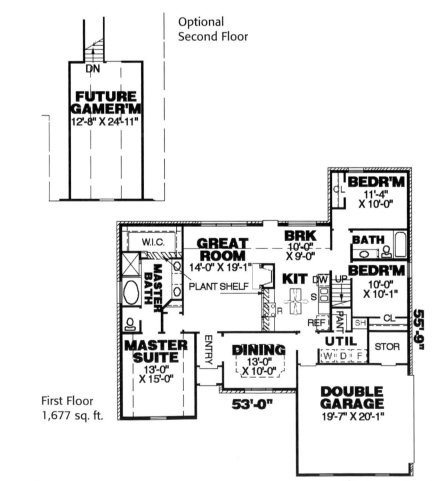

Optional Second Floor

FUTURE GAMER'M
12'-8" X 24'-11"

DN

BEDR'M
11'-4" X 10'-0"

W.I.C.

MASTER BATH

GREAT ROOM
14'-0" X 19'-1"

PLANT SHELF

BRK
10'-0" X 9'-0"

BATH

KIT

BEDR'M
10'-0" X 10'-1"

MASTER SUITE
13'-0" X 15'-0"

ENTRY

DINING
13'-0" X 10'-0"

UTIL

STOR

DOUBLE GARAGE
19'-7" X 20'-1"

First Floor
1,677 sq. ft.

53'-0"

55'-9"

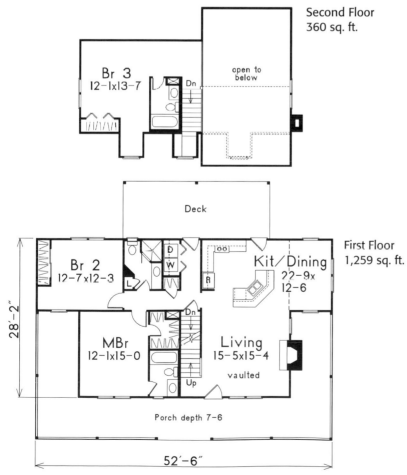

Second Floor
360 sq. ft.

Br 3
12-1x13-7

open to
below

Dn

Deck

First Floor
1,259 sq. ft.

Br 2
12-7x12-3

D

W

L

Kit/Dining
22-9x
12-6

R

28'-2"

MBr
12-1x15-0

Dn

Living
15-5x15-4

vaulted

Up

Porch depth 7-6

52'-6"

Special features

1,619 total square feet of living area

- Private second floor bedroom and bath
- Kitchen features a snack bar and adjacent dining area
- Master bedroom has a private bath
- Centrally located washer and dryer
- 3 bedrooms, 3 baths
- Basement foundation, drawings also include crawl space and slab foundations

Special features

1,453 total square feet of living area

- Decorative vents, window trim, shutters and brick blend to create dramatic curb appeal
- Energy efficient home with 2" x 6" exterior walls
- Kitchen opens to the living area and includes a salad sink in the island as well as a pantry and handy laundry room
- Exquisite master bedroom is highlighted by a vaulted ceiling, dressing area with walk-in closet, private bath and spa tub/shower
- 3 bedrooms, 2 baths, 2-car garage
- Basement foundation, drawings also include crawl space foundation

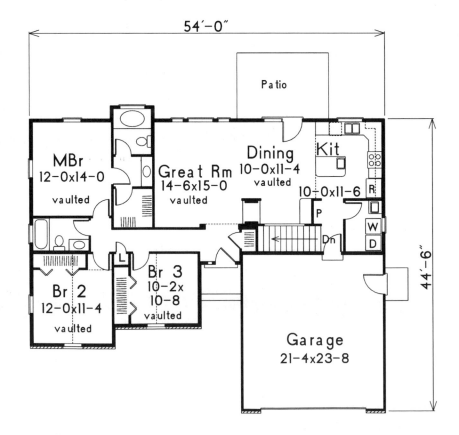

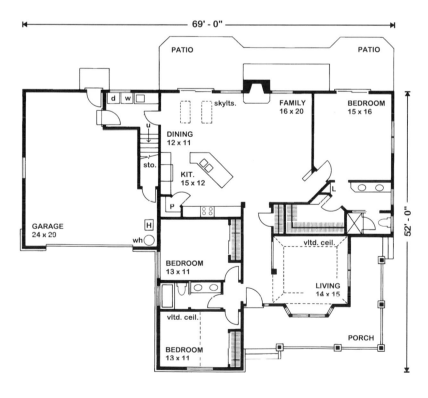

Special features

2,000 total square feet of living area

- Energy efficient home with 2" x 6" exterior walls
- The bright foyer leads to an oversized living area supplied with a vaulted ceiling, skylights, hearth fireplace and sliding doors to the rear patio
- The convenient kitchen boasts a large pantry, breakfast bar and has the laundry area nearby
- The master bedroom is located at the rear of the home and enjoys a vaulted ceiling, luxury bath and patio access
- 3 bedrooms, 2 baths, 2-car garage
- Crawl space foundation

Special features

1,595 total square feet of living area

- Large great room features a tray ceiling and French doors to a screened porch
- Dining room and bedroom #2 have bay windows
- Master bedroom has a tray ceiling and a bay window
- 3 bedrooms, 2 baths, 2-car side entry garage
- Basement, crawl space, slab or walk-out basement foundation, please specify when ordering

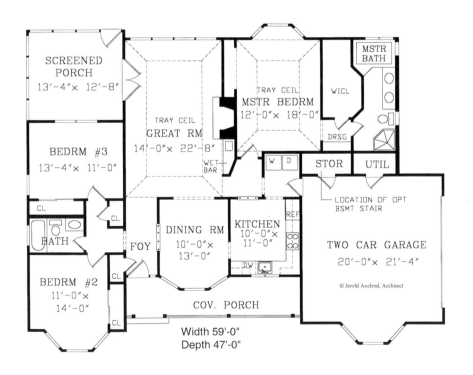

SCREENED PORCH
13'-4" x 12'-8"

MSTR BATH

TRAY CEIL
MSTR BEDRM
12'-0" x 18'-0"

WICL

TRAY CEIL
GREAT RM
14'-0" x 22'-8"

DRSG

BEDRM #3
13'-4" x 11'-0"

WET-BAR

W   D

STOR   UTIL

CL

CL

BATH

FOY

DINING RM
10'-0" x 13'-0"

KITCHEN
10'-0" x 11'-0"

REF

LOCATION OF OPT
BSMT STAIR

TWO CAR GARAGE
20'-0" x 21'-4"

BEDRM #2
11'-0" x 14'-0"

CL

DW

© Jerold Axelrod, Architect

CL

COV. PORCH

Width 59'-0"
Depth 47'-0"

Special features

2,133 total square feet of living area

- Master suite is separate from other bedrooms for privacy
- Large hearth room shares a see-through fireplace with an open, airy great room
- Efficiently designed kitchen
- 3 bedrooms, 2 baths, 2-car side entry garage
- Crawl space or slab foundation, please specify when ordering

Special features

1,599 total square feet of living area

- Spacious entry leads to the great room featuring a vaulted ceiling, fireplace and an octagon-shaped dining area with views to the covered patio
- The kitchen enjoys a snack counter open to the dining area, a breakfast area with bay window and a built-in pantry
- Master bedroom has a sitting area, large walk-in closet and a luxury bath
- The laundry room has a convenient half bath and access to the garage with storage area
- 4 bedrooms, 2 1/2 baths, 2-car garage
- Basement foundation

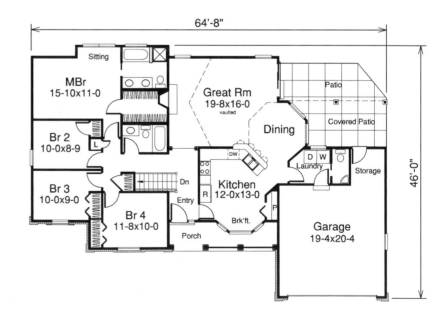

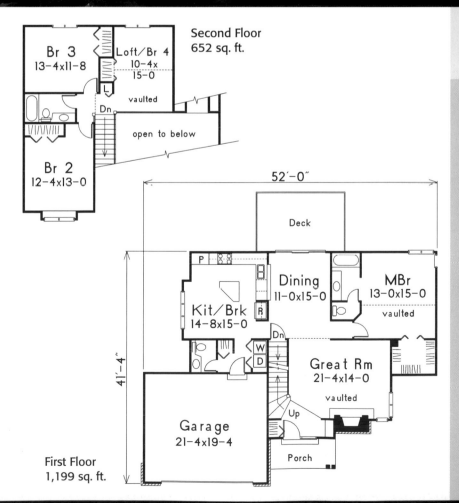

Second Floor
652 sq. ft.

Br 3
13-4x11-8

Loft/Br 4
10-4x
15-0

vaulted

Dn

open to below

Br 2
12-4x13-0

52'-0"

Deck

41'-4"

P

Kit/Brk
14-8x15-0

R

Dining
11-0x15-0

MBr
13-0x15-0

vaulted

Dn

W
D

Great Rm
21-4x14-0

vaulted

Garage
21-4x19-4

Up

Porch

First Floor
1,199 sq. ft.

Special features

1,851 total square feet of living area

- High-impact entrance to great room also leads directly to the second floor
- First floor master bedroom suite with corner window and walk-in closet
- Kitchen/breakfast room has a center work island and pass-through to the dining room
- Second floor bedrooms share a bath
- 4 bedrooms, 2 1/2 baths, 2-car garage
- Basement foundation

Special features

1,143 total square feet of living area

- Energy efficient home with 2" x 6" exterior walls
- Enormous stone fireplace in the family room adds warmth and character
- Spacious kitchen with breakfast bar overlooks the family room
- Separate dining area is great for entertaining
- Vaulted family room and kitchen create an open atmosphere
- 2 bedrooms, 1 bath
- Crawl space foundation

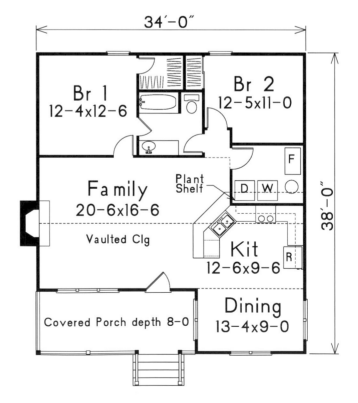

34'-0"

Br 1
12-4x12-6

Br 2
12-5x11-0

Family
20-6x16-6

Plant Shelf

F

D W

Vaulted Clg

Kit
12-6x9-6

R

38'-0"

Covered Porch depth 8-0

Dining
13-4x9-0

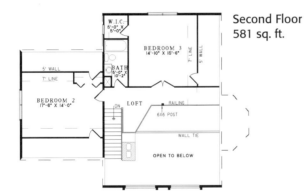

Second Floor
581 sq. ft.

First Floor
1,556 sq. ft.

Special features

2,137 total square feet of living area

- Bay windowed sitting area is a cheerful nook located near main living areas
- Large counter creates plenty of dining area for a large crowd
- Private loft area on the second floor overlooks to the great room below
- 3 bedrooms, 2 1/2 baths
- Crawl space, basement or walk-out basement foundation, please specify when ordering

QUICK FACT - Oak is the most common type of flooring in the United States. Red oak has salmon tones while white oak is more ashen. Oak accepts just about every finish, installs easily and withstands heavy foot traffic. Oak floor boards can blacken if exposed to moisture, so do not install it in kitchens or bathrooms.

Special features

576 total square feet of living area

- Perfect country retreat features vaulted living room and entry with skylights and a plant shelf above
- A double-door entry leads to the vaulted bedroom with bath access
- Kitchen offers generous storage and a pass-through breakfast bar
- 1 bedroom, 1 bath
- Crawl space foundation

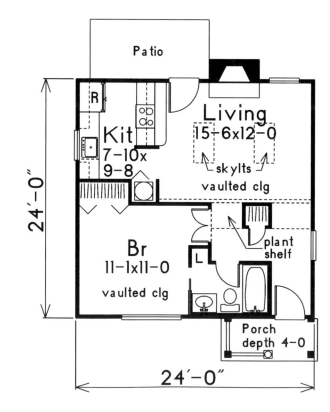

Patio

Kit
7-10x
9-8

Living
15-6x12-0
skylts
vaulted clg

Br
11-1x11-0
vaulted clg

plant shelf

24'-0"

24'-0"

Porch
depth 4-0

Second Floor
527 sq. ft.

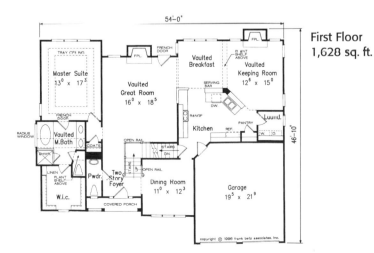

First Floor
1,628 sq. ft.

Special features

2,155 total square feet of living area

- Vaulted breakfast and keeping rooms create an informal area off the kitchen
- All bedrooms have walk-in closets
- Optional bonus room on the second floor has an additional 207 square feet of living area
- 3 bedrooms, 2 1/2 baths, 2-car garage
- Walk-out basement, slab or crawl space foundation, please specify when ordering

Special features

1,260 total square feet of living area

- Spacious kitchen and dining area features a large pantry, storage area and easy access to the garage and laundry room
- Pleasant covered front porch adds a practical touch
- Master bedroom with a private bath adjoins two other bedrooms, all with plenty of closet space
- 3 bedrooms, 2 baths, 2-car garage
- Basement foundation, drawings also include crawl space and slab foundations

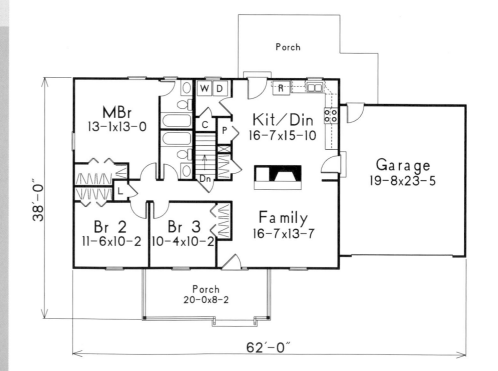

Plan #596-069D-0012

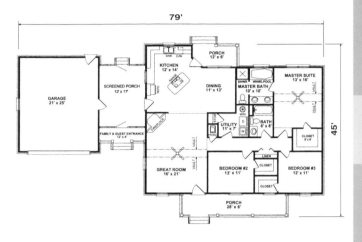

Special features

1,594 total square feet of living area

- Corner fireplace in the great room creates a cozy feel
- Spacious kitchen combines with the dining room creating a terrific gathering place
- A handy family and guest entrance is a casual and convenient way to enter the home
- 3 bedrooms, 2 baths, 2-car garage
- Slab or crawl space foundation, please specify when ordering

Plan #596-077D-0023

Price Code B

Width: 54'-0"
Depth: 47'-0"

Special features

1,426 total square feet of living area

- The charming front porch welcomes visitors
- The efficiently shaped kitchen makes it easy to prepare meals
- The roomy storage closet in the garage keeps the area organized
- 3 bedrooms, 2 baths, 2-car garage
- Slab or crawl space foundation, please specify when ordering

Special features

1,700 total square feet of living area

- Energy efficient home with 2" x 6" exterior walls
- Cozy living area has plenty of space for entertaining
- Snack bar in kitchen provides extra dining area
- 3 bedrooms, 1 1/2 baths
- Basement foundation

QUICK FACT - Flowers of one type in a vase will last longer than a bouquet of mixed varieties. Also, a single bloom will survive longer than many blossoms of the same type.

Second Floor
840 sq. ft.

11'-8" X 11'-0"
3,50 X 3,30

13'-0" X 14'-0"
3,90 X 4,20

11'-0" X 11'-0"
3,30 X 3,30

11'-0" X 10'-0"
3,30 X 3,00

9'-0" X 14'-4"
2,70 X 4,30

28'-0"
8,4 m

14'-0" X 14'-0"
4,20 X 4,20

11'-0" X 12'-0"
3,30 X 3,60

First Floor
860 sq. ft.

30'-0"
9,0 m

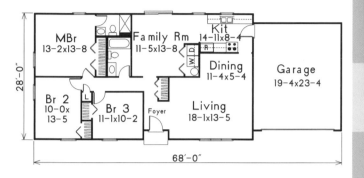

Special features

1,343 total square feet of living area

- Separate and convenient family, living and dining areas
- Master bedroom enjoys a large closet and private bath
- Foyer with convenient coat closet opens into combined living and dining rooms
- Family room has access to the outdoors through sliding glass doors
- 3 bedrooms, 2 baths, 2-car garage
- Crawl space foundation, drawings also include basement foundation

Plan #596-069D-0005

Price Code A

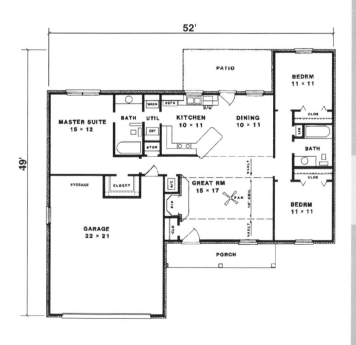

Special features

1,267 total square feet of living area

- 10' vaulted ceiling in the great room
- Open floor plan creates a spacious feeling
- Master suite is separated from the other bedrooms for privacy
- 3 bedrooms, 2 baths, 2-car garage
- Slab or crawl space foundation, please specify when ordering

Special features

809 total square feet of living area

- This attractive earth berm home is perfectly designed for a vacation retreat
- Nestled in a hillside with only one exposed exterior wall, this home offers efficiency, protection and affordability
- A large porch creates an ideal space for lazy afternoons and quiet evenings
- All rooms are very spacious and three closets plus the laundry room provide abundant storage
- 1 bedroom, 1 bath
- Slab foundation

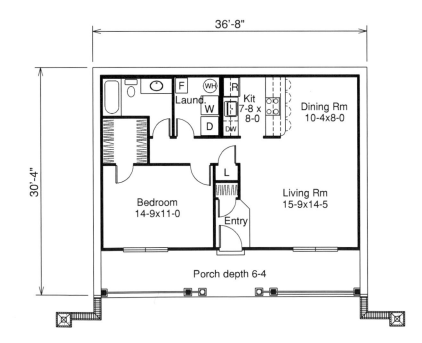

36'-8"

30'-4"

Laund.

F

WH

R

Kit 7-8 x 8-0

W

DW

D

Dining Rm 10-4x8-0

Bedroom 14-9x11-0

L

Living Rm 15-9x14-5

Entry

Porch depth 6-4

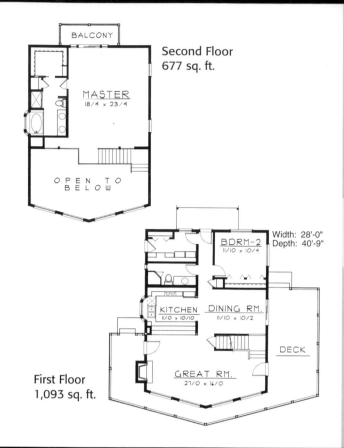

Second Floor
677 sq. ft.

BALCONY

MASTER
18/4 x 23/4

OPEN TO BELOW

Width: 28'-0"
Depth: 40'-9"

BDRM-2
11/10 x 10/4

KITCHEN
11/0 x 10/10

DINING RM.
11/10 x 10/2

DECK

GREAT RM.
27/0 x 16/0

First Floor
1,093 sq. ft.

Special features

1,770 total square feet of living area

- Energy efficient home with 2" x 6" exterior walls
- Private master bedroom on second floor has balcony, bath and large walk-in closet
- Oversized laundry room has extra storage and counterspace
- Dining room is adjacent to the kitchen making entertaining easy
- 2 bedrooms, 2 baths
- Basement or walk-out basement foundation, please specify when ordering

LAUNDRY CHUTE

HALL

GARAGE
21'-0"x22'-0"
(CARPORT OR NO GARAGE OPTIONAL)

16' OVERHEAD DOOR

WORK BENCH/STORAGE

59'-0"

PATIO
20'-0"x12'-0"

WALK-IN CLOSET

PANTRY

KITCHEN
13'-0"x10'-0"

DINING
11'-0"x10'-0"

BEDROOM #3
13'-0"x11'-10"

HALL

MSTR BATH

WDR

FRIG

COLUMNS

OPTIONAL PRIVACY DOOR (POCKET)

BATH

SITTING AREA

MASTER BEDROOM
15'-5"x16'-0"
(9' TRAY CLG)

GREAT ROOM
24'-0"x20'-0"
(9'-5" CLG)

OPTIONAL ROOM DIVIDER

BEDROOM #2
13'-0"x11'-10"

COVERED PORCH
25'-0"x8'-0"
(10' CLG)

Special features

1,698 total square feet of living area

- Large and open great room adds spaciousness to the living area
- Cheerful bayed sitting area in the master bedroom
- Compact, yet efficient kitchen
- 3 bedrooms, 2 1/2 baths, 2-car side entry garage
- Basement, crawl space or slab foundation, please specify when ordering

QUICK FACT - Counters run a close second to floors in the amount of punishment they withstand, so choose your material wisely. Plastic tops run from moderately priced laminate to costly solid acrylic that looks like marble or granite. For slicing, chopping and pounding, hardwood counters or inserts are the gourmet chef's favorite. Small scratches and nicks add character or are easy to smooth out. Hard-surface counters include tile, granite, organic glass, stainless steel and natural and synthetic marble. Any will make a good-looking heat and scratch-proof surface.

Special features

1,978 total square feet of living area

- Energy efficient home with 2" x 6" exterior walls
- Designed for a sloping lot, this multi-level home intrigues the eye
- Sunlight filters into the grand two-story foyer and living room from tall windows
- Master suite has elegant front-facing windows and a private bath
- 3 bedrooms, 2 1/2 baths, 2-car drive under garage
- Basement foundation

Second Floor
872 sq. ft.

BR. 3
11/0 X 10/8

BR. 2
11/0 X 10/0

LOFT

FOYER BELOW

LIVING BELOW

VAULTED
MASTER
15/2 X 12/0

©Alan Mascord Design Associates, Inc.

First Floor
1,106 sq. ft.

DINING
10/6 X 12/0+

NOOK
13/10 X 8/4

2 STORY
LIVING
13/0 X 14/0

FAMILY
13/10 X 20/8

DECK

38'

35'

Lower Level

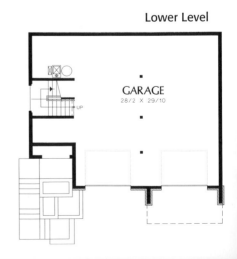

GARAGE
28/2 X 29/10

Plan #596-001D-0053

Price Code A

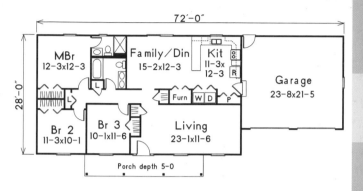

Special features

1,344 total square feet of living area

- Family/dining room has sliding glass doors to the outdoors
- Master bedroom features a private bath
- Hall bath includes a double-bowl vanity for added convenience
- U-shaped kitchen features a large pantry and laundry area
- 2" x 6" exterior walls available, please order plan #596-001D-0108
- 3 bedrooms, 2 baths, 2-car garage
- Crawl space foundation, drawings also include basement and slab foundations

Plan #596-007D-0172

Price Code B

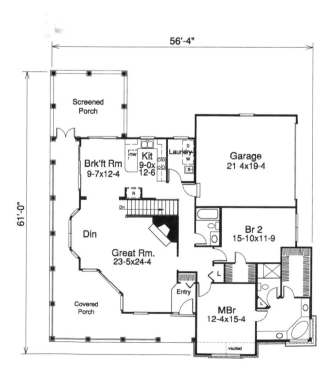

Special features

1,646 total square feet of living area

- Attractive cottage features two large porch areas
- A U-shaped kitchen with snack counter is open to the breakfast room and enjoys access to the side and rear porch
- The master bedroom has a luxury bath with corner tub, double vanities and a huge walk-in closet
- 2 bedrooms, 2 baths, 2-car side entry garage
- Basement foundation, drawings also include slab and crawl space foundations

Special features

1,440 total square feet of living area

- Foyer adjoins massive-sized great room with sloping ceiling and tall masonry fireplace
- The kitchen connects to the spacious dining room and features a pass-through to the breakfast bar
- Master bedroom enjoys a private bath and two closets
- An oversized two-car side entry garage offers plenty of storage for bicycles, lawn equipment, etc.
- 3 bedrooms, 2 baths, 2-car side entry garage
- Basement foundation, drawings also include crawl space and slab foundations

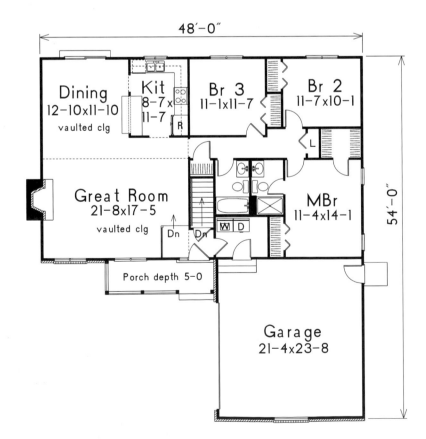

48'-0"

Dining
12-10x11-10
vaulted clg

Kit
8-7x
11-7

Br 3
11-1x11-7

Br 2
11-7x10-1

Great Room
21-8x17-5
vaulted clg

MBr
11-4x14-1

W D

Dn   Dn

54'-0"

Porch depth 5-0

Garage
21-4x23-8

Plan #596-007D-0161

Price Code A

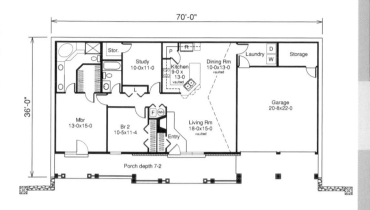

70'-0"

36'-0"

Stor.

Study 10-0x11-0

Kitchen 9-0 x 13-0 vaulted

Dining Rm 10-0x13-0 vaulted

Laundry

Storage

Garage 20-8x22-0

Mbr 13-0x15-0

Br 2 10-5x11-4

Living Rm 18-0x15-0 vaulted

Entry

Porch depth 7-2

Special features

1,480 total square feet of living area

- Home has great looks and lots of space
- Nestled in a hillside with only one exposed exterior wall, this home offers efficiency, protection and affordability
- Triple patio doors with an arched transom bathe the living room with sunlight
- The kitchen features a snack bar open to the living room, large built-in pantry and adjoins a spacious dining area
- 2 bedrooms, 2 baths, 2-car garage
- Slab foundation

Plan #596-062D-0031

Price Code AA

Width: 24'-0"
Depth: 36'-0"

br3
10'8 X 9'

8'4 X 8'
k

11'10 X 14'6
liv

8'4 X 8'
din

DECK

First Floor
672 sq. ft.

STORAGE

br2
13'8 X 9'

STORAGE

STORAGE

13'8 X 10'
mbr

BALCONY

Second Floor
401 sq. ft.

Special features

1,073 total square feet of living area

- The front-facing deck and covered balcony add to the outdoor living areas
- The fireplace is the main focus in the living room and effectively separates the living room from the dining room
- Three large storage areas are found on the second floor
- 3 bedrooms, 1 1/2 baths
- Basement or crawl space foundation, please specify when ordering

Special features

1,776 total square feet of living area

- Master bedroom has a double-door entry into the formal living room
- Large foyer has plenty of room for greeting guests
- Great room is open to the second floor and features a fireplace flanked by windows
- 3 bedrooms, 2 1/2 baths, 2-car side entry garage
- Walk-out basement foundation

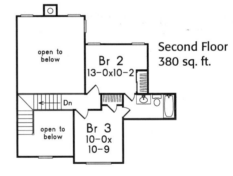

Second Floor
380 sq. ft.

Br 2
13-0x10-2

Br 3
10-0x
10-9

open to below

open to below

Dn

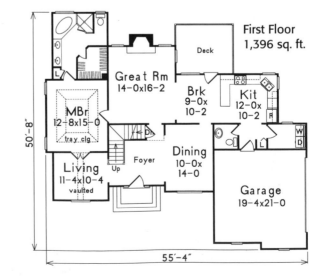

First Floor
1,396 sq. ft.

Deck

Great Rm
14-0x16-2

Brk
9-0x
10-2

Kit
12-0x
10-2

MBr
12-8x15-0
tray clg

Living
11-4x10-4
vaulted

Foyer

Up

Dining
10-0x
14-0

Garage
19-4x21-0

50'-8"

55'-4"

Plan #596-058D-0030

Price Code AA

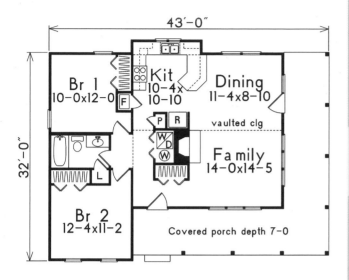

Special features

990 total square feet of living area

- Wrap-around porch creates a relaxing retreat
- Combined family and dining rooms boast a vaulted ceiling
- Space for an efficiency washer and dryer unit offers convenience
- 2" x 6" exterior walls available, please order plan #596-058D-0086
- 2 bedrooms, 1 bath
- Crawl space foundation

Plan #596-077D-0004

Price Code D

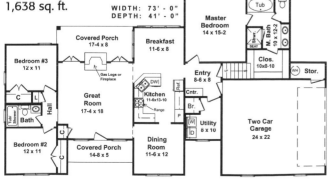

Special features

2,024 total square feet of living area

- Covered porches offer a relaxing atmosphere
- Bedrooms are separated for privacy
- The dining room provides an elegant space for entertaining
- The second floor living area and optional bath are ideal for a guest suite
- 3 bedrooms, 2 baths, 2-car side entry garage
- Basement, crawl space or slab foundation, please specify when ordering

Special features

1,707 total square feet of living area

- The formal living room off the entry hall has a high sloping ceiling and prominent fireplace
- Kitchen and breakfast area allow access to an oversized garage and rear porch
- Master bedroom has an impressive vaulted ceiling, luxurious bath, large walk-in closet and separate tub and shower
- Utility room is conveniently located near the bedrooms
- 3 bedrooms, 2 baths, 2-car garage
- Slab foundation

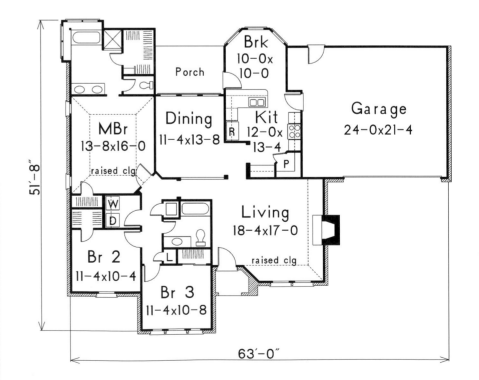

Special features

1,118 total square feet of living area

- Energy efficient home with 2" x 6" exterior walls
- Convenient kitchen has direct access into garage and looks out onto front covered porch
- The covered patio is enjoyed by both the living room and master suite
- Octagon-shaped dining room adds interest to the front exterior while the interior is sunny and bright
- 2 bedrooms, 2 baths, 2-car garage
- Slab foundation

Plan #596-076D-0009

Price Code B

Special features

1,251 total square feet of living area

- A grand corner fireplace graces the vaulted family room
- Secondary bedrooms are generously sized and are secluded from the main living area
- The bonus room on the second floor has 261 square feet of additional living area
- 3 bedrooms, 2 baths, 2-car garage
- Crawl space or slab foundation, please specify when ordering

Special features

1,484 total square feet of living area

- Energy efficient home with 2" x 6" exterior walls
- Useful screened porch is ideal for dining and relaxing
- Corner fireplace warms the living room
- Snack bar adds extra counterspace in kitchen
- 3 bedrooms, 2 baths
- Basement foundation

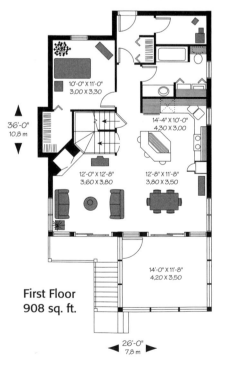

First Floor
908 sq. ft.

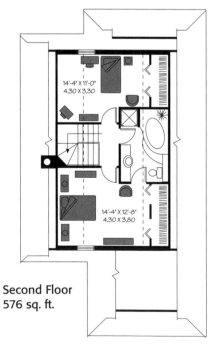

Second Floor
576 sq. ft.

Plan #596-045D-0009

Price Code B

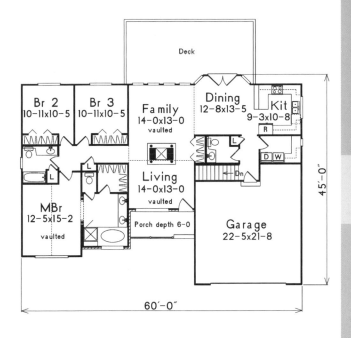

Special features

1,684 total square feet of living area

- The bayed dining area boasts convenient double-door access onto the large deck
- The family room features several large windows for brightness
- Bedrooms are separate from living areas for privacy
- Master bedroom offers a bath with walk-in closet, double-bowl vanity and both a shower and a whirlpool tub
- 3 bedrooms, 2 1/2 baths, 2-car garage
- Basement foundation

Plan #596-055D-0114

Price Code C

Special features

2,050 total square feet of living area

- Open living spaces allow for the dining area, great room and breakfast room to flow together
- Bedroom #4 has a unique design with double closets and a built-in desk
- Plenty of closet space throughout
- 4 bedrooms, 2 baths, 2-car garage
- Crawl space or slab foundation, please specify when ordering

Special features

2,100 total square feet of living area

- A large courtyard with stone walls, lantern columns and covered porch welcomes you into open spaces
- The great room features a stone fireplace, built-in shelves, vaulted ceiling and atrium with dramatic staircase and a two and a half story window wall
- Two walk-in closets, vaulted ceiling with plant shelf and a luxury bath adorn the master bedroom suite
- 1,391 square feet of optional living area on the lower level with family room, walk-in bar, sitting area, bedroom #3 and a bath
- 2 bedrooms, 2 baths, 3-car side entry garage
- Walk-out basement foundation

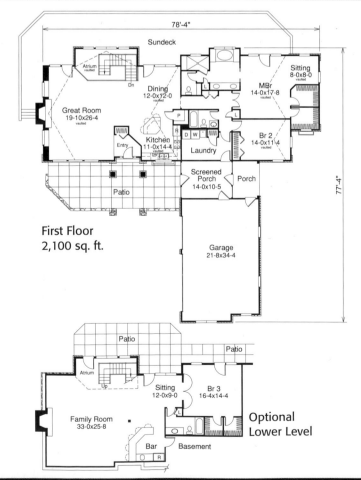

First Floor
2,100 sq. ft.

Optional
Lower Level

Plan #596-001D-0092

Price Code B

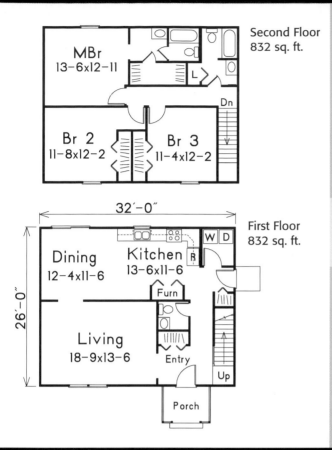

Second Floor
832 sq. ft.

MBr
13-6x12-11

Br 2
11-8x12-2

Br 3
11-4x12-2

Dn
L

32'-0"

26'-0"

Dining
12-4x11-6

Kitchen
13-6x11-6

W D
R

Furn

Living
18-9x13-6

Entry

Up

Porch

First Floor
832 sq. ft.

Special features

1,664 total square feet of living area

- Master bedroom includes private bath, dressing area and walk-in closet
- Spacious rooms throughout
- Kitchen features handy side entrance, adjacent laundry room and coat closet
- 3 bedrooms, 2 1/2 baths
- Crawl space foundation, drawings also include basement and slab foundations

---

Plan #596-038D-0034

Price Code B

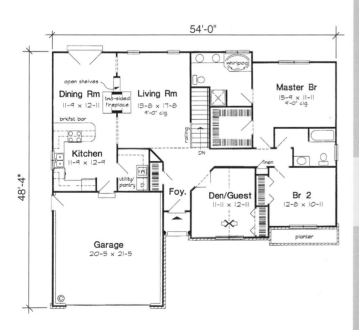

54'-0"

open shelves

Dining Rm
11-9 x 12-11

two-sided fireplace

Living Rm
13-8 x 17-8
9'-0" clg.

Master Br
15-9 x 11-11
9'-0" clg.

brkfst bar

railing

Kitchen
11-9 x 12-9

DN

linen

utility/pantry

48'-4"

Foy.

Den/Guest
11-11 x 12-11

Br 2
12-8 x 10-11

planter

Garage
20-5 x 21-5

Special features

1,625 total square feet of living area

- An interesting double-door entry leads to the den/guest room
- Spacious master bath has both a whirlpool tub and a shower
- Welcoming planter boxes in front add curb appeal
- 3 bedrooms, 2 baths, 2-car garage
- Basement or crawl space foundation, please specify when ordering

---

Special features

2,094 total square feet of living area

- Mediterranean style accentuates the facade of this lovely ranch
- The foyer leads to the combined living and dining rooms that enjoy a grand fireplace and nearby den with French door access
- A second fireplace warms the family room that is open to the kitchen with access onto the delightful covered patio
- 3 bedrooms, 2 baths, 3-car garage
- Crawl space foundation

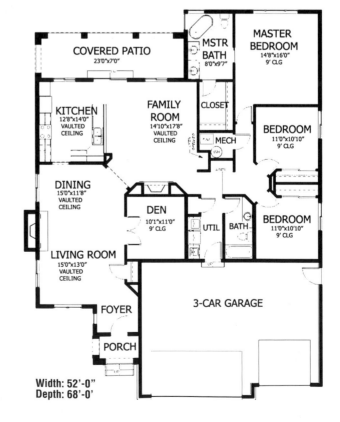

COVERED PATIO
23'0"x7'0"

MSTR BATH
8'0"x9'7"

MASTER BEDROOM
14'8"x16'0"
9' CLG

KITCHEN
12'8"x14'0"
VAULTED CEILING

FAMILY ROOM
14'10"x17'8"
VAULTED CEILING

CLOSET

MECH

BEDROOM
11'0"x10'10"
9' CLG

DINING
15'0"x11'8"
VAULTED CEILING

DEN
10'1"x11'0"
9' CLG

UTIL

BATH

BEDROOM
11'0"x10'10"
9' CLG

LIVING ROOM
15'0"x13'0"
VAULTED CEILING

FOYER

3-CAR GARAGE

PORCH

Width: 52'-0"
Depth: 68'-0'

Plan #596-007D-0041

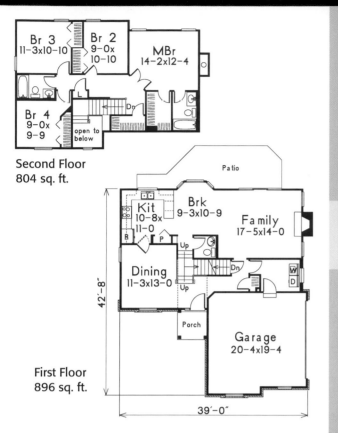

Second Floor
804 sq. ft.

First Floor
896 sq. ft.

Special features

1,700 total square feet of living area

- Two-story entry with T-stair is illuminated with a decorative oval window
- Skillfully designed U-shaped kitchen has a built-in pantry
- All bedrooms have generous closet storage and are common to a spacious hall with a walk-in cedar closet
- 4 bedrooms, 2 1/2 baths, 2-car side entry garage
- Basement foundation

Plan #596-030D-0005

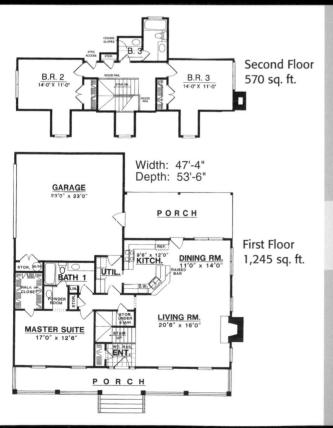

Second Floor
570 sq. ft.

Width: 47'-4"
Depth: 53'-6"

First Floor
1,245 sq. ft.

Special features

1,815 total square feet of living area

- Well-designed kitchen opens to the dining room and features a raised breakfast bar
- First floor master suite has a walk-in closet
- Front and back porches unite this home with the outdoors
- 3 bedrooms, 2 baths, 2-car side entry garage
- Basement, crawl space or slab foundation, please specify when ordering

Special features

1,799 total square feet of living area

- The vaulted ceiling in the great room creates a dynamic living space
- The garage offers an extra storage area with room to create a shop, bonus room or separate porch
- The bonus room with half bath has the potential to be a great guest room or play room and provides an additional 394 square feet of living area
- 3 bedrooms, 2 1/2 baths, 2-car garage
- Crawl space or slab foundation, please specify when ordering

Optional Second Floor

Bonus Room
14-8 x 19-6

First Floor
1,799 sq. ft.

Bedroom 2
12-2 x 11-10
9-0 Ceiling

Covered or
Screened-in Porch
16-2 x 8-0

Dining
12-0 x 17-4
9-0 Ceiling

Jet Tub

Master
Bedroom
14-4 x 17-6
9-0 Ceiling

Optional
Office, Shop,
Bonus, Porch, or
Storage
11-4 x 12-6

Great Room
16-0 x 26-0

Raised Bar

Stairs Option

Storage
11-4 x 5-0

Bedroom 3
12-0 x 11-4
9-0 Ceiling

Kitchen
13-4 x 12-8
Island

Utility
7-10 x 5-10

Optional Side
Entrance
Garage

Covered Porch
41-6 x 6-0

Two or Three-Car
Garage
24-0 x 24-0

Width: 78'-0"
Depth: 46'-0"

Plan #596-055D-0027

Special features

1,353 total square feet of living area

- All bedrooms are located together and away from living areas
- Dining room overlooks great room with fireplace
- Kitchen has counterspace for eating as well as plenty of storage
- 3 bedrooms, 2 baths, 2-car garage
- Basement, walk-out basement, slab or crawl space foundation, please specify when ordering

Plan #596-025D-0006

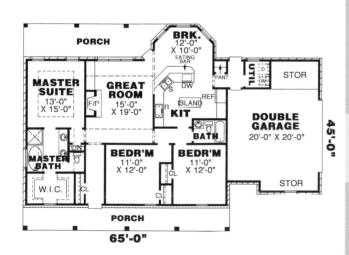

Special features

1,612 total square feet of living area

- Covered porch in rear of home creates an outdoor living area
- Master suite is separated from other bedrooms for privacy
- Eating bar in kitchen extends into breakfast area for additional seating
- 3 bedrooms, 2 baths, 2-car side entry garage
- Slab foundation

Special features

1,944 total square feet of living area

- Spacious surrounding porch, covered patio and stone fireplace create an expansive ponderosa appearance
- The large entry leads to a grand-sized great room featuring a vaulted ceiling, fireplace, wet bar and access to the porch through three patio doors
- The U-shaped kitchen is open to the hearth room and enjoys a snack bar, fireplace and patio access
- 3 bedrooms, 2 baths, 3-car detached garage
- Basement foundation

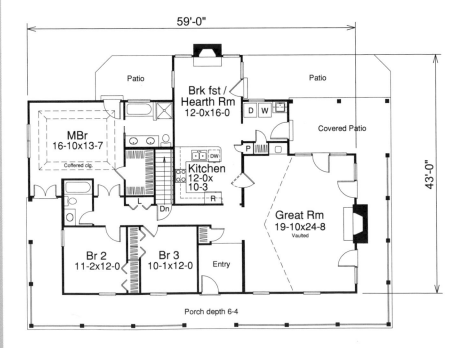

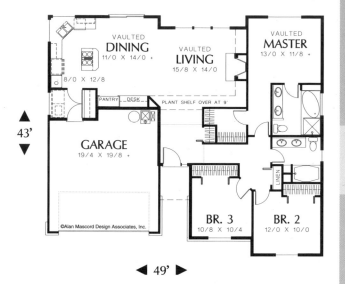

Special features

1,467 total square feet of living area

- Energy efficient home with 2" x 6" exterior walls
- Vaulted ceilings, an open floor plan and a wealth of windows create an inviting atmosphere
- Efficiently arranged kitchen has an island with built-in cooktop and a snack counter
- Plentiful storage and closet space throughout this home
- 3 bedrooms, 2 baths, 2-car garage
- Crawl space foundation

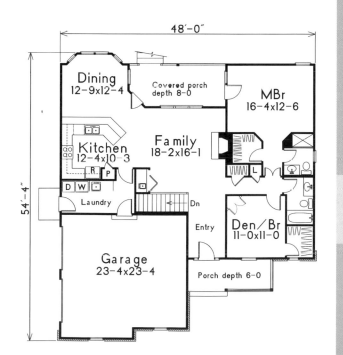

Special features

1,440 total square feet of living area

- Open floor plan with access to covered porches in front and back
- Lots of linen, pantry and closet space throughout
- Laundry/mud room between kitchen and garage is a convenient feature
- 2 bedrooms, 2 baths, 2-car side entry garage
- Basement foundation

Special features

1,540 total square feet of living area

- Energy efficient home with 2" x 6" exterior walls
- Spacious master bedroom has a large walk-in closet and sweeping windows overlooking the yard
- First floor laundry is conveniently located between the garage and kitchen
- Living room features a cathedral ceiling and corner fireplace
- 3 bedrooms, 2 baths, 2-car garage
- Basement foundation

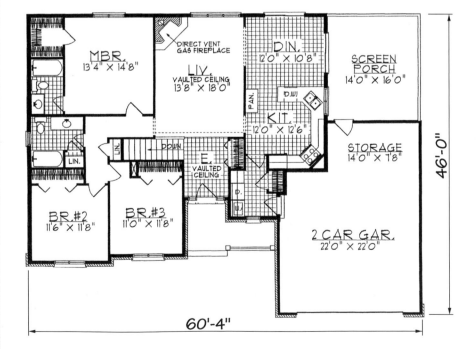

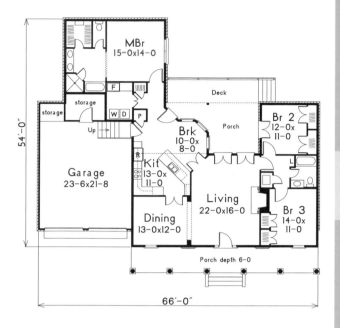

Special features

1,800 total square feet of living area

- The stylish kitchen and breakfast area feature large windows
- Covered front and rear porches provide an added dimension to this home's living space
- Generous storage areas and a large utility room
- Energy efficient home with 2" x 6" exterior walls
- Large separate master bedroom with adjoining bath has a large tub and corner shower
- 3 bedrooms, 2 baths, 2-car garage
- Crawl space foundation, drawings also include slab foundation

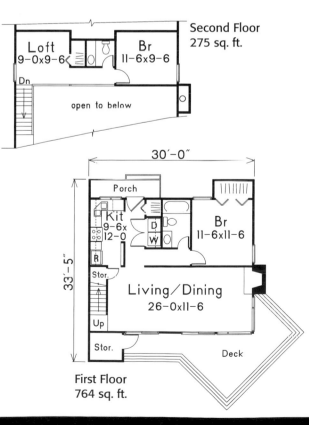

Special features

1,039 total square feet of living area

- Cathedral construction provides the maximum in living area openness
- Expansive glass viewing walls
- Two decks, front and back
- Charming second story loft arrangement
- Simple, low-maintenance construction
- 2 bedrooms, 1 1/2 baths
- Crawl space foundation

Special features

1,312 total square feet of living area

- Energy efficient home with 2" x 6" exterior walls
- A beamed ceiling and fireplace create an exciting feel to the living room
- Box window behind the double sink in the kitchen is a nice added feature
- Private bath and generous closet space in the master bedroom
- 3 bedrooms, 2 baths, 2-car garage
- Basement or crawl space foundation, please specify when ordering

Plan #596-014D-0005

Price Code A

Special features

1,314 total square feet of living area

- Energy efficient home with 2" x 6" exterior walls
- Covered porch adds immediate appeal and welcoming charm
- Open floor plan combined with a vaulted ceiling offers spacious living
- Functional kitchen is complete with a pantry and eating bar
- Cozy fireplace in the living room
- Private master bedroom features a large walk-in closet and bath
- 3 bedrooms, 2 baths, 2-car garage
- Basement foundation

Plan #596-035D-0004

Price Code A

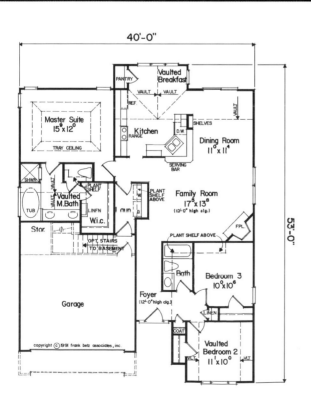

Special features

1,425 total square feet of living area

- Kitchen and vaulted breakfast room are the center of activity
- A corner fireplace warms the spacious family room
- Oversized serving bar extends seating in dining room
- 3 bedrooms, 2 baths, 2-car garage
- Crawl space, slab or walk-out basement foundation, please specify when ordering

Special features

1,698 total square feet of living area

- An extra-large island with seating enhances the kitchen and opens to the spacious great room and breakfast area
- Retreat to the master bedroom that features a large bay window and private bath with two walk-in closets, two vanities and a whirlpool tub
- The expansive rear porch offers a great place to relax or entertain guests
- 3 bedrooms, 2 baths, 2-car side entry garage
- Crawl space, basement, or slab foundation, please specify when ordering

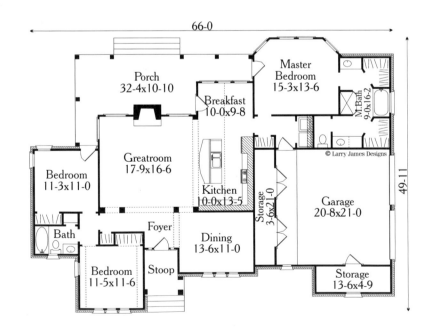

Porch
32-4x10-10

Breakfast
10-0x9-8

Master Bedroom
15-3x13-6

M. Bath
9-0x16-2

Greatroom
17-9x16-6

© Larry James Designs

Bedroom
11-3x11-0

Kitchen
10-0x13-5

Storage
3-6x21-0

Garage
20-8x21-0

Bath

Foyer

Dining
13-6x11-0

Bedroom
11-5x11-6

Stoop

Storage
13-6x4-9

66-0

49-11

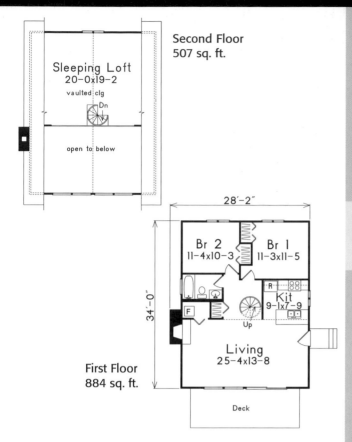

Second Floor
507 sq. ft.

Sleeping Loft
20-0x19-2
vaulted clg

Dn

open to below

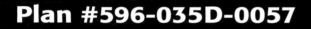

28'-2"

34'-0"

Br 2
11-4x10-3

Br 1
11-3x11-5

Kit
9-1x7-9

Up

Living
25-4x13-8

First Floor
884 sq. ft.

Deck

Special features

1,391 total square feet of living area

- Large living room with masonry fireplace features a soaring vaulted ceiling
- A spiral staircase in the hall leads to a huge loft area overlooking the living room below
- Two first floor bedrooms share a full bath
- 2 bedrooms, 1 bath
- Pier foundation, drawings also include crawl space foundation

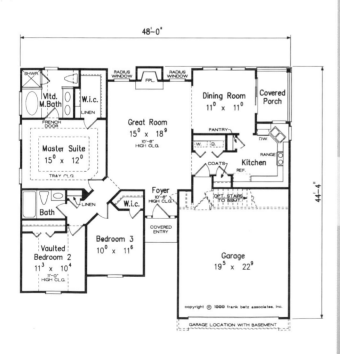

48'-0"

SHWR

Vltd.
M.Bath

W.i.c.

LINEN

RADIUS
WINDOW

FPL.

RADIUS
WINDOW

Dining Room
11⁰ x 11⁰

Covered
Porch

FRENCH
DOOR

Master Suite
15⁰ x 12⁰

TRAY CLG.

Great Room
15⁰ x 18⁹
10'-8"
HIGH CLG.

PANTRY

W. D.

DW

RANGE

COATS

Kitchen

REF.

LINEN

Bath

W.i.c.

Foyer
10'-8"
HIGH CLG.

OPT. STAIRS
TO BSMT.

44'-4"

Vaulted
Bedroom 2
11³ x 10⁴
11'-0"
HIGH CLG.

Bedroom 3
10⁰ x 11⁶

COVERED
ENTRY

Garage
19⁵ x 22⁹

copyright © 1999 frank betz associates, inc.

GARAGE LOCATION WITH BASEMENT

Special features

1,324 total square feet of living area

- Appealing French door in the master suite leads to a private bath with oversized tub and separate shower
- Corner sink in the kitchen has surrounding windows
- Enormous great room is centrally located and features a fireplace flanked by windows
- 3 bedrooms, 2 baths, 2-car garage
- Crawl space, slab or walk-out basement foundation, please specify when ordering

Special features

1,905 total square feet of living area

- Energy efficient home with 2" x 6" exterior walls
- Bright and airy living and dining rooms are created with a vaulted ceiling and two pairs of French doors that open onto the front porch
- Kitchen features an abundance of counterspace, vaulted ceiling and island counter
- Oversized utility room contains a coat closet, pantry and access to the garage
- A spiral stairway in the living/dining area leads to a charming loft which has an additional 323 square feet of living area
- 3 bedrooms, 2 baths, 3-car rear entry garage
- Crawl space foundation

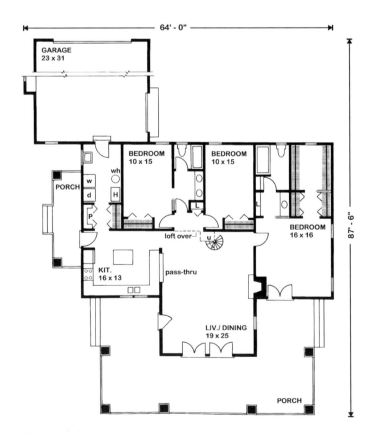

Plan #596-008D-0026

Price Code AA

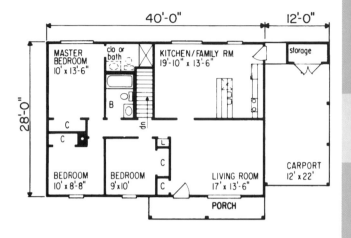

Special features

1,120 total square feet of living area

- Kitchen/family room creates a useful spacious area
- Rustic, colonial design is perfect for many surroundings
- Oversized living room is ideal for entertaining
- Carport includes a functional storage area
- 3 bedrooms, 2 baths, 1-car carport
- Basement foundation, drawings also include crawl space and slab foundations

Plan #596-047D-0020

Price Code B

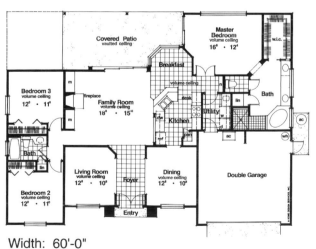

Width: 60'-0"
Depth: 45'-0"

Special features

1,783 total square feet of living area

- Formal living and dining rooms in the front of the home
- Kitchen overlooks breakfast area
- Conveniently located laundry area is near the kitchen and master bedroom
- Plans include a version with 4 bedrooms, 3 baths and an additional 206 square feet of living area
- 3 bedrooms, 2 baths, 2-car garage
- Slab foundation

Special features

1,304 total square feet of living area

- Energy efficient home with 2" x 6" exterior walls
- Second floor features a sitting area near the bedroom creating a relaxing retreat from the living area below
- Large dining area combines with living area for maximum comfort and space
- 2 bedrooms, 1 bath
- Crawl space foundation

First Floor
945 sq. ft.

Second Floor
359 sq. ft.

11'-4" X 13'-0"
3,40 X 3,90

11'-0" X 17'-0"
3,30 X 5,10

38'-4"
11,5 m

12'-0" X 10'-0"
3,60 X 3,00

9'-0" X 10'-0"
2,70 X 3,00

11'-4" X 18'-4"
3,40 X 5,50

12'-0" X 11'-0"
3,60 X 3,30

OPEN TO BELOW

24'-8"
7,4 m

Plan #596-037D-0003

Price Code D

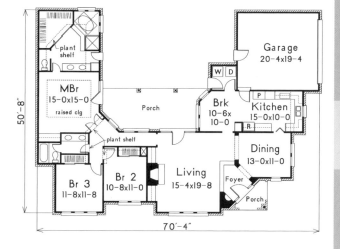

Special features

1,996 total square feet of living area

- Garden courtyard comes with a large porch and direct access to the master bedroom suite, breakfast room and garage
- Sculptured entrance has plant shelves and niche in foyer
- Master bedroom boasts French doors, garden tub, desk with bookshelves and generous storage
- Plant shelves and a high ceiling grace the hallway
- 3 bedrooms, 2 baths, 2-car side entry garage
- Slab foundation, drawings also include crawl space foundation

Plan #596-053D-0053

Price Code B

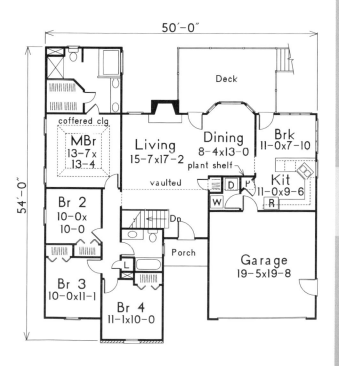

Special features

1,609 total square feet of living area

- Kitchen includes a corner pantry and adjacent laundry room
- Breakfast room boasts plenty of windows and opens onto a rear deck
- Master bedroom features a tray ceiling and private deluxe bath
- Entry opens into large living area with fireplace
- 4 bedrooms, 2 baths, 2-car garage
- Basement foundation

Special features

1,270 total square feet of living area

- Spacious living area features angled stairs, vaulted ceiling, exciting fireplace and deck access
- Master bedroom includes a walk-in closet and private bath
- Dining and living rooms join to create an open atmosphere
- Eat-in kitchen has a convenient pass-through to the dining room
- 3 bedrooms, 2 baths, 2-car garage
- Basement foundation

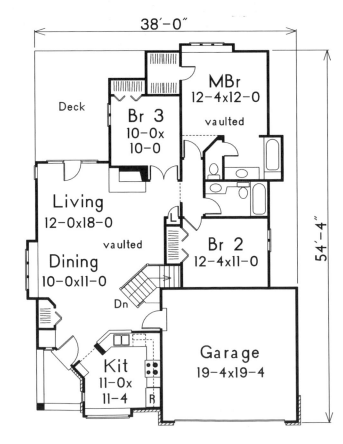

38'-0"

54'-4"

Deck

MBr
12-4x12-0
vaulted

Br 3
10-0x
10-0

Living
12-0x18-0
vaulted

Dining
10-0x11-0

Br 2
12-4x11-0

Dn

Kit
11-0x
11-4

Garage
19-4x19-4

Special features

2,196 total square feet of living area

- Energy efficient home with 2" x 6" exterior walls
- Covered front porch leads to the vaulted foyer which invites guests into the great room
- Master bedroom features a walk-in closet, private bath with double vanity, spa tub and linen closet
- Large open kitchen
- 3 bedrooms, 2 1/2 baths, 3-car garage
- Basement foundation

Plan #596-070D-0001

Price Code A

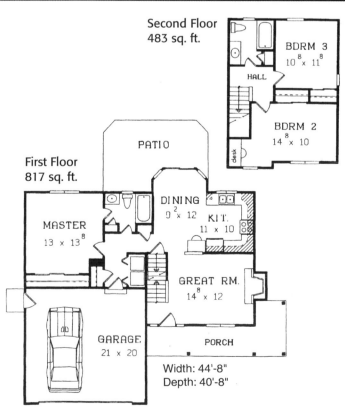

Second Floor
483 sq. ft.

First Floor
817 sq. ft.

Width: 44'-8"
Depth: 40'-8"

Special features

1,300 total square feet of living area

- Bayed dining room has sliding glass doors that open onto an outdoor patio
- Large bedroom #2 has a built-in desk
- Charming wrap-around front porch adds curb appeal
- 3 bedrooms, 2 baths, 2-car garage
- Basement foundation

Special features

1,580 total square feet of living area

- Energy efficient home with 2" x 6" exterior walls
- A covered porch extends the great room to the outdoors
- Secluded master bedroom enjoys a vaulted ceiling, private bath with double vanity and a large walk-in closet
- Built-in bookshelves flank one wall of the dining room and are perfect for collectibles or cookbooks
- 3 bedrooms, 2 1/2 baths, 2-car garage
- Crawl space foundation

Plan #596-041D-0004

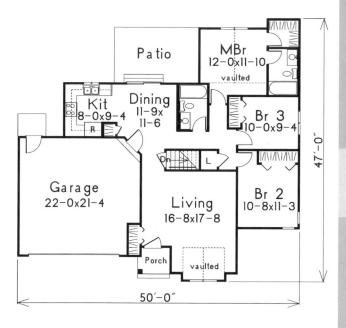

Special features

1,195 total square feet of living area

- Dining room opens onto the patio
- Master bedroom features a vaulted ceiling, private bath and walk-in closet
- Coat closets are located by both the entrances
- Convenient secondary entrance is located at the back of the garage
- 3 bedrooms, 2 baths, 2-car garage
- Basement foundation

Plan #596-058D-0004

Price Code AA

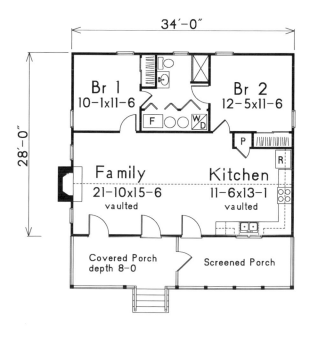

Special features

962 total square feet of living area

- Both the kitchen and family room share warmth from the fireplace
- Charming facade features a covered porch on one side, screened porch on the other and attractive planter boxes
- L-shaped kitchen boasts a convenient pantry
- 2 bedrooms, 1 bath
- Crawl space foundation

Special features

1,339 total square feet of living area

- Energy efficient home with 2" x 6" exterior walls
- Full-length covered porch enhances front facade
- Vaulted ceiling and stone fireplace add drama to the family room
- Walk-in closets in the bedrooms provide ample storage space
- Combined kitchen/dining area adjoins the family room for the perfect entertaining space
- 3 bedrooms, 2 1/2 baths
- Crawl space foundation

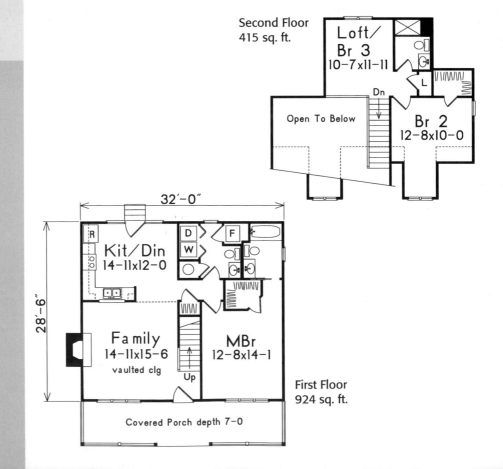

Second Floor
415 sq. ft.

Loft/ Br 3
10-7x11-11

Open To Below

Dn

Br 2
12-8x10-0

32'-0"

28'-6"

Kit/Din
14-11x12-0

R

D   F
W

Family
14-11x15-6
vaulted clg

Up

MBr
12-8x14-1

First Floor
924 sq. ft.

Covered Porch depth 7-0

Plan #596-001D-0093

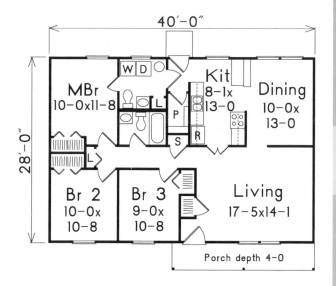

40'-0"

28'-0"

| W D | | Kit 8-1x 13-0 | Dining 10-0x 13-0 |

MBr 10-0x11-8

P
L
S
R

Br 2 10-0x 10-8

Br 3 9-0x 10-8

Living 17-5x14-1

Porch depth 4-0

Special features

1,120 total square feet of living area

- Master bedroom includes a half bath with laundry area, linen closet and kitchen access
- Kitchen has charming double-door entry, breakfast bar and a convenient walk-in pantry
- Welcoming front porch opens to a large living room with coat closet
- 3 bedrooms, 1 1/2 baths
- Crawl space foundation, drawings also include basement and slab foundations

Plan #596-038D-0018

Price Code B

56'-0"

32'-0"

Deck

Kitchen 12 x 11-4

Dining Rm 9 x 11-4

W D

Ldry

pantry

MBr 1 14-2 x 14-4

Living Rm 21-6 x 19-4

decor. beams

Br 3 12 x 12-6

Br 2 12 x 12-6

slope

lin.

Special features

1,792 total square feet of living area

- Energy efficient home with 2" x 6" exterior walls
- Master bedroom has a private bath and large walk-in closet
- A central stone fireplace and windows on two walls are focal points in the living room
- Decorative beams and sloped ceilings add interest to the kitchen, living and dining rooms
- 3 bedrooms, 2 baths, 2-car drive under garage
- Basement foundation

Special features

1,914 total square feet of living area

- Great room features a vaulted ceiling, dining area, entry foyer, corner fireplace and 9' wide sliding doors to the rear patio
- The secluded secondary bedrooms offer walk-in closets and share a Jack and Jill bath
- A multi-purpose room has a laundry alcove and can easily be used as a hobby room, sewing room or small office
- Bedroom #4 can be open to the master bedroom suite and utilized as a private study or nursery
- 4 bedrooms, 3 baths, 2-car garage
- Basement foundation

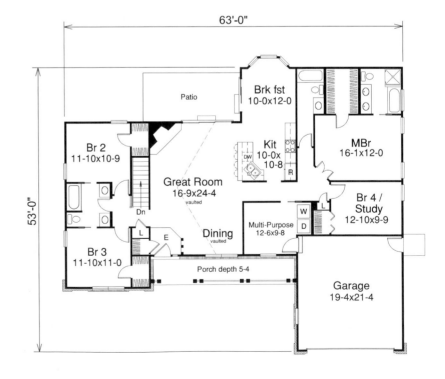

63'-0"

53'-0"

Patio

Brk fst
10-0x12-0

Br 2
11-10x10-9

Kit
10-0x
10-8

MBr
16-1x12-0

Great Room
16-9x24-4
vaulted

Dn

Dining
vaulted

Br 4 /
Study
12-10x9-9

Multi-Purpose
12-6x9-8

Br 3
11-10x11-0

Porch depth 5-4

Garage
19-4x21-4

First Floor 787 sq. ft.

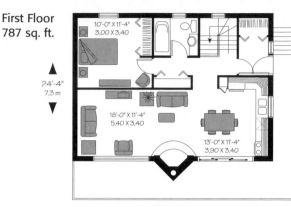

10'-0" X 11'-4"
3,00 X 3,40

18'-0" X 11'-4"
5,40 X 3,40

13'-0" X 11'-4"
3,90 X 3,40

24'-4"
7,3 m

32'-4"
9,7 m

Lower Level 787 sq. ft.

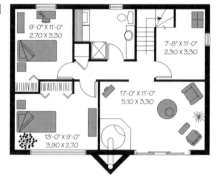

9'-0" X 11'-0"
2,70 X 3,30

7'-8" X 11'-0"
2,30 X 3,30

17'-0" X 11'-0"
5,10 X 3,30

13'-0" X 9'-0"
3,90 X 2,70

Special features

1,574 total square feet of living area

- Energy efficient home with 2" x 6" exterior walls
- Secluded bedroom on first floor has plenty of privacy
- Lower level includes another living area in addition to the secondary bedrooms
- 3 bedrooms, 2 baths
- Basement foundation

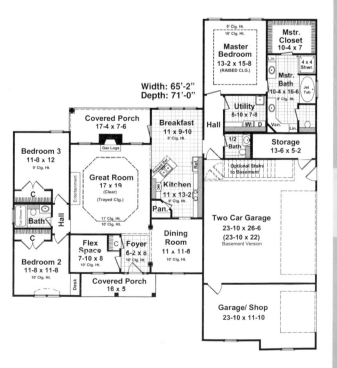

Width: 65'-2"
Depth: 71'-0"

9' Clg. Ht.
10' Clg. Ht.

Master Bedroom
13-2 x 15-8
(RAISED CLG.)

Mstr. Closet
10-4 x 7

4 x 4
Shwr.

Mstr. Bath
10-4 x 15-6

Jet Tub

9' Clg. Ht.

Covered Porch
17-4 x 7-6

Breakfast
11 x 9-10
9' Clg. Ht.

Hall

Utility
8-10 x 7-8

W D   Van.

Lin.

Gas Logs

Great Room
17 x 19
(Clear)
(Trayed Clg.)

11" Clg. Ht.
10' Clg. Ht.

Bedroom 3
11-8 x 12
9' Clg. Ht.

C

Bath

C

Bedroom 2
11-8 x 11-8
10' Clg. Ht.

Hall

Kitchen
11 x 13-2
9' Clg. Ht.

DW
Pan.

1/2 Bath

Storage
13-6 x 5-2

Two Car Garage
23-10 x 26-6
(23-10 x 22)
Basement Version

Flex Space
7-10 x 8
10' Clg. Ht.

C

Foyer
6-2 x 8
10' Clg. Ht.

Dining Room
11 x 11-6
10' Clg. Ht.

Desk

Covered Porch
16 x 5

Garage/ Shop
23-10 x 11-10

Optional Stairs to Basement

Special features

2,005 total square feet of living area

- The trayed ceiling adds a point of visual interest to the great room as well as increasing the sense of space
- The covered back porch has plenty of space to lounge
- High ceilings throughout the house enhance the spaciousness
- 3 bedrooms, 2 1/2 baths, 3-car side entry garage
- Slab or crawl space foundation, please specify when ordering

Special features

1,823 total square feet of living area

- Vaulted living room is spacious and easily accesses the dining area
- The master bedroom boasts a tray ceiling, large walk-in closet and a private bath with a corner whirlpool tub
- Cheerful dining area is convenient to the U-shaped kitchen and also enjoys patio access
- Centrally located laundry room connects the garage to the living areas
- 3 bedrooms, 2 baths, 2-car garage
- Basement foundation

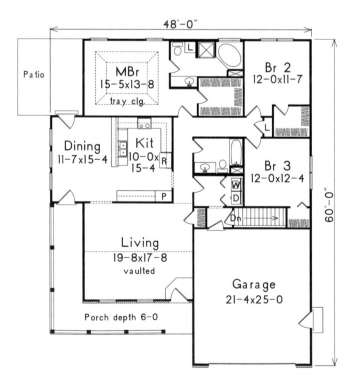

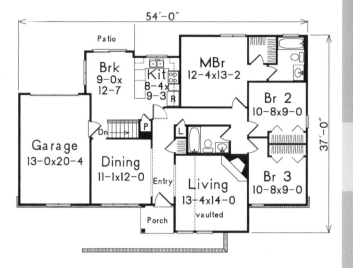

Special features

1,321 total square feet of living area

- Rear entry garage and elongated brick wall add to the appealing facade
- Dramatic vaulted living room includes corner fireplace and towering feature windows
- Breakfast room is immersed in light from two large windows and glass sliding doors
- 3 bedrooms, 2 baths, 1-car rear entry garage
- Basement foundation

Plan #596-068D-0010

Price Code C

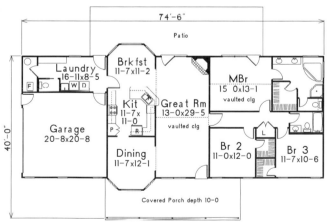

Special features

1,849 total square feet of living area

- Lavish master bath has a corner whirlpool tub, double sinks, separate shower and walk-in closet
- Secondary bedrooms include walk-in closets
- Kitchen has a wrap-around counter and is positioned between the formal dining area and breakfast room for convenience
- 3 bedrooms, 2 1/2 baths, 2-car side entry garage
- Slab foundation, drawings also include crawl space foundation

Special features

2,198 total square feet of living area

- Great room features a warm fireplace flanked by bookshelves for storage
- Double French doors connect the formal dining room to the kitchen
- An oversized laundry room has extra counterspace
- The second floor bonus room has an additional 385 square feet of living area
- 4 bedrooms, 2 1/2 baths, 2-car side entry garage with shop/storage
- Basement, crawl space or slab foundation, please specify when ordering

Second Floor
997 sq. ft.

First Floor
1,201 sq. ft.

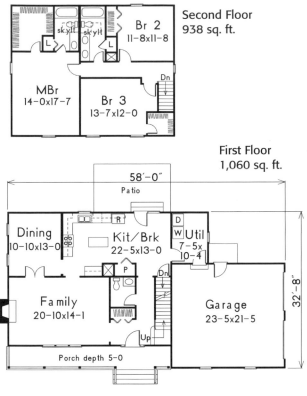

Second Floor
938 sq. ft.

Br 2
11-8x11-8

MBr
14-0x17-7

Br 3
13-7x12-0

Dn

First Floor
1,060 sq. ft.

58'-0"

Patio

Dining
10-10x13-0

Kit/Brk
22-5x13-0

Util
7-5x
10-4

Family
20-10x14-1

Garage
23-5x21-5

32'-8"

Porch depth 5-0

Special features

1,998 total square feet of living area

- Large family room features a fireplace and access to the kitchen and dining area
- Skylights add daylight to the second floor baths
- Utility room is located near the garage and kitchen
- Kitchen/breakfast area includes a pantry, island workspace and easy access to the patio
- 3 bedrooms, 2 1/2 baths, 2-car side entry garage
- Basement foundation, drawings also include crawl space and slab foundations

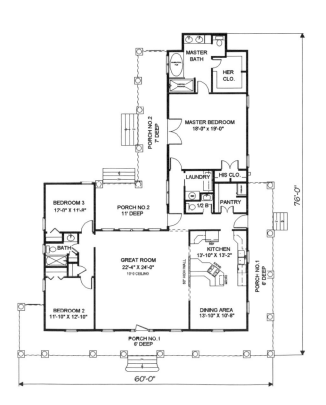

MASTER BATH

HER CLO.

MASTER BEDROOM
18'-0" X 19'-0"

PORCH NO.2
7' DEEP

BEDROOM 3
12'-0" X 11'-8"

PORCH NO.2
11' DEEP

LAUNDRY

HIS CLO.

1/2 B

PANTRY

76'-0"

BATH

GREAT ROOM
22'-4" X 24'-0"
10'-0" CEILING

KITCHEN
13'-10" X 13'-2"

PORCH NO.1
6' DEEP

BEDROOM 2
11'-10" X 12'-10"

DINING AREA
13'-10" X 10'-8"

PORCH NO.1
6' DEEP

60'-0"

Special features

2,123 total square feet of living area

- L-shaped porch extends the entire length of this home creating lots of extra space for outdoor living
- Master bedroom has two closets, double vanity in bath and a double-door entry onto covered porch
- The kitchen is designed for efficiency
- 3 bedrooms, 2 1/2 baths
- Crawl space or slab foundation, please specify when ordering

Special features

2,159 total square feet of living area

- Energy efficient home with 2" x 6" exterior walls
- Covered entry opens into the large foyer with a skylight and coat closet
- Master bedroom includes a private bath with angled vanity, separate spa and shower and walk-in closet
- Family and living rooms feature vaulted ceilings and sunken floors for added openness
- Kitchen features an island counter and convenient pantry
- 3 bedrooms, 2 baths, 2-car garage
- Basement foundation, drawings also include crawl space and slab foundations

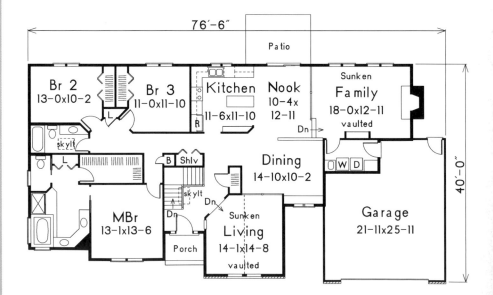

Canned Goods

Armored with Design Plan In A Can™ you can conquer the battle of interior decorating and give even the smallest of spaces a pulled-together look.

Building a home from the ground up is a huge investment of time and money. There is no need to add stress to the process by fretting over the additional investment of decorating your new home. Residential Color Specialist Edith Snell has developed a product to make the world of interior decorating as simple and painless as possible. By taking all the guesswork out of how to a create complete designed look, and for only $99, her Design Plan In A Can™ will ease the task and help turn your home into a retreat that looks like a million bucks.

DESIGN

"Design Plan In A Can offers everything you need to design your entire home, simple and painless," says Snell, a 20-year-veteran of the interior design industry from Jonesboro, Arkansas. It is a unique product that will help save time and money for everyone in the home industry, including builders, realtors, developers and consumers.

Over the years, Snell has put together an abundance of color boards for builders and individuals, complete with a design concept for an entire house, from floor coverings to paint finishes. Struggling to balance these time-consuming projects and the needs of her family, she decided that coordinated collections could be created and duplicated many times to suit the needs of many people rather than design each one separately.

Design Plan In A Can was the solution. Once Snell had the vision, she partnered with Stephanie Nelson, a friend in the home building community, to create Interior Solutions Group, LLC and produce Design Plan In A Can.

Complete with swatches of everything one needs to style their home, these innovative cans are the answer to stressful, time-consuming and expensive design consultations.

For $99, and the time it takes you to open the can, you will receive expert design suggestions. Just pry open the lid to find swatches for your countertops, grout, cabinets, floors, paint colors and finishes, fabrics, and wall coverings.

"Traditionally it could take the first several hours just to gain a direction for a client's home design," Snell explains. "When interior designers can charge into the hundreds for one hour of service, Design Plan In A Can will instantly save you money and time."

By flipping through the catalogue, which can be found at www.designplaninacan.com, it is easy to select your favorite color palette. Snell has spent hours of research creating each can, "making sure that you have the most current and innovative colors available in the market today." She has fashioned more than 70 different coordinated designs, sectioned into collections including Island Tones, Neutrals, Mid-Tones, Traditional, Spices, Jewel Tones, Metro, Arts & Crafts, Tuscan and Retro.

"I strive to achieve a timeless palette that you and

your family will think is beautiful now as well as 15 years from now," Snell says. "These palettes are also easy for builders who are fearful of making wrong choices or getting stuck in the 'builder's white' rut."

Specific suppliers and item codes further simplify the process, giving users the exact information they need to purchase the suggested item. Current suppliers include Sherwin Williams Paints, Anderson Wood Floors, DalTile Wall and Floor Tile, Shaw Carpets, Kemiko Concrete Stain, Laticrete Grout, LG Hi-Macs Acrylic Solid Surface, Woodharbor Doors & Cabinetry, Seabrook Wallcoverings, and Wilsonart Laminate. Snell created the fabric selections herself with Interior Solutions Group.

"I've chosen vendors that are the best at what they're known for, and with national suppliers, they can be found everywhere," Snell says.

The key to the can is the Color Placement Recommendation Guide. This guide lists every surface suggestion, room-by-room, going as far as to suggest the paint finish for each room. Of course, you can venture out of the guide if you must, but at the very least it gives you an excellent starting point.

"These cans give you 90 percent of the design to start with and allows 10 percent freedom to style your home with your own creativity," Snell says.

Further simplifying the design process, Design Plan In A Can is available for every level of home.

A Level (starter homes) cans include laminate countertops, resilient tile flooring, resilient laminate wood flooring and modest carpet samples.

B Level (moderate homes) cans specify solid surface countertops, ceramic or porcelain tiles, hardwood flooring and moderate carpet.

C Level (luxury homes) cans feature quartz, ceramic porcelain tiles or natural stone, as well as an additional carpet selection for basement or media areas. For every home level, the colors and paints remain the same in each palette.

For builders and developers, Design Plan In A Can goes the extra step of offering customized labels. For a small set-up fee, they will put your logo on the side profile of the paint can, allowing you to create a design library for your clients.

"Our cans can help a builder close a sale on a house because it shows clients they are thinking all the way from start to finish on building their home," Snell explains.

Snell truly hopes her product will be the guidance needed to design a home, a place for comfort, beauty and function. For more information on her revolutionary product, and to order your Design Plan In A Can, please visit www.designplaninacan.com, or call toll-free 1-800-590-2423.

Images courtesy of Interior Solutions Group, LLC

Special features

1,643 total square feet of living area

- Family room has a vaulted ceiling, open staircase and arched windows allowing for plenty of light
- Kitchen captures full use of space, with a pantry, storage, ample counterspace and work island
- Large closets and storage areas throughout
- Roomy master bath has a skylight for natural lighting plus a separate tub and shower
- Rear of house provides ideal location for future screened-in porch
- 3 bedrooms, 2 baths, 2-car side entry garage
- Basement foundation, drawings also include slab and crawl space foundations

Deck

72'-0"

Dining
11-0x11-7

Kit
11-1x11-7

R

skylt

MBr
17-2x15-2

Dn

Brm

P

34'-0"

Garage
21-8x23-5

Family
22-5x13-11
vaulted

W
D

Br 2
10-0x
12-9

Br 3
13-11x9-10

Porch

Second Floor
665 sq. ft.

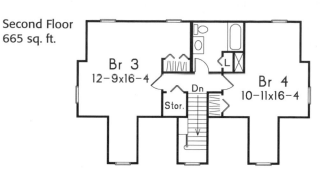

Br 3
12-9x16-4

Dn
Stor.

Br 4
10-11x16-4

L

First Floor
1,040 sq. ft.

40'-0"

26'-0"

Dining
9-5x9-3

Kit
10-4x
9-3

R

Br 2
10-11x10-4

F

Living
18-7x15-10

D W

Up

Br 1
14-7x12-4

Special features

1,705 total square feet of living area

- Cozy design includes two bedrooms on the first floor and two bedrooms on the second floor for added privacy
- L-shaped kitchen provides easy access to the dining room and the outdoors
- Convenient first floor laundry area
- 2" x 6" exterior walls available, please order plan #596-001D-0111
- 4 bedrooms, 2 baths
- Crawl space foundation, drawings also include basement and slab foundations

Optional
Second Floor

OPT'D
BATH
DORMER

BALCONY

CL

BEDRM #3
14'-0" x 12'-0"

DN

BEDRM #4
12'-8" x 12'-0"

WICL

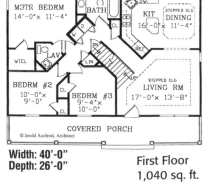

BUILT-IN
OR CLOS.

BATH

MSTR BEDRM
14'-0" x 14'-0"

D

W

CL

DN
LIN

WICL

CL

MSTR
BATH

BEDRM #2
9'-4" x
10'-0"

COV PORCH

MSTR BEDRM
14'-0" x 11'-4"

BATH

D

W

CL

KIT
16'-0"

STEPPED CLG
DINING
11'-4"

LAV

DN
LIN

WICL

REF.

BEDRM #2
10'-0" x
9'-0"

CL

BEDRM #3
9'-4" x
10'-0"

UP

STEPPED CLG
LIVING RM
17'-0" x 13'-8"

COVERED PORCH
© Jerold Axelrod, Architect

Width: 40'-0"
Depth: 26'-0"

First Floor
1,040 sq. ft.

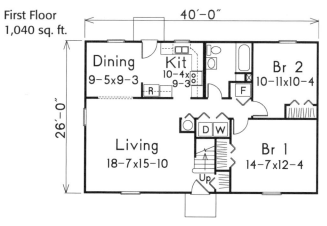

Special features

1,040 total square feet of living area

- A wide archway joins the formal living room to the dramatic angled kitchen and dining room
- Optional second floor has an additional 597 square feet of living area
- Optional first floor design has two bedrooms including a large master bedroom that enjoys a private luxury bath
- 3 bedrooms, 1 1/2 baths
- Basement, crawl space or slab foundation, please specify when ordering

Special features

920 total square feet of living area

- Energy efficient home with 2" x 6" exterior walls
- Bath has extra space for a washer and dryer
- Plenty of seating for dining at the kitchen counter
- 2 bedrooms, 1 bath
- Basement foundation

QUICK FACT - Never run an empty microwave. It can cause overheating and serious damage.

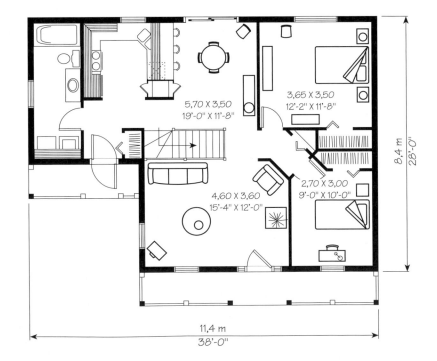

5,70 X 3,50
19'-0" X 11'-8"

3,65 X 3,50
12'-2" X 11'-8"

4,60 X 3,60
15'-4" X 12'-0"

2,70 X 3,00
9'-0" X 10'-0"

8,4 m
28'-0"

11,4 m
38'-0"

Plan #596-007D-0130

Price Code C

Second Floor
1,015 sq. ft.

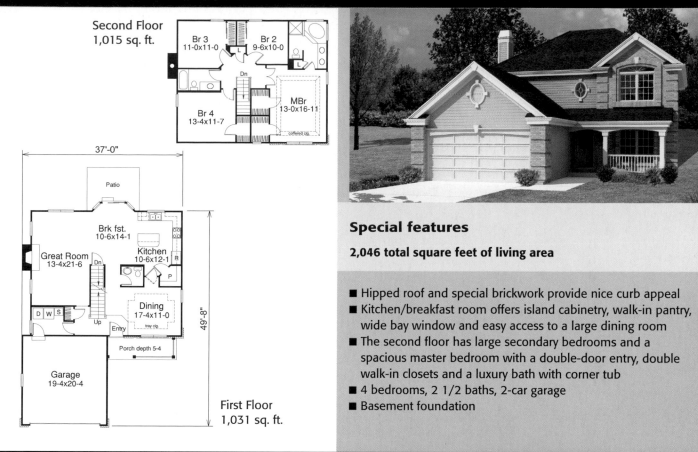

Br 3
11-0x11-0

Br 2
9-6x10-0

Dn

MBr
13-0x16-11

Br 4
13-4x11-7

coffered clg.

37'-0"

Patio

Brk fst.
10-6x14-1

Great Room
13-4x21-6

Kitchen
10-6x12-1

P

R

Dn

D W S

Dining
17-4x11-0

tray clg.

Up

Entry

Porch depth 5-4

49'-8"

Garage
19-4x20-4

First Floor
1,031 sq. ft.

Special features

2,046 total square feet of living area

- Hipped roof and special brickwork provide nice curb appeal
- Kitchen/breakfast room offers island cabinetry, walk-in pantry, wide bay window and easy access to a large dining room
- The second floor has large secondary bedrooms and a spacious master bedroom with a double-door entry, double walk-in closets and a luxury bath with corner tub
- 4 bedrooms, 2 1/2 baths, 2-car garage
- Basement foundation

Plan #596-058D-0014

Price Code AAA

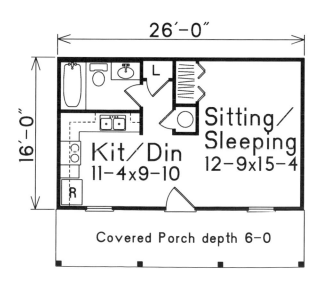

26'-0"

16'-0"

L

Sitting/
Sleeping
12-9x15-4

Kit/Din
11-4x9-10

R

Covered Porch depth 6-0

Special features

416 total square feet of living area

- Covered porch has rustic appeal
- Open floor plan creates a spacious feeling
- The kitchen offers plenty of cabinets and workspace
- Large linen closet is centrally located and close to the bath
- 2" x 6" exterior walls available, please order plan #596-058D-0076
- Sleeping area, 1 bath
- Slab foundation

Special features

1,322 total square feet of living area

- Wrap-around counter connects the kitchen to the dining and family rooms creating an open atmosphere
- The private master bedroom boasts a deluxe bath with a double vanity, whirlpool tub and large walk-in closet
- Bonus room above the garage has an additional 294 square feet of living area
- 3 bedrooms, 2 baths, 2-car garage
- Slab foundation

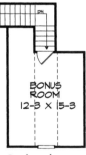

Optional
Second Floor

BONUS
ROOM
12-3 X 15-3

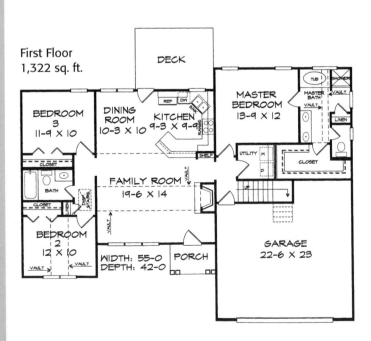

First Floor
1,322 sq. ft.

DECK

BEDROOM 3
11-9 X 10

DINING ROOM
10-3 X 10

KITCHEN
9-3 X 9-9

MASTER BEDROOM
13-9 X 12

MASTER BATH

LINEN

BATH

FAMILY ROOM
19-6 X 14

UTILITY

CLOSET

BEDROOM 2
12 X 10

WIDTH: 55-0
DEPTH: 42-0

PORCH

GARAGE
22-6 X 23

Plan #596-013D-0003

Price Code B

Special features

1,296 total square feet of living area

- Two secondary bedrooms share a bath and have convenient access to the laundry room
- Family room has a large fireplace flanked by sunny windows
- Master bedroom includes privacy as well as an amenity-full bath
- 3 bedrooms, 2 baths, 2-car garage
- Basement, crawl space or slab foundation, please specify when ordering

Plan #596-037D-0002

Price Code C

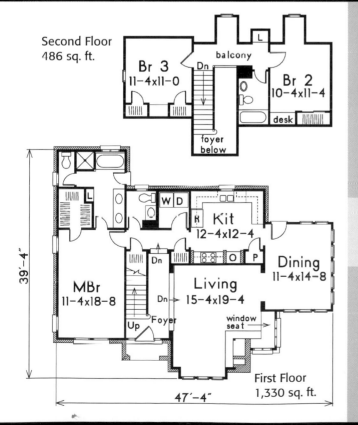

Special features

1,816 total square feet of living area

- The living room features a two-way fireplace
- Wrap-around dining room windows create a sunroom appearance
- Master bedroom has abundant closet and storage space
- Rear dormers, closets and desk areas create an interesting and functional second floor
- 3 bedrooms, 2 1/2 baths, 2-car detached garage
- Slab foundation, drawings also include crawl space foundation

Special features

2,070 total square feet of living area

- Great room enjoys a fireplace, wet bar and rear views through two-story vaulted atrium
- The U-shaped kitchen opens to the breakfast area and features a walk-in pantry, computer center and atrium overlook
- Master bath has a Roman whirlpool tub, TV alcove, separate shower/toilet area and linen closet
- Extra storage in garage
- Atrium opens to 1,062 square feet of optional living area below
- 3 bedrooms, 2 baths, 2-car drive-under garage with storage area
- Walk-out basement foundation

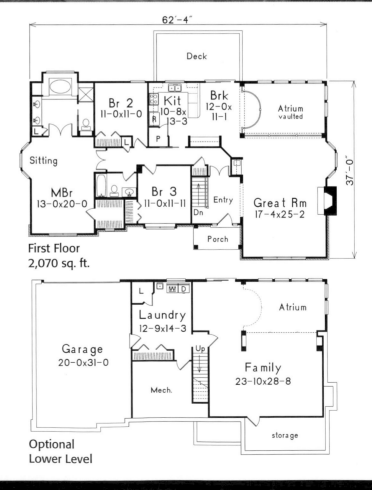

First Floor
2,070 sq. ft.

Optional
Lower Level

Plan #596-022D-0005

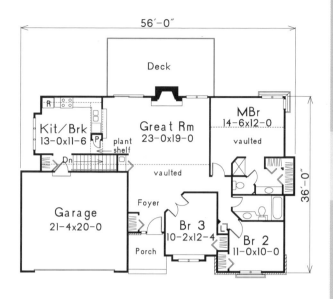

Special features

1,360 total square feet of living area

- Double-gabled front facade frames large windows
- The foyer opens to the vaulted great room with a fireplace
- Vaulted ceiling and large windows add openness to the kitchen/breakfast room
- Bedroom #3 easily converts to a den
- Plan easily adapts to crawl space or slab construction, with the utilities replacing the stairs
- 3 bedrooms, 2 baths, 2-car garage
- Basement foundation

Plan #596-053D-0058

Price Code C

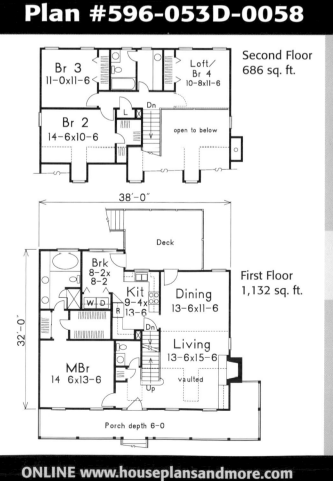

Special features

1,818 total square feet of living area

- Breakfast room is tucked behind the kitchen and has a laundry closet and deck access
- Living and dining areas share a vaulted ceiling and fireplace
- Master bedroom has two closets, a large double-bowl vanity and a separate tub and shower
- Large front porch wraps around the home
- 4 bedrooms, 2 1/2 baths, 2-car drive under garage
- Basement foundation

Special features

1,584 total square feet of living area

- Energy efficient home with 2" x 6" exterior walls
- Kitchen overlooks family room creating a natural gathering place
- Double vanity in master bath
- Dining room flows into living room
- 3 bedrooms, 2 1/2 baths, 2-car rear entry garage
- Crawl space foundation

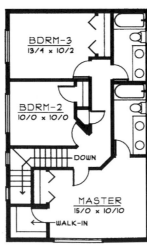
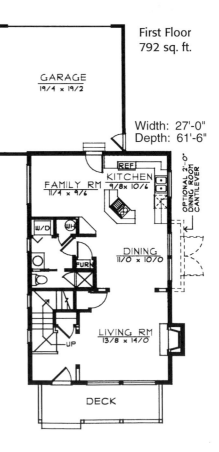

First Floor
792 sq. ft.

GARAGE
19/4 x 19/2

Width: 27'-0"
Depth: 61'-6"

Second Floor
792 sq. ft.

BDRM-3
13/4 x 10/2

BDRM-2
10/0 x 10/0

MASTER
15/0 x 10/10

WALK-IN

DOWN

FAMILY RM
11/4 x 9/6

KITCHEN
9/8 x 10/6

REF

DINING
11/0 x 10/0

LIVING RM
13/8 x 14/0

UP

W/D WH

FUR.

DECK

OPTIONAL 2'-0"
DINING ROOM
CANTILEVER

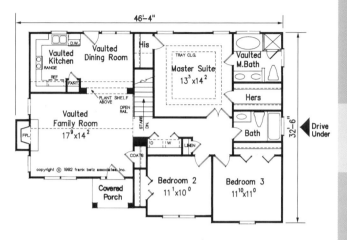

Special features

1,281 total square feet of living area

- Spacious master suite has a tray ceiling, double closets and a private bath
- Vaulted family room has lots of sunlight from multiple windows and a fireplace
- Plant shelf above kitchen and dining room is a nice decorative touch
- 3 bedrooms, 2 baths, 2-car drive under garage
- Walk-out basement foundation

Plan #596-058D-0008

Price Code A

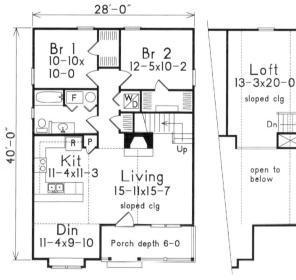

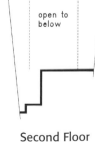

First Floor
1,032 sq. ft.

Second Floor
253 sq. ft.

Special features

1,285 total square feet of living area

- Second floor loft is perfect for a recreation space or office hideaway
- Kitchen, dining and living areas combine making a perfect gathering place
- Bedrooms include walk-in closets for extra storage space
- Dining nook creates a warm feeling with sunny bay window
- 2 bedrooms, 1 bath
- Crawl space foundation

Special features

1,290 total square feet of living area

- The kitchen is located conveniently between the dining room and breakfast area
- Master suite has a private luxurious bath with walk-in closet
- Decorative plant shelves throughout this plan add style
- 3 bedrooms, 2 baths, 2-car side entry garage
- Slab, crawl space or walk-out basement foundation, please specify when ordering

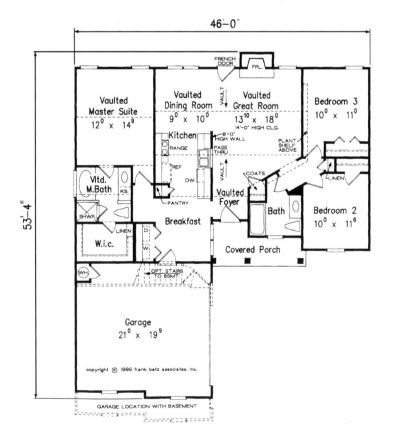

46'-0"

53'-4"

FRENCH DOOR

FPL

Vaulted Master Suite
12⁰ x 14⁹

Vaulted Dining Room
9⁰ x 10⁰

VAULT

Vaulted Great Room
13¹⁰ x 18⁰
14'-0" HIGH CLG.

Bedroom 3
10⁰ x 11⁰

Kitchen
RANGE
8'-0" HIGH WALL
PASS THRU
REF
DW.
VAULT
PLANT SHELF ABOVE
PLANT SHELF ABOVE

Mtd. M.Bath
KS.
COATS
LINEN

SHWR.
LINEN
PANTRY
Vaulted Foyer
Bath

Breakfast
Bedroom 2
10⁰ x 11⁶

W.i.c.
D.
W.

WH
OPT. STAIRS TO BSMT.
Covered Porch

Garage
21⁰ x 19⁹

copyright © 1999 frank betz associates, inc.

GARAGE LOCATION WITH BASEMENT

Plan #596-007D-0013

Price Code A

Second Floor
732 sq. ft.

MBr
11-0x14-8

Br 2
12-0x11-0

Dn

Br 3
12-0x9-9

raised
ceiling

35'-0"

Deck

Brk
9-0x
11-0

Dining
12-0x9-4

Kit
10-9x14-6

Dn

Living
15-8x14-0

Up

41'-8"

Porch

Garage
19-4x21-4

First Floor
760 sq. ft.

Special features

1,492 total square feet of living area

- Cleverly angled entry spills into the living and dining rooms which share warmth from the fireplace flanked by arched windows
- Master bedroom includes a double-door entry, huge walk-in closet, shower and bath with picture window
- Stucco and dutch-hipped roofs add warmth and charm to facade
- 3 bedrooms, 2 1/2 baths, 2-car garage
- Basement foundation

Plan #596-040D-0029

Price Code AA

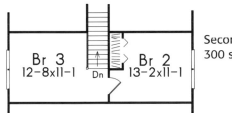

Second Floor
300 sq. ft.

Br 3
12-8x11-1

Dn

Br 2
13-2x11-1

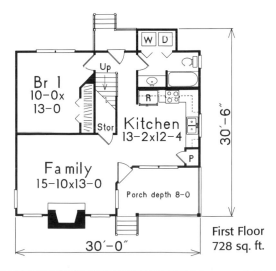

Up

W D

Br 1
10-0x
13-0

Stor

Kitchen
13-2x12-4

R

P

Family
15-10x13-0

Porch depth 8-0

30'-6"

30'-0"

First Floor
728 sq. ft.

Special features

1,028 total square feet of living area

- Well-designed bath contains laundry facilities
- L-shaped kitchen has a handy pantry
- Tall windows flank family room fireplace
- Cozy covered porch provides unique angled entry into home
- 3 bedrooms, 1 bath
- Crawl space foundation

Special features

1,768 total square feet of living area

- Uniquely designed vaulted living and dining rooms combine making great use of space
- Informal family room has a vaulted ceiling, plant shelf accents and kitchen overlook
- Sunny breakfast area conveniently accesses the kitchen
- 3 bedrooms, 2 baths, 2-car garage
- Slab foundation

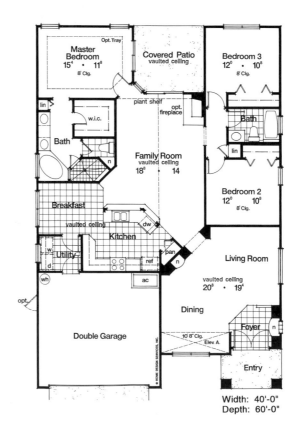

Master Bedroom 15⁴ • 11⁸

Covered Patio vaulted ceiling

Bedroom 3 12⁰ • 10⁸

w.i.c.

Bath

plant shelf   opt. fireplace

Family Room vaulted ceiling 18⁸ • 14

Bath

Bedroom 2 12⁰ • 10⁸

Breakfast

vaulted ceiling

Kitchen

Living Room vaulted ceiling 20⁸ • 19⁴

Utility

Dining

Double Garage

Foyer

Entry

Width: 40'-0"
Depth: 60'-0"

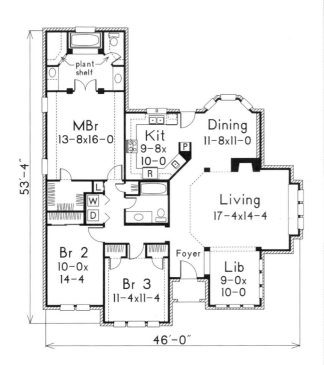

Special features

1,824 total square feet of living area

- Living room features a 10' ceiling, fireplace and media center
- Dining room includes a bay window and convenient kitchen access
- Master bedroom features a large walk-in closet and luxurious bath with a double-door entry
- Modified U-shaped kitchen features pantry and bar
- 3 bedrooms, 2 baths, 2-car detached garage
- Slab foundation

Special features

1,821 total square feet of living area

- 9' ceilings throughout the first floor
- Master suite is secluded for privacy and has a spacious bath
- Sunny breakfast room features a bay window
- Bonus room on the second floor has an additional 191 square feet of living area
- 3 bedrooms, 2 baths, 2-car side entry garage
- Slab foundation

Special features

1,680 total square feet of living area

- Enormous and luxurious master suite
- Kitchen and dining room have vaulted ceilings creating an open feeling
- Double sinks grace the secondary bath
- 3 bedrooms, 2 baths, 2-car garage
- Walk-out basement, basement, crawl space or slab foundation, please specify when ordering

Plan #596-007D-0087

Price Code A

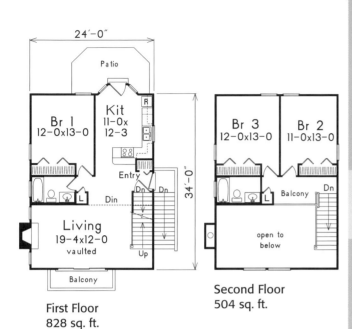

24'-0"

Patio

Br 1
12-0x13-0

Kit
11-0x
12-3

R

Entry

Dn

Din

Dn Dn

L

Living
19-4x12-0
vaulted

Up

Balcony

34'-0"

First Floor
828 sq. ft.

Br 3
12-0x13-0

Br 2
11-0x13-0

L

Balcony

Dn

open to
below

Second Floor
504 sq. ft.

Special features

1,332 total square feet of living area

- Home offers both basement and first floor entry locations
- A dramatic living room features a vaulted ceiling, fireplace, exterior balcony and dining area
- An L-shaped kitchen offers spacious cabinetry, breakfast area with bay window and access to the rear patio
- 3 bedrooms, 2 baths, 4-car tandem garage
- Walk-out basement foundation

Plan #596-032D-0016

Price Code AA

9'-0"x 11'-0"
2,70 x 3,30

14'-0"x 11'-0"
4,20 x 3,30

Second Floor
533 sq. ft.

24'-0"
7,2 m

10'-0"x 12'-0"
3,00 x 3,60

8'-0"x 11'-0"
2,40 x 3,30

11'-0"x 14'-0"
3,30 x 4,20

First Floor
587 sq. ft.

26'-0"
8,0 m

Special features

1,120 total square feet of living area

- Energy efficient home with 2" x 6" exterior walls
- Dining and cooking island in the kitchen makes food preparation easy
- All bedrooms are located on the second floor for privacy from the living area
- Convenient laundry closet on the first floor
- 2 bedrooms, 1 1/2 baths
- Slab foundation

Special features

1,295 total square feet of living area

- Energy efficient home with 2" x 6" exterior walls
- Wrap-around porch is a lovely place for dining
- A fireplace gives a stunning focal point to the great room that is heightened with a sloped ceiling
- The master suite is full of luxurious touches such as a walk-in closet and a lush private bath
- 2 bedrooms, 2 baths, 2-car garage
- Basement foundation

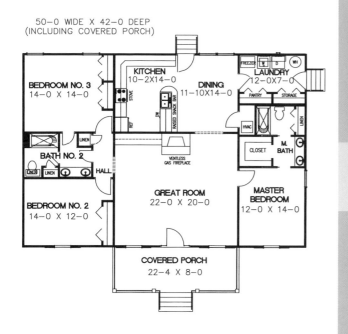

50-0 WIDE X 42-0 DEEP
(INCLUDING COVERED PORCH)

BEDROOM NO. 3
14-0 X 14-0

KITCHEN
10-2X14-0

DINING
11-10X14-0

LAUNDRY
12-0X7-0

FREEZER

PANTRY   STORAGE

STOVE   RAISED SNACK BAR   REF   DW

HWAC

LINEN

BATH NO. 2

LINEN   LINEN

HALL

BEDROOM NO. 2
14-0 X 12-0

VENTLESS
GAS FIREPLACE

CLOSET

M.
BATH

GREAT ROOM
22-0 X 20-0

MASTER
BEDROOM
12-0 X 14-0

COVERED PORCH
22-4 X 8-0

Special features

1,700 total square feet of living area

- Oversized laundry room has a large pantry and storage area as well as access to the outdoors
- Master bedroom is separated from other bedrooms for privacy
- Raised snack bar in kitchen allows extra seating for dining
- 3 bedrooms, 2 baths
- Crawl space or slab foundation, please specify when ordering

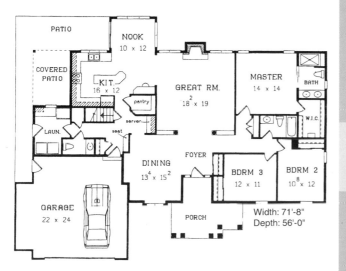

PATIO

NOOK
10 x 12

COVERED
PATIO

KIT.
16 x 12

pantry

server

GREAT RM.
18^2 x 19

MASTER
14 x 14

BATH

W.I.C.

LAUN.

seat

DINING
13^4 x 15^2

FOYER

BDRM 3
12 x 11

BDRM 2
10^8 x 12

GARAGE
22 x 24

PORCH

Width: 71'-8"
Depth: 56'-0"

Special features

2,083 total square feet of living area

- Energy efficient home with 2" x 6" exterior walls
- A handy server counter located between the kitchen and formal dining room is ideal for entertaining
- Decorative columns grace the entrance into the great room
- A large island in the kitchen aids in food preparation
- 3 bedrooms, 2 1/2 baths, 2-car garage
- Basement foundation

Special features

1,575 total square feet of living area

- Energy efficient home with 2" x 6" exterior walls
- Two secondary bedrooms share a full bath
- The formal dining room features column accents
- Breakfast room has sliding glass doors leading to an outdoor deck
- 3 bedrooms, 2 baths, 2-car garage
- Basement foundation

Plan #596-025D-0005

Price Code A

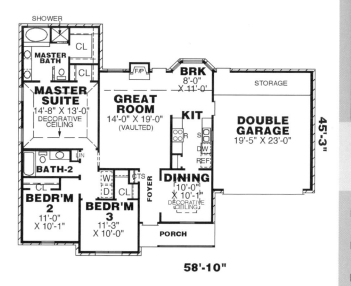

SHOWER

MASTER BATH — CL — CL

MASTER SUITE 14'-8" X 13'-0" DECORATIVE CEILING

F/P

GREAT ROOM 14'-0" X 19'-0" (VAULTED)

KIT

BRK 8'-0" X 11'-0"

STORAGE

DOUBLE GARAGE 19'-5" X 23'-0"

45'-3"

BATH-2

CL

BEDR'M 2 11'-0" X 10'-1"

W D — CL

BEDR'M 3 11'-3" X 10'-0"

CTS

FOYER

DINING 10'-0" X 10'-1" DECORATIVE CEILING

PORCH

58'-10"

Special features

1,429 total square feet of living area

- Master bedroom features a spacious private bath and double walk-in closets
- Formal dining room has convenient access to the kitchen which is perfect for entertaining
- Additional storage can be found in the garage
- 3 bedrooms, 2 baths, 2-car garage
- Slab foundation

Plan #596-087D-0065

Price Code E

DINING 10 x 8

PAN.

KITCHEN 11 x 10

F/P

"VAULTED" FAMILY ROOM 14 x 21

"VAULTED" MASTER BEDROOM 13 x 15

CLOSET 5 x 7

L.

48'

BATH #2 — UTIL.

HALL

MSTR. BATH 9 x 15

CLO. 4 x 7

HALL

CLOS.

CTS

STOR 5 x 3

F.

CLOS.

L.

BEDROOM #3 10 x 10

BEDROOM #2 10 x 12

ENTRY 4 x 8

PORCH 4 x 5

DOUBLE GARAGE 18 x 20

45'

© Sullivan & Assoc.

Special features

1,384 total square feet of living area

- The entry leads into the large vaulted family room that enjoys a corner fireplace and access to the rear yard
- The U-shaped kitchen has an abundance of counterspace and opens to the bayed dining room
- Split bedrooms ensure privacy for all
- 3 bedrooms, 2 baths, 2-car garage
- Slab foundation

Special features

2,153 total square feet of living area

- Secluded first floor study would make an ideal home office
- Breakfast room flows into the great room creating an open feel
- Bonus room on the second floor has an additional 486 square feet of living area
- 3 bedrooms, 2 1/2 baths, 2-car side entry garage
- Basement foundation

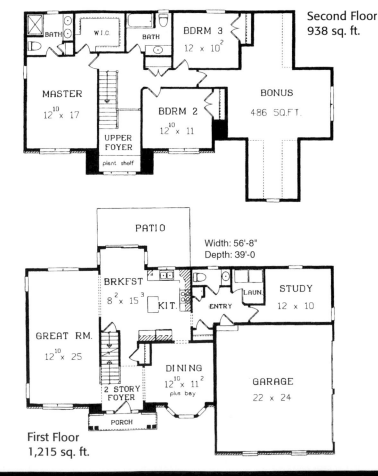

Second Floor
938 sq. ft.

BATH

W.I.C.

BATH

BDRM 3
12 x 10²

MASTER
12¹⁰ x 17

BONUS
486 SQ.FT.

BDRM 2
12¹⁰ x 11

UPPER
FOYER
plant shelf

PATIO

Width: 56'-8"
Depth: 39'-0

BRKFST
8² x 15³

KIT.

LAUN.

STUDY
12 x 10

ENTRY

GREAT RM.
12¹⁰ x 25

DINING
12¹⁰ x 11²
plus bay

GARAGE
22 x 24

2 STORY
FOYER

PORCH

First Floor
1,215 sq. ft.

Plan #596-013D-0001

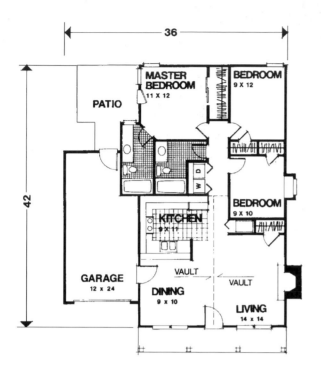

Special features

1,050 total square feet of living area

- Master bedroom has its own private bath and access to the outdoors onto a private patio
- Vaulted ceilings in the living and dining areas create a feeling of spaciousness
- The laundry closet is convenient to all bedrooms
- Efficient U-shaped kitchen
- 3 bedrooms, 2 baths, 1-car garage
- Basement or slab foundation, please specify when ordering

Plan #596-076D-0017

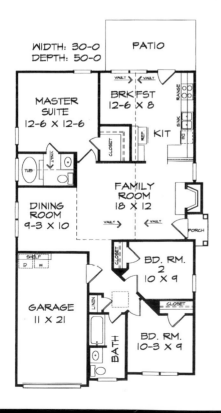

Special features

1,123 total square feet of living area

- Spacious kitchen and breakfast area feature vaulted ceilings and patio access
- Fireplace warms the adjoining family and dining rooms
- Secondary bedrooms are secluded and share a bath
- 3 bedrooms, 2 baths, 1-car garage
- Crawl space or slab foundation, please specify when ordering

Special features

632 total square feet of living area

- Porch leads to a vaulted entry and stair with feature window, coat closet and access to garage/laundry
- Cozy living room offers a vaulted ceiling, fireplace, large palladian window and pass-through to kitchen
- A garden tub with arched window is part of a very roomy bath
- 1 bedroom, 1 bath, 2-car garage
- Slab foundation

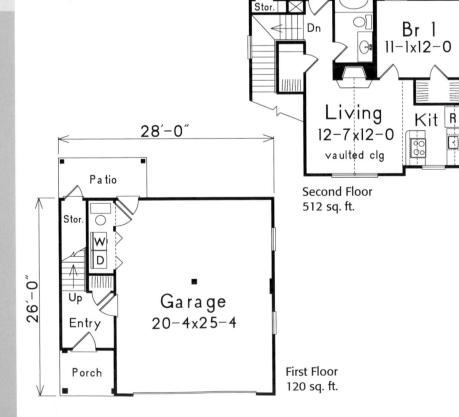

Second Floor
512 sq. ft.

First Floor
120 sq. ft.

Plan #596-016D-0007

Special features

1,207 total square feet of living area

- Triple sets of sliding glass doors leading to the deck brighten the living room
- Oversized mud room has lots of extra closet space for convenience
- Centrally located heat circulating fireplace creates a focal point while warming the home
- 3 bedrooms, 2 baths
- Basement or crawl space foundation, please specify when ordering

Plan #596-077D-0109

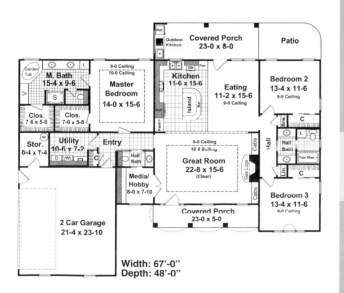

Special features

2,000 total square feet of living area

- A unique media/hobby room off the great room keeps household projects organized
- The great room, eating area and kitchen combine for a large family center complete with a fireplace
- The master bedroom enjoys a decorative ceiling, two walk-in closets and a plush bath designed to pamper
- 3 bedrooms, 2 1/2 baths, 2-car side entry garage
- Slab or crawl space foundation, please specify when ordering

Special features

991 total square feet of living area

- Energy efficient home with 2" x 6" exterior walls
- Master bedroom has a large walk-in closet
- Large and open kitchen is well organized
- 2 bedrooms, 2 baths
- Basement foundation

QUICK FACT - A colored ceiling can make a room much more interesting. If the walls have been painted, but the ceiling is still white, the eye is drawn to the white ceiling because of the contrast. Why not make the contrast an unexpected color to complement the space creating an element of surprise?

Second Floor
395 sq. ft.

11'-0" X 10'-4"
3,30 X 3,10

11'-8" X 11'-8"
3,50 X 3,50

First Floor
596 sq. ft.

9'-4" X 10'-4"
2,80 X 3,10

8'-0" X 14'-4"
2,40 X 4,30

13'-0" X 12'-0"
3,90 X 3,60

10'-0" X 24'-0"
3,00 X 7,20

26'-8"
8,0 m

22'-8"
6,8 m

Plan #596-007D-0133

Price Code A

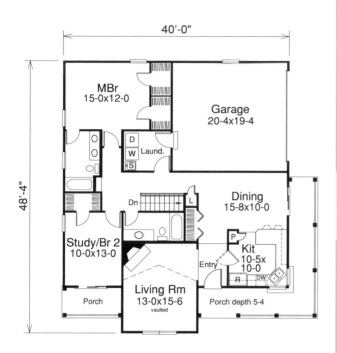

40'-0"

48'-4"

MBr
15-0x12-0

Garage
20-4x19-4

D
W
S
Laund.

Dn

L

Dining
15-8x10-0

Study/Br 2
10-0x13-0

P

Kit
10-5x
10-0

Entry

R
DW

Living Rm
13-0x15-6
vaulted

Porch

Porch depth 5-4

Special features

1,316 total square feet of living area

- Porches are accessible from entry, dining room and bedroom #2
- The living room enjoys a vaulted ceiling, corner fireplace and twin windows with an arched transom above
- A kitchen is provided with corner windows, an outdoor plant shelf, a built-in pantry and opens to a large dining room
- Bedrooms are very roomy and feature walk-in closets
- 2 bedrooms, 2 baths, 2-car side entry garage
- Basement foundation, drawings also include crawl space and slab foundations

Plan #596-008D-0139

Price Code A

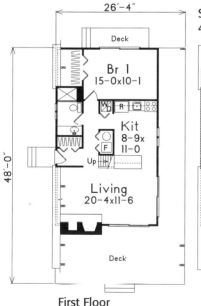

26'-4"

Second Floor
480 sq. ft.

Deck

Br 1
15-0x10-1

W
D
R

Kit
8-9x
11-0

F

Up

Living
20-4x11-6

Deck

48'-0"

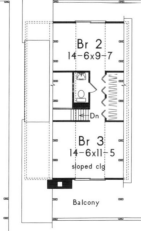

Br 2
14-6x9-7

Dn

Br 3
14-6x11-5
sloped clg

Balcony

First Floor
792 sq. ft.

Special features

1,272 total square feet of living area

- Stone fireplace accents living room
- Spacious kitchen includes snack bar overlooking the living room
- First floor bedroom is roomy and secluded
- Plenty of closet space for second floor bedrooms plus a generous balcony which wraps around the second floor
- 3 bedrooms, 1 1/2 baths
- Crawl space foundation

Special features

1,800 total square feet of living area

- Energy efficient home with 2" x 6" exterior walls
- Covered front and rear porches add outdoor living area
- 12' ceilings in the kitchen, breakfast area, dining and living rooms
- Private master bedroom features an expansive bath
- Side entry garage has two storage areas
- Pillared styling with brick and stucco exterior finish
- 3 bedrooms, 2 baths, 2-car side entry garage
- Crawl space foundation, drawings also include slab foundation

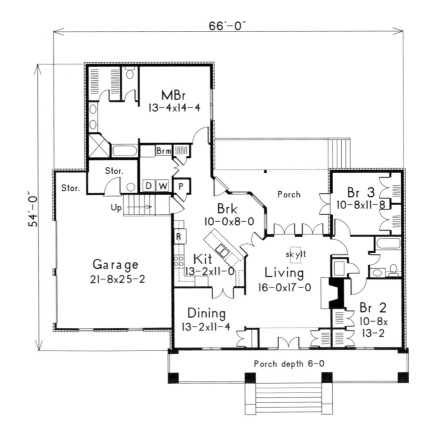

Plan #596-013D-0010

Price Code C

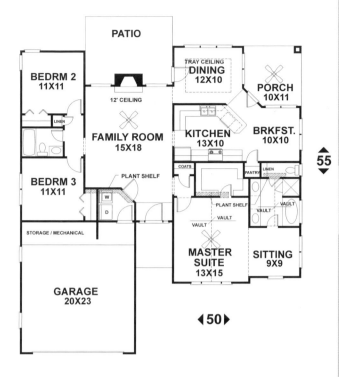

Special features

1,593 total square feet of living area

- Large sitting area is enjoyed by the master bedroom which also features a walk-in closet and bath
- Centrally located kitchen accesses the family, dining and breakfast rooms with ease
- Storage/mechanical area is ideal for seasonal storage or hobby supplies
- 3 bedrooms, 2 baths, 2-car garage
- Basement, crawl space or slab foundation, please specify when ordering

Plan #596-035D-0027

Price Code B

Special features

1,544 total square feet of living area

- Well-designed floor plan has a vaulted family room
- Decorative columns separate the dining area from the foyer
- A vaulted ceiling adds spaciousness to the master bath
- Bonus room above garage has an additional 284 square feet of living area
- 3 bedrooms, 2 baths, 2-car garage
- Walk-out basement or crawl space foundation, please specify when ordering

Special features

1,560 total square feet of living area

- Cozy breakfast room is tucked at the rear of this home and features plenty of windows for natural light
- Large entry has easy access to the secondary bedrooms, utility area, dining and living rooms
- Private master bedroom
- Kitchen overlooks the living room which features a fireplace and patio access
- 3 bedrooms, 2 baths, 2-car garage
- Slab foundation

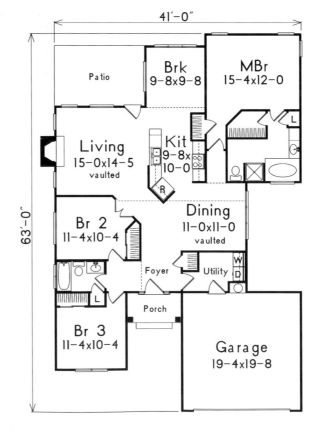

Plan #596-087D-0071

Price Code E

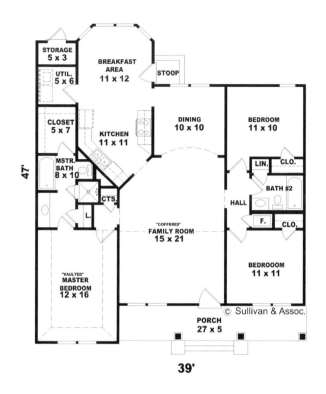

Special features

1,437 total square feet of living area

- The covered front porch opens into the massive family room
- The private master bedroom enjoys a vaulted ceiling, dressing area and bath with walk-in closet
- Two secondary bedrooms are located in a separate wing and share a full bath
- 3 bedrooms, 2 baths
- Slab foundation

Floor plan labels: STORAGE 5 x 3, UTIL. 5 x 6, BREAKFAST AREA 11 x 12, STOOP, CLOSET 5 x 7, KITCHEN 11 x 11, DINING 10 x 10, BEDROOM 11 x 10, MSTR. BATH 8 x 10, CTS., LIN., CLO., BATH #2, HALL, "COFFERED" FAMILY ROOM 15 x 21, F., CLO., "VAULTED" MASTER BEDROOM 12 x 16, BEDROOOM 11 x 11, © Sullivan & Assoc., PORCH 27 x 5, 47', 39'

Plan #596-055D-0012

Price Code A

Special features

1,381 total square feet of living area

- Plenty of closet space in all bedrooms
- Kitchen has a large eating bar for extra dining
- Great room has a sunny wall of windows creating a cheerful atmosphere
- 3 bedrooms, 2 baths, 2-car garage
- Slab, crawl space, walk-out basement or basement foundation, please specify when ordering

Floor plan labels: 48' 0", MASTER SUITE 13'-6" X 13'-6", 9' BOXED CEILING, GREAT ROOM 17'-0" X 13'-6", GAS FIREPLACE, 9' BOXED CEILING, BEDROOM 3 11'-4" X 11'-8", BATH, DW, REF, KITCHEN, RG, DINING 11'-2" X 13'-8", FOYER, LIN, BATH, HVAC, BEDROOM 2 11'-4" X 11'-6", VAULTED CEILING, PRCH, W, D, STRG., GARAGE 19'-4" X 21'-6", 48' 0"

Special features

990 total square feet of living area

- Covered front porch adds a charming feel
- Vaulted ceilings in the kitchen, family and dining rooms create a spacious feel
- Large linen, pantry and storage closets throughout
- 2 bedrooms, 1 bath
- Crawl space foundation

QUICK FACT - Painting the cabinets in the kitchen with a high gloss paint bounces even more light around making the space seem bigger.

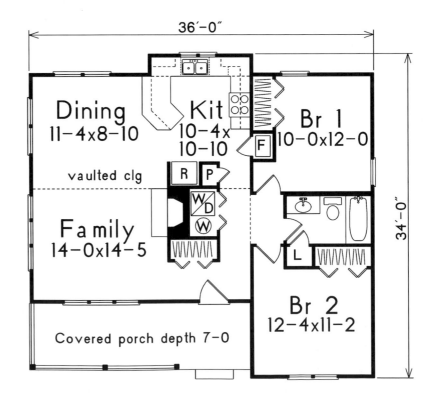

36'-0"

Dining
11-4x8-10

Kit
10-4x
10-10

Br 1
10-0x12-0

F

vaulted clg

R   P

W D

W

Family
14-0x14-5

L

34'-0"

Br 2
12-4x11-2

Covered porch depth 7-0

Plan #596-035D-0006

Price Code B

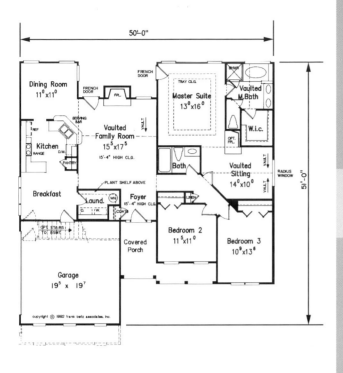

Special features

1,671 total square feet of living area

- Kitchen is conveniently located between the breakfast and dining rooms
- Vaulted family room is centrally located
- Laundry room is located near the garage for easy access
- 3 bedrooms, 2 baths, 2-car side entry garage
- Slab, crawl space or walk-out basement foundation, please specify when ordering

Plan #596-045D-0017

Price Code AA

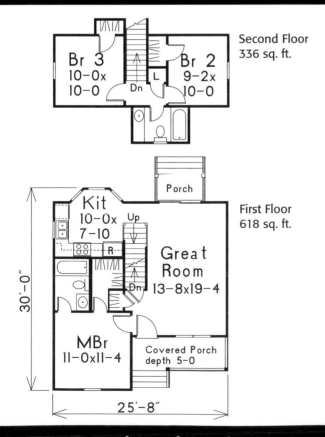

Second Floor
336 sq. ft.

First Floor
618 sq. ft.

Special features

954 total square feet of living area

- Kitchen has a cozy bayed eating area
- Master bedroom has a walk-in closet and private bath
- Large great room has access to the back porch
- Convenient coat closet is near the front entry
- 3 bedrooms, 2 baths
- Basement foundation

Special features

1,299 total square feet of living area

- Large porch for enjoying relaxing evenings
- First floor master bedroom has a bay window, walk-in closet and roomy bath
- Two generous bedrooms with lots of closet space, a hall bath, linen closet and balcony overlook comprise the second floor
- 3 bedrooms, 2 1/2 baths
- Basement foundation

24'-0"

Patio

Kit
12-0x14-10

MBr
13-0x13-6

40'-0"

Dn

Living Rm
12-1x18-3

Up

Porch depth 6-0

First Floor
834 sq. ft.

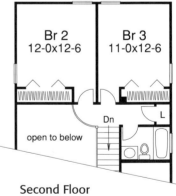

Br 2
12-0x12-6

Br 3
11-0x12-6

open to below

Dn

Second Floor
465 sq. ft.

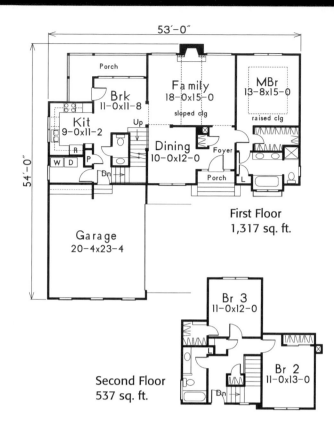

53'-0"

54'-0"

Porch

Brk
11-0x11-8

Family
18-0x15-0
sloped clg

MBr
13-8x15-0
raised clg

Kit
9-0x11-2

Up

Dining
10-0x12-0

Foyer

R

W D P

Dn

Porch

L

Garage
20-4x23-4

First Floor
1,317 sq. ft.

Br 3
11-0x12-0

Br 2
11-0x13-0

Dn

Second Floor
537 sq. ft.

Special features

1,854 total square feet of living area

- Front entrance is enhanced by arched transom windows and rustic stone
- Isolated master bedroom includes a dressing area and walk-in closet
- Family room features a high sloped ceiling and large fireplace
- Breakfast area accesses the covered rear porch
- 3 bedrooms, 2 1/2 baths, 2-car side entry garage
- Basement foundation

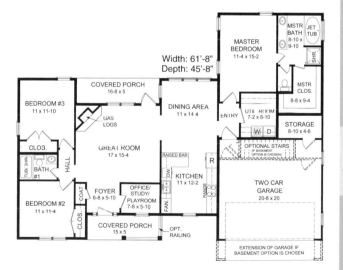

Width: 61'-8"
Depth: 45'-8"

BEDROOM #3
11 x 11-10

COVERED PORCH
16-8 x 5

GAS LOGS

CLO3.

TUB/SHR.

BATH #1

HALL

BEDROOM #2
11 x 11-4

CLOS.

COAT

FOYER
6-8 x 5-10

OFFICE/STUDY/PLAYROOM
7-8 x 5-10

GREAT ROOM
17 x 15-4

RAISED BAR

DINING AREA
11 x 14 4

KITCHEN
11 x 12-2

DW

RANGE

R

COVERED PORCH
15 x 5

OPT. RAILING

ENTRY

UTIL ROOM
7-2 x 8-10

W D

OPTIONAL STAIRS
(IF BASEMENT OPTION IS CHOSEN)

MASTER BEDROOM
11-4 x 15-2

MSTR BATH
8-10 x 9-10

JET TUB

SHR.

MSTR CLOS.
8-8 x 9-4

STORAGE
8-10 x 4-6

TWO CAR GARAGE
20-8 x 20

EXTENSION OF GARAGE IF BASEMENT OPTION IS CHOSEN

Special features

1,600 total square feet of living area

- Energy efficient home with 2" x 6" exterior walls
- The office/study/playroom is a flexible space that can adapt to any need
- The covered back porch is set into the house making it a lovely sheltered retreat
- 3 bedrooms, 2 baths, 2-car garage
- Basement, crawl space or slab foundation, please specify when ordering

Special features

1,840 total square feet of living area

- All bedrooms are located on the second floor for privacy
- Counter dining space is provided in the kitchen
- Formal dining room connects to the kitchen through French doors
- 4 bedrooms, 2 1/2 baths, 2-car side entry garage with shop/storage
- Basement, crawl space or slab foundation, please specify when ordering

Second Floor
826 sq. ft.

BEDROOM #3
11'-8"x11'-9"

HALL BATH

MSTR BATH

W.I.C.

BEDROOM #2
10'-8"x10'-0"

6'-7"

MASTER BEDROOM
11'-8"x16'-0"
(10' TRAY CLG)

SITTING AREA
(VAULTED)

First Floor
1,014 sq. ft.

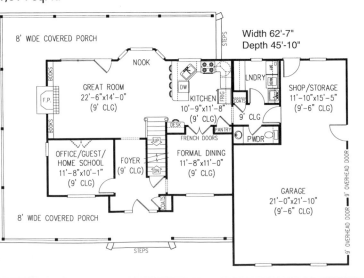

8' WIDE COVERED PORCH

NOOK

GREAT ROOM
22'-6"x14'-0"
(9' CLG)

F.P.

KITCHEN
10'-9"x11'-8"
(9' CLG)

LNDRY

SHOP/STORAGE
11'-10"x15'-5"
(9'-6" CLG)

Width 62'-7"
Depth 45'-10"

OFFICE/GUEST/
HOME SCHOOL
11'-8"x10'-1"
(9' CLG)

FOYER
(9' CLG)

FORMAL DINING
11'-8"x11'-0"
(9' CLG)

FRENCH DOORS

PWDR

GARAGE
21'-0"x21'-10"
(9'-6" CLG)

8' WIDE COVERED PORCH

9' OVERHEAD DOOR

9' OVERHEAD DOOR

STEPS

Br 1
10-0x
13-8
vaulted

Kit

R

Dn

Second Floor
528 sq. ft.

plant shelf

Living
15-8x10-8
vaulted

Balcony

29'-0"

Furn

24'-0"

Garage
21-4x23-4

Up

Entry

First Floor
126 sq. ft.

Special features

654 total square feet of living area

- Two-story vaulted entry has a balcony overlook and large windows to welcome the sun
- Vaulted living room is open to a pass-through kitchen and breakfast bar with an overhead plant shelf and features sliding glass doors to an outdoor balcony
- The bedroom with vaulted ceiling offers a private bath and walk-in closet
- 1 bedroom, 1 bath, 2-car garage
- Slab foundation

64'-8"

56'-0"

MBr
13-4x14-0

Living
17-4x17-4

Brk
12-0x11-0

W D

Storage

Kit
12-0x
12-0

R

P

Garage
20-4x21-4

Br 3
13-4x11-8

Br 2
11-4x14-8

sloped clg

Foyer

Dining
11-8x13-0

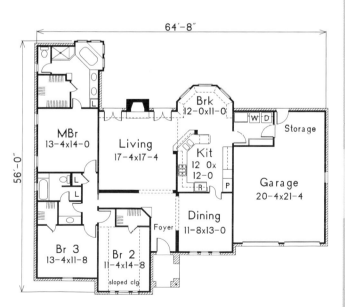

Special features

1,994 total square feet of living area

- Convenient entrance from the garage into the main living area through the utility room
- Bedroom #2 features a 12' vaulted ceiling and the dining room boasts a 10' ceiling
- Entry leads to the formal dining room and attractive living room with double French doors and fireplace
- 3 bedrooms, 2 baths, 2-car garage
- Slab foundation

Special features

2,128 total square feet of living area

- Versatile kitchen has plenty of space for entertaining with large dining area and counter seating
- Luxurious master bedroom has a double-door entry and private bath with whirlpool tub, double sinks and large walk-in closet
- Secondary bedrooms include spacious walk-in closets
- Coat closet in front entry is a nice added feature
- 4 bedrooms, 2 baths, 2-car garage
- Slab foundation, drawings also include crawl space foundation

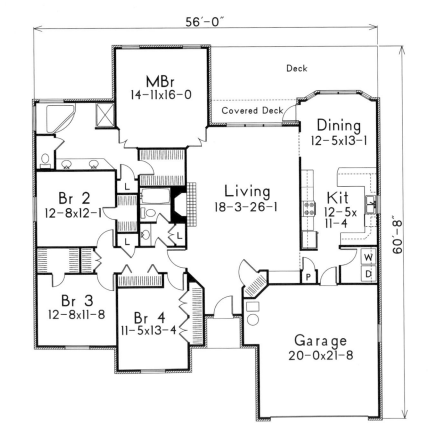

56'-0"

MBr
14-11x16-0

Deck

Covered Deck

Dining
12-5x13-1

Br 2
12-8x12-1

Living
18-3-26-1

Kit
12-5x
11-4

60'-8"

Br 3
12-8x11-8

Br 4
11-5x13-4

Garage
20-0x21-8

Plan #596-001D-0030

Price Code A

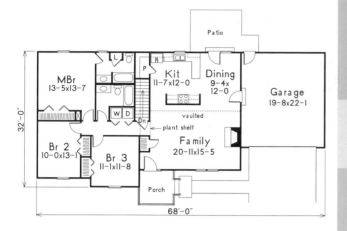

Special features

1,416 total square feet of living area

- Family room includes fireplace, elevated plant shelf and vaulted ceiling
- Patio is accessible from the dining area and garage
- Centrally located laundry area
- Oversized walk-in pantry in the kitchen
- 3 bedrooms, 2 baths, 2-car garage
- Basement foundation, drawings also include crawl space and slab foundations

Plan #596-007D-0103

Price Code A

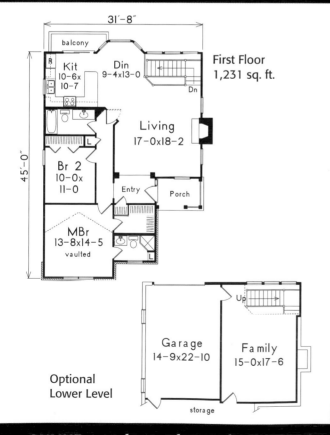

Special features

1,231 total square feet of living area

- Dutch gables and stone accents provide an enchanting exterior
- The spacious living room offers a masonry fireplace, atrium with window wall and is open to a dining area
- Kitchen has a breakfast counter, lots of cabinet space and glass sliding doors to a balcony
- 380 square feet of optional living area on the lower level
- 2 bedrooms, 2 baths, 1-car drive under garage
- Walk-out basement foundation

Special features

1,344 total square feet of living area

- Kitchen has side entry, laundry area, pantry and joins family/dining area
- Master bedroom includes a private bath
- Linen and storage closets in hall
- Covered porch opens to the spacious living room with a handy coat closet
- 3 bedrooms, 2 baths
- Crawl space foundation, drawings also include basement and slab foundations

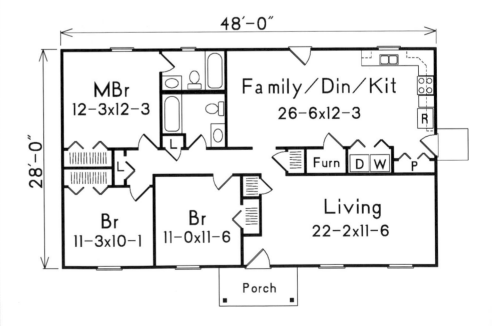

48'-0"

28'-0"

MBr
12-3x12-3

Family/Din/Kit
26-6x12-3

R

Furn | D | W | P

Br
11-3x10-1

Br
11-0x11-6

Living
22-2x11-6

Porch

Plan #596-035D-0013

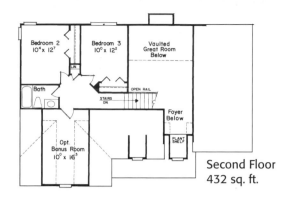

Second Floor
432 sq. ft.

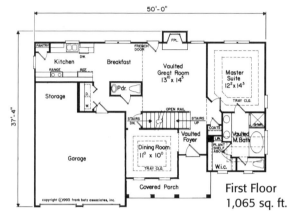

First Floor
1,065 sq. ft.

Special features

1,497 total square feet of living area

- Master suite has a private luxurious bath with spacious walk-in closet
- Formal dining room has a tray ceiling and views onto the front covered porch
- Bonus room on the second floor has an additional 175 square feet of living area
- 3 bedrooms, 2 1/2 baths, 2-car garage
- Crawl space or walk-out basement foundation, please specify when ordering

Plan #596-040D-0008

Price Code B

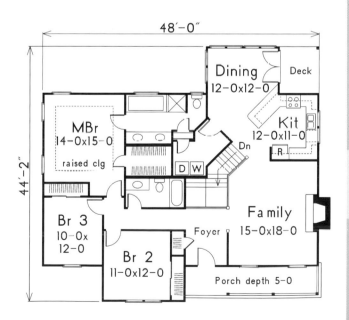

Special features

1,631 total square feet of living area

- 9' ceilings throughout this home
- Utility room is conveniently located near the kitchen
- Roomy kitchen and dining area boast a breakfast bar and deck access
- A raised ceiling accents the master bedroom
- 3 bedrooms, 2 baths, 2-car drive under garage
- Basement foundation

Special features

902 total square feet of living area

- Vaulted entry with laundry room leads to a spacious second floor apartment
- The large living room features an entry coat closet, L-shaped kitchen with pantry and dining area/balcony overlooking atrium window wall
- Roomy bedroom with walk-in closet is convenient to hall bath
- 1 bedroom, 1 bath, 2-car side entry garage
- Slab foundation

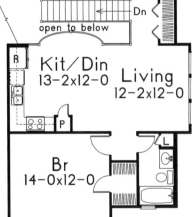

open to below   Dn

Kit/Din
13-2x12-0

Living
12-2x12-0

R

P

Br
14-0x12-0

Second Floor
664 sq. ft.

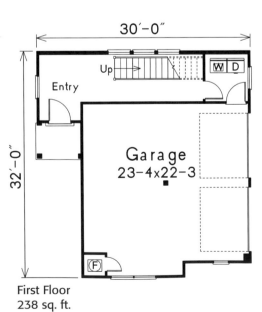

30'-0"

Up

W   D

Entry

32'-0"

Garage
23-4x22-3

F

First Floor
238 sq. ft.

Plan #596-047D-0032

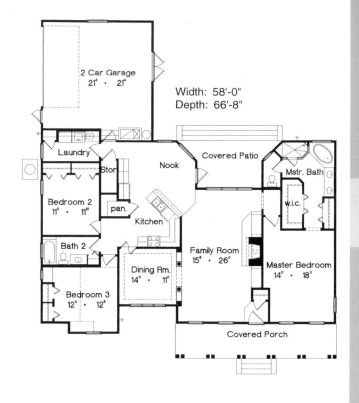

Width: 58'-0"
Depth: 66'-8"

Special features

1,963 total square feet of living area

- Spacious breakfast nook is a great gathering place
- Master bedroom has its own wing with a private bath and lots of closet space
- Large laundry room with closet and sink
- Framing - only concrete block available
- 3 bedrooms, 2 baths, 2-car side entry garage
- Slab or crawl space foundation, please specify when ordering

Plan #596-058D-0023

Price Code C

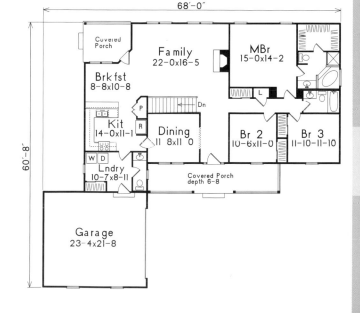

Special features

1,883 total square feet of living area

- Energy efficient home with 2" x 6" exterior walls
- Large laundry room located off the garage has a half bath
- Large family room with fireplace and access to the covered porch is a great central gathering room
- U-shaped kitchen has breakfast bar, large pantry and swing door to dining room for convenient serving
- 3 bedrooms, 2 1/2 baths, 2-car side entry garage
- Basement foundation

Special features

1,618 total square feet of living area

- Wrap-around porch offers a covered passageway to the garage
- Dramatic two-story entry, with balcony above and staircase provide an expansive feel with an added decorative oval window
- Dazzling kitchen features walk-in pantry, convenient laundry and covered rear porch
- 3 bedrooms, 2 1/2 baths, 1-car garage
- Basement foundation

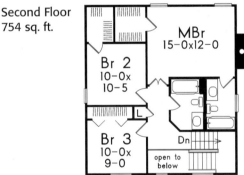

Second Floor
754 sq. ft.

MBr
15-0x12-0

Br 2
10-0x
10-5

Br 3
10-0x
9-0

Dn

open to below

L

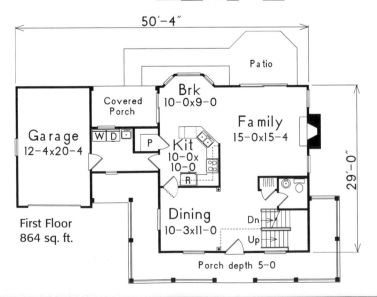

50'-4"

Patio

Brk
10-0x9-0

Covered Porch

Family
15-0x15-4

Garage
12-4x20-4

W D

P

Kit
10-0x
10-0

R

29'-0"

Dining
10-3x11-0

Dn

Up

First Floor
864 sq. ft.

Porch depth 5-0

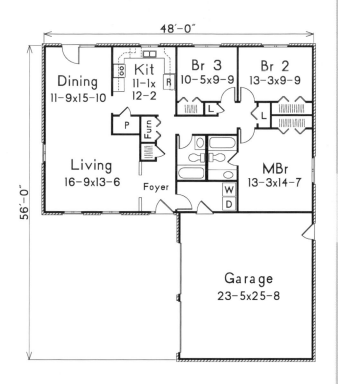

Special features

1,440 total square feet of living area

- Entry foyer features a coat closet and half wall leading into the living area
- Spaciousness is created with open living and dining areas
- Walk-in pantry adds convenience to the U-shaped kitchen
- Spacious utility room is adjacent to the garage
- 3 bedrooms, 2 baths, 2-car side entry garage
- Crawl space foundation, drawings also include basement and slab foundations

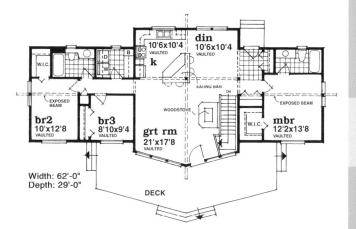

Special features

1,405 total square feet of living area

- Energy efficient home with 2" x 6" exterior walls
- An expansive wall of glass gives a spectacular view to the great room and accentuates the vaulted ceilings
- Great room is open to the dining room and L-shaped kitchen
- Triangular snack bar graces the kitchen
- 3 bedrooms, 2 baths
- Basement or crawl space foundation, please specify when ordering

Special features

1,516 total square feet of living area

- Energy efficient home with 2" x 6" exterior walls
- Warm fireplace adds coziness to living areas
- Dining area and kitchen are convenient to each other making entertaining easy
- 3 bedrooms, 2 baths
- Basement foundation

QUICK FACT - Cedar is a light, reddish-brown, rather soft wood used from the 18th century for drawer linings, boxes, chests (inside and out), and wardrobes. It was, and still is, much valued for its moth and insect repelling qualities.

Second Floor
454 sq. ft.

14'-0" X 17'-4"
4,20 X 5,20

OPEN TO BELOW

First Floor
1,062 sq. ft.

9'-8" X 10'-4"
2,90 X 3,10

10'-8" X 13'-4"
3,20 X 4,00

9'-2" X 10'-0"
2,75 X 3,00

17'-4" X 13'-0"
5,20 X 3,90

8'-4" X 12'-8"
2,50 X 3,80

28'-0"
8,4 m

40'-0"
12,0 m

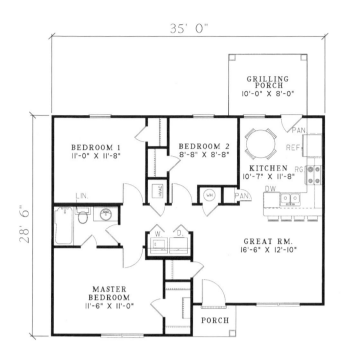

Special features

930 total square feet of living area

- Kitchen overlooks the great room and includes space for counter dining
- Convenient laundry closet
- Master bedroom has walk-in closet and direct access to hall bath
- 3 bedrooms, 1 bath
- Slab or crawl space foundation, please specify when ordering

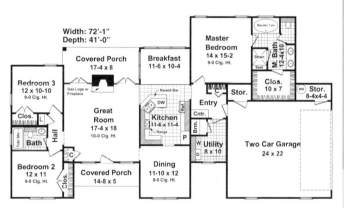

First Floor
1,638 sq. ft.

Optional
Stair Location

Special features

1,638 total square feet of living area

- Great room features a fireplace with flanking doors that access the covered porch
- The centrally located kitchen serves the breakfast and dining areas with ease
- Plenty of storage area is located in the garage
- 3 bedrooms, 2 baths, 2-car side entry garage
- Basement, crawl space or slab foundation, please specify when ordering

Special features

2,012 total square feet of living area

- Gables, cantilevers, and box-bay windows all contribute to an elegant exterior
- Two-story entry leads to an efficient kitchen and bayed breakfast area with morning room
- Garage contains extra space for a shop, bicycles and miscellaneous storage
- 5 bedrooms, 2 1/2 baths, 2-car garage
- Basement foundation

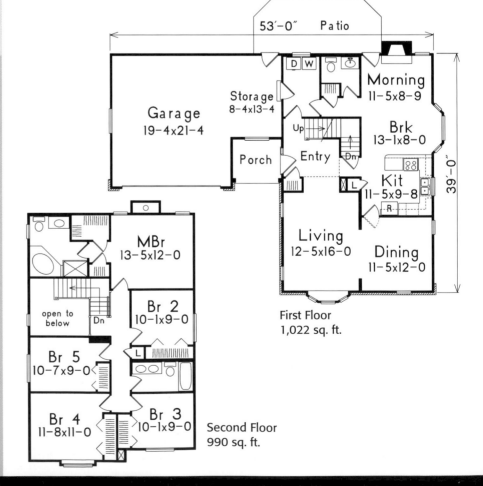

53'-0"   Patio

Garage
19-4x21-4

Storage
8-4x13-4

Morning
11-5x8-9

Brk
13-1x8-0

Up

Entry   Dn

Porch

Kit
11-5x9-8

39'-0"

Living
12-5x16-0

Dining
11-5x12-0

First Floor
1,022 sq. ft.

MBr
13-5x12-0

open to
below   Dn

Br 2
10-1x9-0

Br 5
10-7x9-0

Br 4
11-8x11-0

Br 3
10-1x9-0

Second Floor
990 sq. ft.

Special features

2,104 total square feet of living area

- Energy efficient home with 2" x 6" exterior walls
- 9' ceilings on the first floor
- Living room opens onto the deck through double French doors
- Second floor includes a large storage room
- 3 bedrooms, 2 baths, 2-car garage
- Crawl space foundation

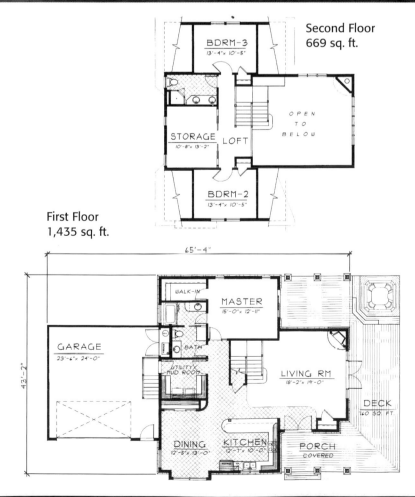

Second Floor
669 sq. ft.

First Floor
1,435 sq. ft.

BDRM-3
13'-4" x 10'-5"

STORAGE
10'-8" x 13'-2"

LOFT

OPEN TO BELOW

BDRM-2
13'-4" x 10'-5"

65'-4"

43'-2"

GARAGE
23'-6" x 24'-0"

WALK-IN

MASTER
15'-0" x 12'-11"

BATH

UTILITY & MUD ROOM

LIVING RM
18'-2" x 19'-0"

DECK
160 SQ. FT.

DINING
12'-5" x 13'-0"

KITCHEN
12'-7" x 10'-0"

PORCH
COVERED

Special features

1,810 total square feet of living area

- Enormous master bath has a double vanity, corner whirlpool tub and separate shower
- French doors in dining room lead to a handy grilling porch
- Convenient mud room leads to laundry closet
- 3 bedrooms, 2 1/2 baths
- Crawl space foundation

Second Floor
534 sq. ft.

BEDROOM 2
13'-6" X 12'-10"

BATH
7'-3" X 5'-0"

LOFT
7'-6" X 11'-2"

WALL TIES

6X6 POST

DN.

7' LINE

5' LINE

BEDROOM 3
16'-0" X 14'-8"

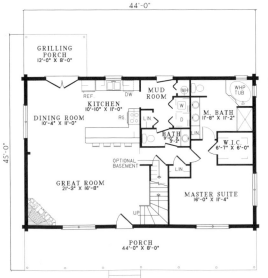

44'-0"

45'-0"

GRILLING PORCH
12'-0" X 8'-0"

MUD ROOM

KITCHEN
10'-10" X 11'-0"

WH

WHP TUB

DINING ROOM
10'-4" X 11'-0"

REF.   DW

RG.

LIN

W

D

M. BATH
11'-8" X 11'-2"

BATH
9'-3"
X
5'-0"

W.I.C.
6'-7" X 6'-0"

OPTIONAL BASEMENT

LIN.

LIN.

GREAT ROOM
21'-3" X 16'-8"

MASTER SUITE
16'-0" X 11'-4"

UP

First Floor
1,276 sq. ft.

PORCH
44'-0" X 8'-0"

Second Floor
809 sq. ft.

MASTER
12/0 X 13/0

LINEN

BR. 3
10/8 X 10/0

DN

FOYER
BELOW

BR. 2
11/0 X 11/8

DINING
10/0 X 10/0

RANGE

REF

GREAT RM.
15/0 X 13/0
(9' CLG.)

P

STOR.

GARAGE
19/0 X 19/6 +

UP

First Floor
655 sq. ft.

©Alan Mascord Design Associates, Inc.

42'

30'

Special features

1,464 total square feet of living area

- Energy efficient home with 2" x 6" exterior walls
- Contemporary styled home has a breathtaking two-story foyer and a lovely open staircase
- U-shaped kitchen is designed for efficiency
- Elegant great room has a cozy fireplace
- 3 bedrooms, 2 1/2 baths, 2-car garage
- Crawl space foundation

Special features

1,760 total square feet of living area

- Energy efficient home with 2" x 6" exterior walls
- Second floor master bedroom is large enough for a sitting area and features a luxury bath
- 9' ceilings on the first floor
- Bonus room on the second floor has an additional 256 square feet of living area
- 3 bedrooms, 2 1/2 baths, 1-car garage
- Basement foundation

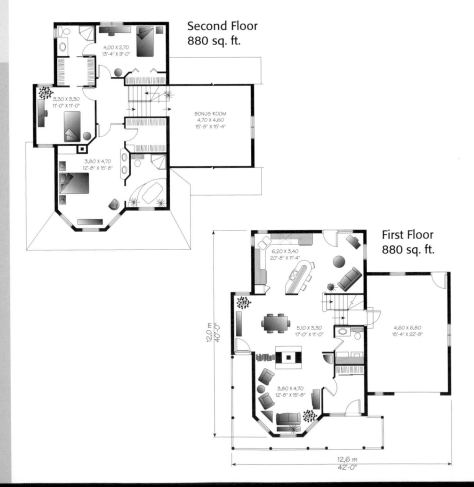

Second Floor
880 sq. ft.

First Floor
880 sq. ft.

Special features

1,902 total square feet of living area

- Great room with fireplace is easily viewable from the kitchen and breakfast area
- Luxury master bedroom has a bay window and two walk-in closets
- Formal living and dining rooms create a wonderful entertaining space
- 3 bedrooms, 2 baths, 2-car side entry garage
- Basement, crawl space or slab foundation, please specify when ordering

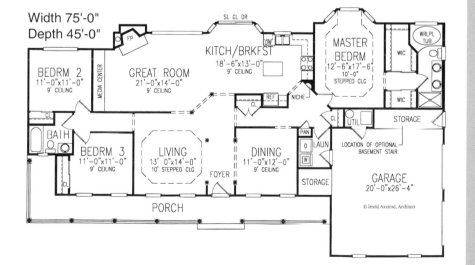

Special features

1,978 total square feet of living area

- Energy efficient home with 2" x 6" exterior walls
- A cheerful breakfast nook is a great place to start the day
- An enormous walk-in pantry permits easy organization
- Large enough for entertaining, the dining room is a great gathering place
- 2 bedrooms, 2 baths, 1-car garage
- Basement foundation

Second Floor
803 sq. ft.

First Floor
1,175 sq. ft.

53'-4"
16,0 m

43'-0"
12,9 m

14'-0" X 18'-0"
4,20 X 5,40

14'-4" X 17'-4"
4,30 X 5,20

13'-4" X 12'-0"
4,00 X 3,60

16'-8" X 20'-4"
5,00 X 6,10

16'-0" X 14'-0"
4,80 X 4,20

14'-4" X 11'-0"
4,30 X 3,30

QUICK FACT - Garden furniture can be found in a variety of materials. Consider the pros and cons of each before selecting. Wicker has a traditional look and moderate cost but needs protection from weather. Metal is highly durable, usually needs cushions and can be cold to the touch. Resin is an inexpensive and light material and is easily cleaned with soap and water. Weather-resistant hardwood can be left natural for low maintenance and is durable but costly. Regular hardwood or treated softwood is inexpensive but will need regular painting or staining.

Second Floor
831 sq. ft.

Bath

Bedroom
11'x 10'

Master
Bath

Bedroom
10'6"x 10'6"

Study
9'x 7'3"

Master
Bedroom
13'x 14'

Balcony
13'6"x 5'

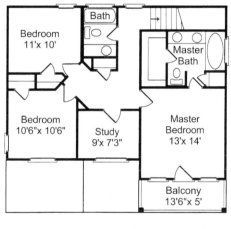

First Floor
912 sq. ft.

Utility
9'7"x 6'10"

1/2 Ba

Kitchen
12'8"x 12'2"

Living
14'2"x 19'6"

Dining
11'4"x 12'

Porch
22'x8'

Width: 34'-0"
Depth: 32'-0"

Special features

1,743 total square feet of living area

- 9' ceilings on the first floor
- Covered porch off living area is spacious enough for entertaining
- Private study on the second floor is ideal for a computer area or office
- 3 bedrooms, 3 baths, 2-car drive under carport
- Pier foundation

Special features

1,365 total square feet of living area

- Home is easily adaptable for physical accessibility featuring no stairs and extra-wide hall baths, laundry and garage
- Living room has separate entry and opens to a spacious dining room with view of rear patio
- L-shaped kitchen is well equipped and includes a built-in pantry
- All bedrooms are spaciously sized and offer generous closet storage
- 3 bedrooms, 2 baths, 1-car garage
- Slab foundation

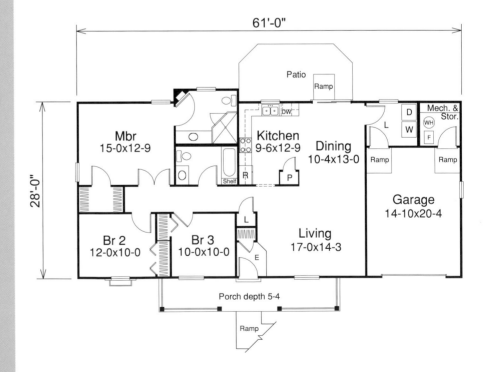

First Floor
2,039 sq. ft.

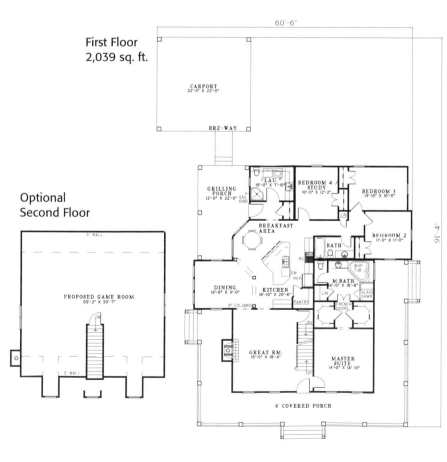

Optional
Second Floor

Special features

2,039 total square feet of living area

- A walk-in pantry and extra-large island add convenience to the open kitchen
- Columns define the formal dining room
- The luxurious master suite features two walk-in closets and French doors leading to the relaxing master bath
- The optional second floor has an additional 1,155 square feet of living space
- 4 bedrooms, 3 baths, 2-car carport
- Slab or crawl space foundation, please specify when ordering

Special features

1,261 total square feet of living area

- Great room, brightened by windows and doors, features a vaulted ceiling, fireplace and access to the deck
- Vaulted master bedroom enjoys a private bath
- Split-level foyer leads to the living space or basement
- Centrally located laundry area is near the bedrooms
- 3 bedrooms, 2 baths, 2-car drive under garage
- Basement foundation

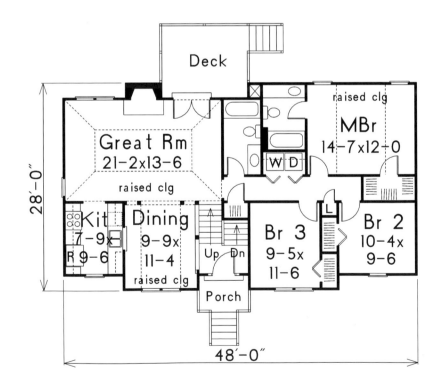

Deck

Great Rm
21-2x13-6
raised clg

MBr
14-7x12-0
raised clg

W D

Kit
7-9x
R 9-6

Dining
9-9x
11-4
raised clg

Br 3
9-5x
11-6

Br 2
10-4x
9-6

Up Dn

L

Porch

28'-0"

48'-0"

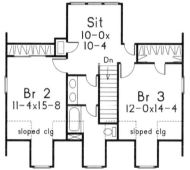

Second Floor
751 sq. ft.

Sit
10-0x
10-4

Dn

Br 2
11-4x15-8

Br 3
12-0x14-4

sloped clg   sloped clg

Special features

2,059 total square feet of living area

- Octagon-shaped breakfast room offers plenty of windows and creates a view to the veranda
- First floor master bedroom has a large walk-in closet and deluxe bath
- 9' ceilings throughout the home
- Secondary bedrooms and bath feature dormers and are adjacent to the cozy sitting area
- 3 bedrooms, 2 1/2 baths, 2-car detached garage
- Slab foundation, drawings also include basement and crawl space foundations

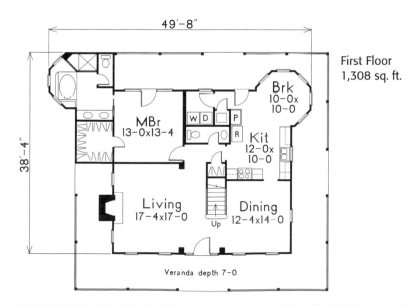

49'-8"

38'-4"

First Floor
1,308 sq. ft.

Brk
10-0x
10-0

MBr
13-0x13-4

W D   P
R

Kit
12-0x
10-0

Living
17-4x17-0

Up

Dining
12-4x14-0

Veranda depth 7-0

Special features

1,680 total square feet of living area

- The covered front porch welcomes guests into the home and offers a cozy place to relax
- A 16'-3" ceiling tops the great room while the other rooms in the house feature 9' ceilings keeping the entire area open and airy
- Plenty of storage can be found with a walk-in closet in each bedroom, large pantry off the dining room and a storage area off the carport
- 3 bedrooms, 2 baths, 2-car carport
- Basement, crawl space or slab foundation, please specify when ordering

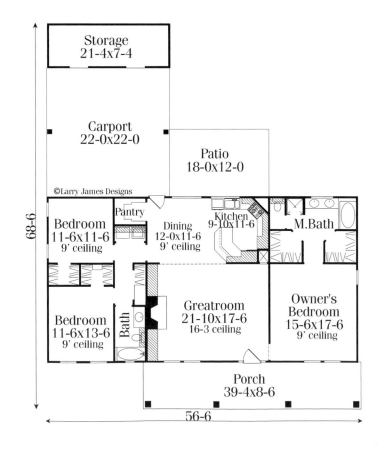

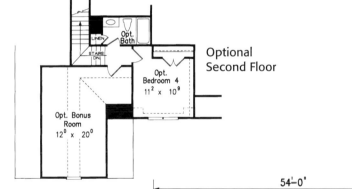

Optional
Second Floor

Special features

1,583 total square feet of living area

- 9' ceilings throughout this home
- Additional bedrooms are located away from the master suite for privacy
- Optional second floor has an additional 544 square feet of living area
- 3 bedrooms, 2 baths, 2-car garage
- Walk-out basement, slab or crawl space foundation, please specify when ordering

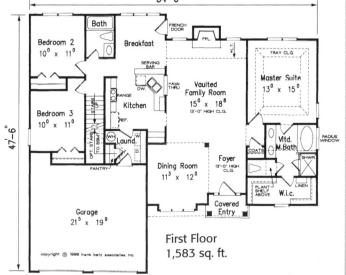

First Floor
1,583 sq. ft.

Special features

1,389 total square feet of living area

- Energy efficient home with 2" x 6" exterior walls
- Formal living room has a warming fireplace and delightful bay window
- U-shaped kitchen shares a snack bar with the bayed family room
- Lovely master bedroom has its own private bath
- 3 bedrooms, 2 baths, 2-car garage
- Slab foundation

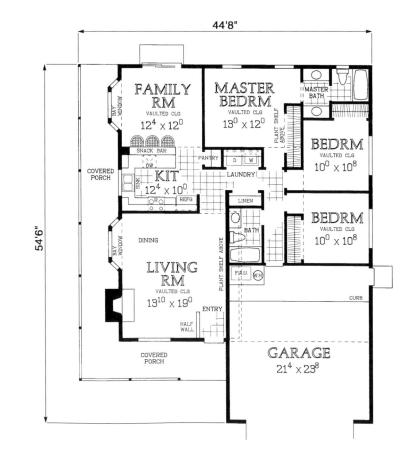

Width 59'-0"
Depth 61'-0"

Special features

1,698 total square feet of living area

- Vaulted master bedroom has a private bath and a walk-in closet
- Decorative columns flank the entrance to the dining room
- Open great room is perfect for gathering family together
- 3 bedrooms, 2 1/2 baths, 2-car side entry garage with storage
- Basement, crawl space or slab foundation, please specify when ordering

Special features

581 total square feet of living area

- Kitchen/living room features space for dining and spiral steps leading to the loft area
- Large loft area can easily be converted to a bedroom or home office
- Entry space has a unique built-in display niche
- 1 bedroom, 1 bath
- Slab foundation

QUICK FACT - Coastal colors, from watery pale aquamarine to dark blue-green, refresh and invigorate. Seek the colors of this palette for their renewing properties. A variety of marine hues are rejuvenating, crisp, clean and ever-popular for the bath and bedrooms.

Second Floor
132 sq. ft.

open to below

Dn

Loft
11-8x9-4
sloped clg

Kit/Living
11-0x17-0
Up

vaulted

Br 1
10-0x10-8

24'-4"

19'-0"

First Floor
449 sq. ft.

Special features

2,003 total square feet of living area

- The kitchen features a large island with a bar facing the eating area
- The screen porch connects to the patio, perfect for relaxing outdoors in any weather
- The master bedroom enjoys two walk-in closets and a deluxe bath
- 3 bedrooms, 2 1/2 baths, 2-car garage
- Crawl space or slab foundation, please specify when ordering

Width: 65'-0"
Depth: 56'-8"

QUICK FACT - Relaxing in a warm, bubbling spa or hot tub can relieve sore muscles, invigorate the skin, and contribute to a sense of calm. Once only available at great expense, many manufacturers now offer kits for home use that are affordable, easy to install, and can be adapted to just about any home. Most spa and hot tub dealers will assist you with delivery and installation of the unit. In most cases, you just place the hot tub, fill it with a water hose, set the controls and you're ready to go.

Special features

1,612 total square feet of living area

- The front porch welcomes guests into this cheerful home designed to fit on a narrow lot
- The garage enters the home to find a convenient mud room, half bath and large laundry room
- A corner fireplace warms the adjoining kitchen, family and dining rooms
- 3 bedrooms, 2 1/2 baths, 2-car garage
- Basement foundation

First Floor
846 sq. ft.

Width: 43'-6"
Depth: 43'-0"

Second Floor
766 sq. ft.

Second Floor
983 sq. ft.

First Floor
1,124 sq. ft.

Special features

2,107 total square feet of living area

- Kitchen has pantry and adjacent dining area
- Master bedroom has a bath and a large walk-in closet
- Second floor bedrooms have attic storage
- Bonus room above the garage has an additional 324 square feet of living area
- 3 bedrooms, 2 1/2 baths, 2-car garage
- Walk-out basement, basement, crawl space or slab foundation, please specify when ordering

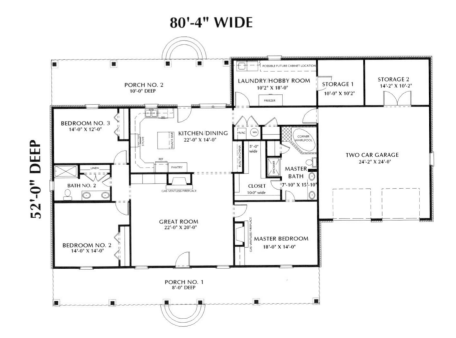

Special features

2,091 total square feet of living area

- The laundry/hobby room offers endless possibilities and accesses a large storage area
- The luxurious master bedroom is warmed by a gas fireplace and includes built-in cabinets, spa-style bath and a walk-in closet
- A ventless gas fireplace highlights the airy great room
- An arched opening leads into the kitchen/dining area which features an island with snack bar and a built-in china cabinet
- 3 bedrooms, 2 baths, 2-car garage
- Crawl space or slab foundation, please specify when ordering

80'-4" WIDE

52'-0" DEEP

PORCH NO. 2
10'-0" DEEP

LAUNDRY/HOBBY ROOM
10'2" X 18'-0"

POSSIBLE FUTURE CABINET LOCATION

FREEZER

STORAGE 1
10'-0" X 10'2"

STORAGE 2
14'-2" X 10'-2"

BEDROOM NO. 3
14'-0" X 12'-0"

KITCHEN/DINING
22'-0" X 14'-0"

SNACK BAR

STOVE

REF

PANTRY

HVAC

5'-0" wide

CORNER WHIRLPOOL

SHOWER

MASTER BATH
17'-10" X 15'-10"

TWO CAR GARAGE
24'-2" X 24'-0"

LINEN

BATH NO. 2

GAS VENTLESS FIREPLACE

CLOSET
10'-0" wide

BEDROOM NO. 2
14'-0" X 14'-0"

GREAT ROOM
22'-0" X 20'-0"

GAS VENTLESS FIREPLACE

MASTER BEDROOM
18'-0" X 14'-0"

PORCH NO. 1
8'-0" DEEP

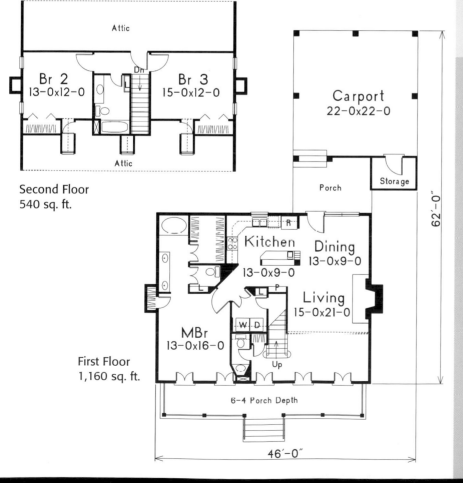

Second Floor
540 sq. ft.

Br 2
13-0x12-0

Br 3
15-0x12-0

Attic

Dn

Attic

Carport
22-0x22-0

Porch

Storage

Kitchen
13-0x9-0

Dining
13-0x9-0

Living
15-0x21-0

MBr
13-0x16-0

W D

P

Up

First Floor
1,160 sq. ft.

6-4 Porch Depth

46'-0"

62'-0"

Special features

1,700 total square feet of living area

- Fully appointed kitchen with wet bar
- Energy efficient home with 2" x 6" exterior walls
- Linen drop from the second floor bath to utility room
- Master bath includes raised marble tub and a sloped ceiling
- 3 bedrooms, 2 1/2 baths, 2-car attached carport
- Crawl space foundation, drawings also include basement and slab foundations

Special features

1,367 total square feet of living area

- Energy efficient home with 2" x 6" exterior walls
- Neat front porch shelters the entrance
- Dining room has a full wall of windows and convenient storage area
- Breakfast area leads to the rear terrace through sliding doors
- The large living room features a high ceiling, skylight and fireplace
- 3 bedrooms, 2 baths, 2-car garage
- Basement foundation, drawings also include slab foundation

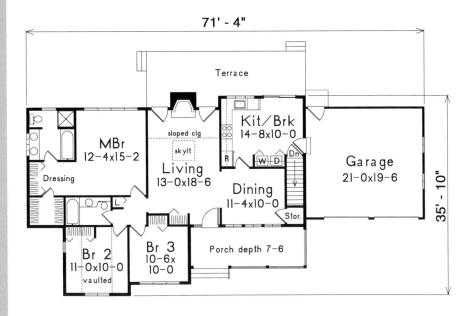

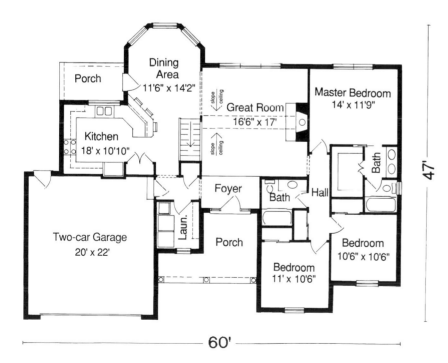

Special features

1,508 total square feet of living area

- Grand opening between rooms creates a spacious effect
- Additional room for quick meals or serving a larger crowd is provided at the breakfast bar
- Sunny dining area accesses the outdoors as well
- 3 bedrooms, 2 baths, 2-car garage
- Basement or crawl space foundation, please specify when ordering

QUICK FACT - Bricks are made from clay and other materials which are formed into shapes and then fired in a kiln to make them durable and strong. Red bricks contain large amounts of iron; yellow bricks contain little iron. Bricks can be sealed or unsealed. If they have been sealed they are easier to keep clean.

Special features

1,000 total square feet of living area

- Large mud room has a separate covered porch entrance
- Full-length covered front porch
- Bedrooms are on opposite sides of the home for privacy
- Vaulted ceiling creates an open and spacious feeling
- 2" x 6" exterior walls available, please order plan #596-058D-0085
- 2 bedrooms, 1 bath
- Crawl space foundation

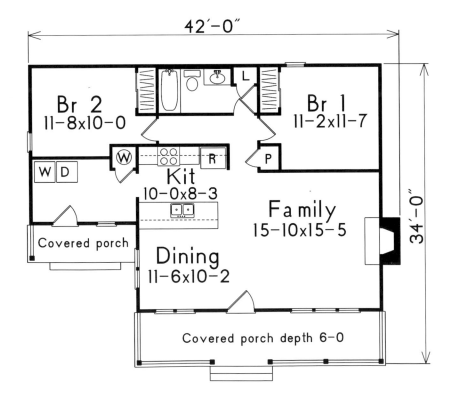

42'-0"

34'-0"

Br 2
11-8x10-0

Br 1
11-2x11-7

Kit
10-0x8-3

W D

Covered porch

Family
15-10x15-5

Dining
11-6x10-2

Covered porch depth 6-0

Special features

1,945 total square feet of living area

- Large gathering room with corner fireplace and 12' high ceiling
- Master suite has a coffered ceiling and French door leading to the patio/deck
- Master bath has a cultured marble seat, separate shower and tub
- All bedrooms have walk-in closets
- 3 bedrooms, 2 baths, 2-car side entry garage
- Slab or crawl space foundation, please specify when ordering

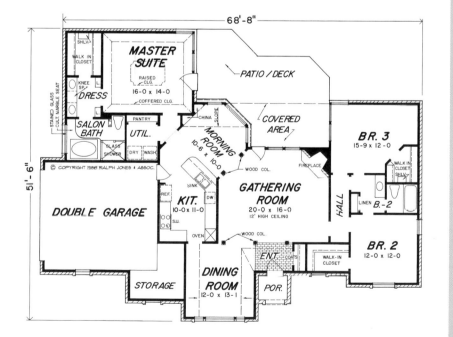

Special features

1,500 total square feet of living area

- Living room features a cathedral ceiling and opens to the breakfast room
- Breakfast room has a spectacular bay window and adjoins a well-appointed kitchen with generous storage
- Laundry room is convenient to the kitchen and includes a large closet
- Large walk-in closet gives the master bedroom abundant storage
- 3 bedrooms, 2 baths, 2-car garage
- Basement foundation

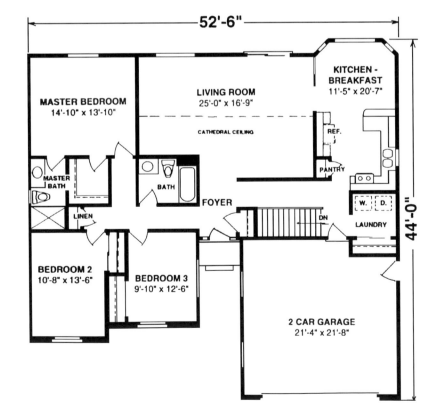

MASTER BEDROOM
14'-10" x 13'-10"

LIVING ROOM
25'-0" x 16'-9"

CATHEDRAL CEILING

KITCHEN - BREAKFAST
11'-5" x 20'-7"

REF.

PANTRY

MASTER BATH

BATH

FOYER

W. D.

LAUNDRY

LINEN

DN

BEDROOM 2
10'-8" x 13'-6"

BEDROOM 3
9'-10" x 12'-6"

2 CAR GARAGE
21'-4" x 21'-8"

52'-6"

44'-0"

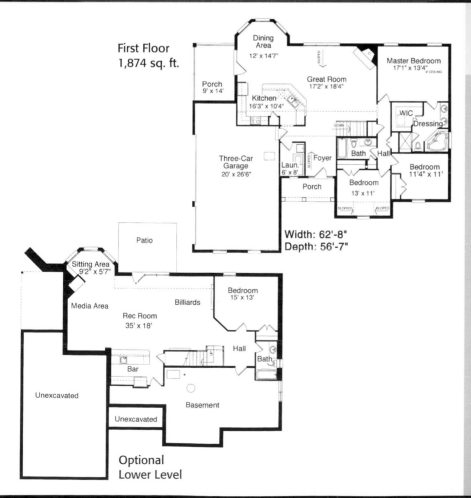

First Floor
1,874 sq. ft.

Dining Area
12' x 14'7"

Porch
9' x 14'

Great Room
17'2" x 18'4"

Kitchen
16'3" x 10'4"

Master Bedroom
17'1" x 13'4"

WIC

Dressing

Three-Car Garage
20' x 26'6"

Laun.
6' x 8'

Foyer

Bath

Hall

Bedroom
11'4" x 11'

Porch

Bedroom
13' x 11'

Width: 62'-8"
Depth: 56'-7"

Patio

Sitting Area
9'2" x 5'7"

Media Area

Rec Room
35' x 18'

Billiards

Bedroom
15' x 13'

Bar

Hall

Bath

Unexcavated

Unexcavated

Basement

Optional
Lower Level

Special features

1,874 total square feet of living area

- The bayed dining area, kitchen and great room with a fireplace combine for an open living area
- The master bedroom pampers with a corner whirlpool tub, double vanity and walk-in closet
- 9' ceilings throughout this home add to the spaciousness
- Optional lower level has an additional 1,175 square feet of living area
- 3 bedrooms, 2 baths, 3-car side entry garage
- Walk-out basement foundation

Special features

929 total square feet of living area

- Spacious living room with dining area has access to 8' x 12' deck through glass sliding doors
- Splendid U-shaped kitchen features a breakfast bar, oval window above sink and impressive cabinet storage
- Master bedroom enjoys a walk-in closet and large elliptical feature window
- Laundry, storage closet and mechanical space are located off the first floor garage
- 2 bedrooms, 1 bath, 3-car side entry garage
- Slab foundation

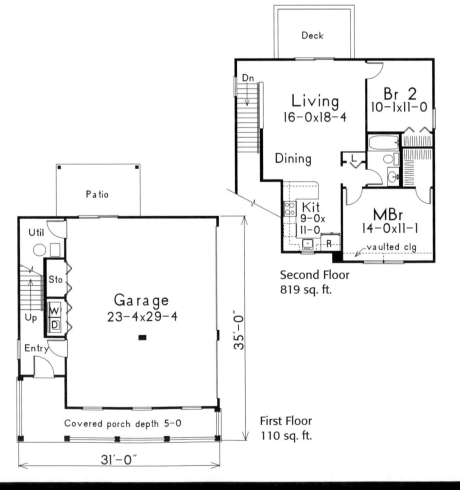

Deck

Dn

Living
16-0x18-4

Br 2
10-1x11-0

Dining

L

Kit
9-0x
11-0

R

MBr
14-0x11-1

vaulted clg

Second Floor
819 sq. ft.

Patio

Util

Sto

Up

W
D

Garage
23-4x29-4

Entry

35'-0"

Covered porch depth 5-0

31'-0"

First Floor
110 sq. ft.

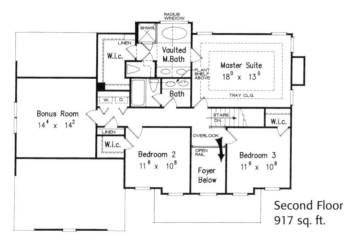

Second Floor
917 sq. ft.

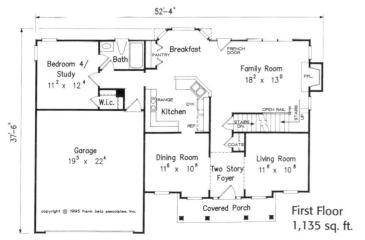

First Floor
1,135 sq. ft.

Special features

2,052 total square feet of living area

- Terrific family room has a fireplace and several windows adding sunlight
- Bedroom #4/study has a private bath making it an ideal in-law suite
- Bonus room on the second floor has an additional 216 square feet of living area
- 4 bedrooms, 3 baths, 2-car garage
- Walk-out basement, crawl space or slab foundation, please specify when ordering

Special features

1,605 total square feet of living area

- Vaulted ceilings in the great room, kitchen and breakfast area
- Spacious great room features a large bay window, fireplace, built-in bookshelves and a convenient wet bar
- The formal dining room and breakfast area are perfect for entertaining or everyday living
- Master bedroom has a spacious bath with oval tub and separate shower
- 3 bedrooms, 2 baths, 2-car garage
- Basement foundation, drawings also include slab and crawl space foundations

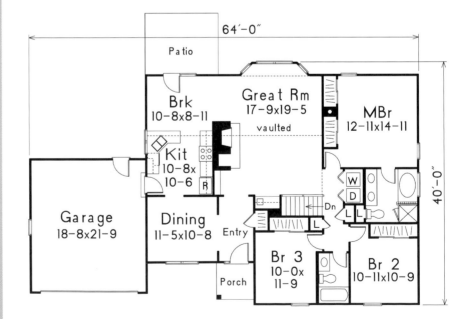

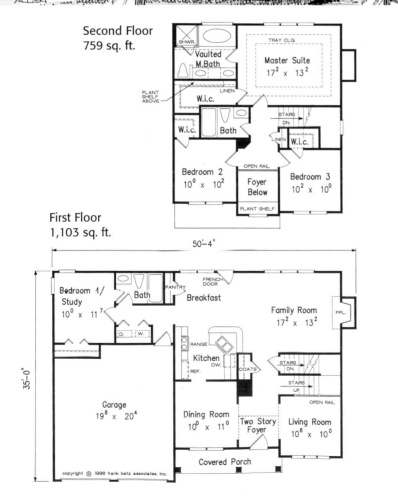

Second Floor
759 sq. ft.

SHWR.

Vaulted M.Bath

TRAY CLG.

Master Suite
17² x 13²

PLANT SHELF ABOVE

LINEN

W.i.c.

STAIRS DN.

W.i.c.   Bath

LINEN   W.i.c.

Bedroom 2
10⁰ x 10²

OPEN RAIL

Foyer Below

Bedroom 3
10² x 10⁰

PLANT SHELF

First Floor
1,103 sq. ft.

50'-4"

35'-0"

Bedroom 4/ Study
10⁰ x 11⁷

Bath

PANTRY

FRENCH DOOR

Breakfast

Family Room
17² x 13²

FPL.

D.   W.

RANGE

Kitchen
DW.

REF.

COATS

STAIRS DN.

STAIRS UP

OPEN RAIL

Garage
19⁸ x 20⁴

Dining Room
10⁰ x 11⁰

Two Story Foyer

Living Room
10⁶ x 10⁰

Covered Porch

copyright © 1996 frank betz associates, inc.

Special features

1,862 total square feet of living area

- Dining and living rooms flank the grand two-story foyer
- Open floor plan combines kitchen, breakfast and family rooms
- Bedroom #4/study is tucked away on the first floor for privacy
- Second floor bedrooms have walk-in closets
- 4 bedrooms, 3 baths, 2-car garage
- Walk-out basement or crawl space foundation, please specify when ordering

Special features

1,487 total square feet of living area

- Energy efficient home with 2" x 6" exterior walls
- Kitchen has a pass-through counter with space for dining
- First floor bedroom/den can easily be converted to an office with spacious walk-in closet and access to deck outdoors
- Second floor bedroom also has a private deck
- 3 bedrooms, 1 1/2 baths
- Basement foundation

Second Floor
576 sq. ft.

First Floor
911 sq. ft.

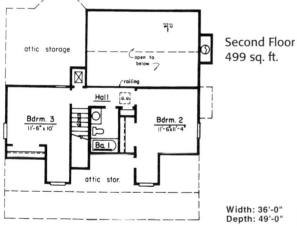

Second Floor
499 sq. ft.

Width: 36'-0"
Depth: 49'-0"

First Floor
1,238 sq. ft.

Special features

1,737 total square feet of living area

- U-shaped kitchen, sunny bayed breakfast room and living area become one large gathering area
- Living area has a sloped ceiling and a balcony overlook from the second floor
- Second floor includes lots of storage area
- 3 bedrooms, 2 1/2 baths
- Slab or crawl space foundation, please specify when ordering

Special features

1,720 total square feet of living area

- Lower level includes large family room with laundry area and half bath
- L-shaped kitchen has a convenient serving bar and pass-through to dining area
- Private half bath in master bedroom
- 3 bedrooms, 1 full bath, 2 half baths, 2-car drive under garage
- Basement foundation

QUICK FACT - Shutters have been used for centuries as practical and aesthetic additions to buildings. The original purpose of exterior shutters was to provide light control, ventilation, and protection against inclement weather. Shutters are still used for those practical purposes, but they are also increasingly used exclusively as a decorative element.

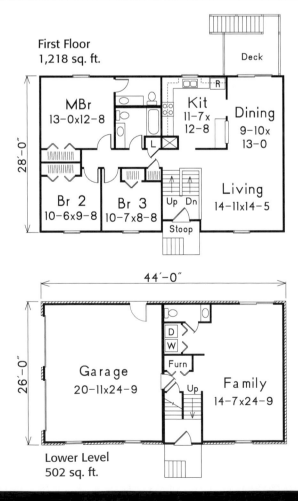

First Floor
1,218 sq. ft.

Deck

MBr
13-0x12-8

Kit
11-7x
12-8

Dining
9-10x
13-0

Living
14-11x14-5

Br 2
10-6x9-8

Br 3
10-7x8-8

Up Dn

Stoop

28'-0"

44'-0"

26'-0"

Garage
20-11x24-9

Family
14-7x24-9

Furn

Up

Lower Level
502 sq. ft.

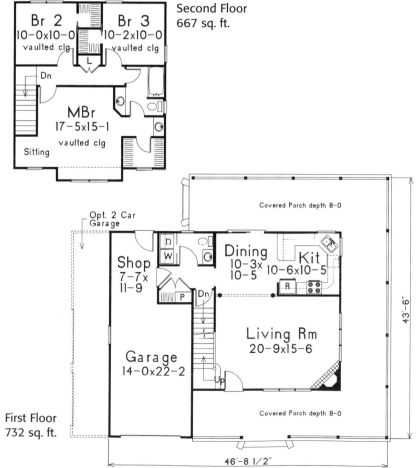

Second Floor
667 sq. ft.

Br 2
10-0x10-0
vaulted clg

Br 3
10-2x10-0
vaulted clg

Dn

MBr
17-5x15-1
vaulted clg

Sitting

Opt. 2 Car
Garage

Shop
7-7x
11-9

Dining
10-3x
10-5

Kit
10-6x10-5

Dn

Covered Porch depth 8-0

Garage
14-0x22-2

Up

Living Rm
20-9x15-6

43'-6"

Covered Porch depth 8-0

First Floor
732 sq. ft.

46'-8 1/2"

Special features

1,399 total square feet of living area

- Living room overlooks the dining area through arched columns
- Laundry room contains a handy half bath
- Spacious master bedroom includes a sitting area, walk-in closet and plenty of sunlight
- 3 bedrooms, 1 1/2 baths, 1-car garage
- Basement foundation, drawings also include crawl space and slab foundations

Special features

1,591 total square feet of living area

- Spacious porch and patio provide outdoor enjoyment
- Large entry foyer leads to a cheery kitchen and breakfast room which welcomes the sun through a wide array of windows
- The great room features a vaulted ceiling, corner fireplace, wet bar and access to the rear patio
- Double walk-in closets, private porch and a luxury bath are special highlights of the vaulted master bedroom suite
- 3 bedrooms, 2 baths, 2-car side entry garage
- Basement foundation

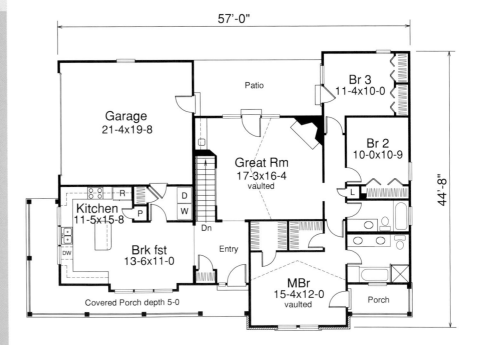

57'-0"

44'-8"

Garage
21-4x19-8

Patio

Br 3
11-4x10-0

Great Rm
17-3x16-4
vaulted

Br 2
10-0x10-9

Kitchen
11-5x15-8

Brk fst
13-6x11-0

Entry

MBr
15-4x12-0
vaulted

Porch

Covered Porch depth 5-0

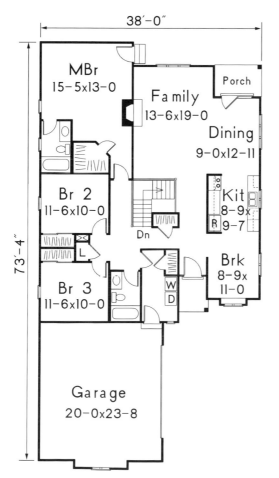

38'-0"

73'-4"

MBr
15-5x13-0

Family
13-6x19-0

Porch

Dining
9-0x12-11

Br 2
11-6x10-0

Dn

Kit
8-9x
9-7

R

Brk
8-9x
11-0

Br 3
11-6x10-0

L

W
D

Garage
20-0x23-8

Special features

1,624 total square feet of living area

- Master bedroom has a private entry from the outdoors
- Garage is adjacent to the utility room with convenient storage closet
- Large family and dining areas feature a fireplace and porch access
- Pass-through kitchen opens directly to cozy breakfast area
- 3 bedrooms, 2 baths, 2-car side entry garage
- Basement foundation, drawings also include crawl space and slab foundations

Special features

1,941 total square feet of living area

- Dramatic, exciting and spacious interior
- Vaulted great room is brightened by a sunken atrium window wall and skylights
- Vaulted U-shaped gourmet kitchen with plant shelf opens to dining room
- First floor half bath features space for a stackable washer and dryer
- 4 bedrooms, 2 1/2 baths, 2-car garage
- Walk-out basement foundation

Lower Level
945 sq. ft.

First Floor
996 sq. ft.

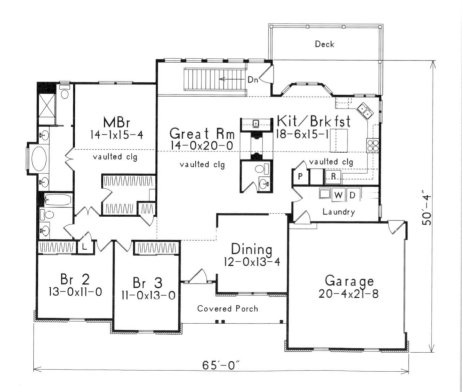

Special features

2,164 total square feet of living area

- Great design for entertaining with a wet bar and see-through fireplace in the great room
- Plenty of closet space
- Vaulted ceilings enlarge the master bedroom, great room and kitchen/breakfast area
- Great room features great view to the rear of the home
- 2" x 6" exterior walls available, please order plan #596-058D-0083
- 3 bedrooms, 2 1/2 baths, 2-car side entry garage
- Basement foundation

Special features

755 total square feet of living area

- Energy efficient home with 2" x 6" exterior walls
- The spacious living/dining area is highlighted with a box-bay window
- The kitchen enjoys French-door access to the deck
- The 3-car garage includes space for a laundry area
- 1 bedroom, 1 bath, 3-car garage
- Slab foundation

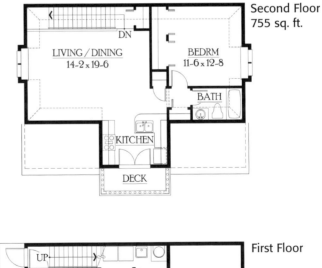

Second Floor
755 sq. ft.

LIVING / DINING
14-2 x 19-6

DN

BEDRM
11-6 x 12-8

BATH

KITCHEN

DECK

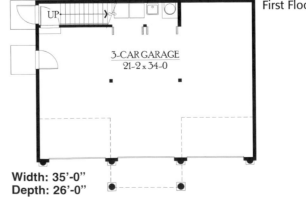

First Floor

UP

3-CAR GARAGE
21-2 x 34-0

Width: 35'-0"
Depth: 26'-0"

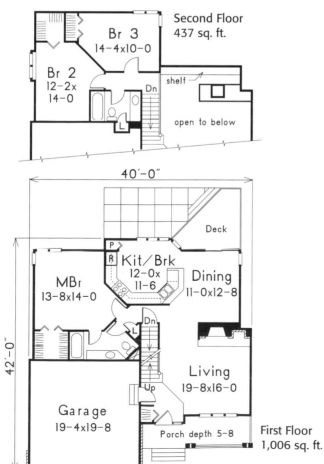

Second Floor 437 sq. ft.

Br 3
14-4x10-0

Br 2
12-2x
14-0

shelf

Dn

L

open to below

40'-0"

42'-0"

Deck

P
R

Kit/Brk
12-0x
11-6

MBr
13-8x14-0

Dining
11-0x12-8

Dn

L

Living
19-8x16-0

Up

Garage
19-4x19-8

Porch depth 5-8

First Floor
1,006 sq. ft.

Special features

1,443 total square feet of living area

- Raised foyer and cathedral ceiling in living room
- Impressive tall-wall fireplace between living and dining rooms
- Open U-shaped kitchen features a cheerful breakfast bay
- Angular side deck accentuates patio and garden
- First floor master bedroom has a walk-in closet and a corner window
- 3 bedrooms, 2 baths, 2-car garage
- Basement foundation

Special features

1,715 total square feet of living area

- Vaulted great room is spacious and bright
- Master suite enjoys a sitting room and private bath
- Kitchen has plenty of counterspace and cabinetry
- 3 bedrooms, 2 baths, 2-car garage
- Walk-out basement, crawl space or slab foundation, please specify when ordering

QUICK FACT - Stucco has been used since the days of Renaissance Italy and was thought to give a building the appearance of being important. It was also used for weather and fire protection.

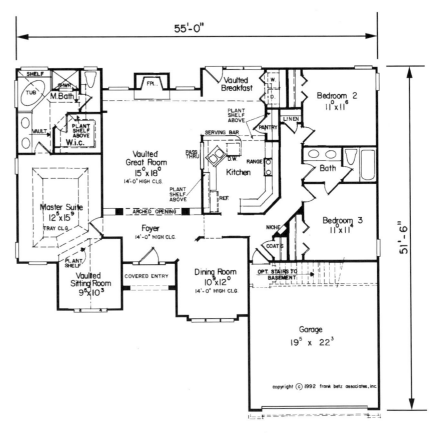

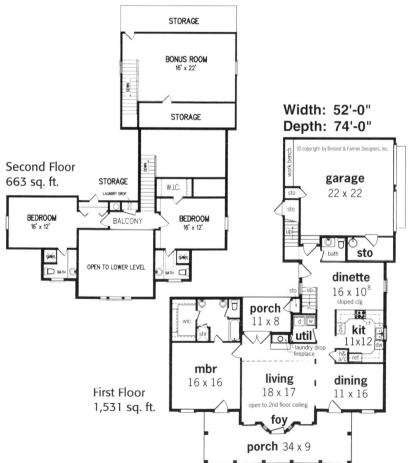

STORAGE

BONUS ROOM
16' x 22'

STORAGE

Width: 52'-0"
Depth: 74'-0"

Second Floor
663 sq. ft.

STORAGE

LAUNDRY DROP

W.I.C.

BEDROOM
16' x 12'

BALCONY

BEDROOM
16' x 12'

OPEN TO LOWER LEVEL

SHWR

BATH

SHWR

BATH

© copyright by Breland & Farmer Designers, Inc.

work bench

garage
22 x 22

sto

sto

up

bath

sto

dinette
16 x 10⁸
sloped clg

sto

up

wic

shr

porch
11 x 8

d   w

util

laundry drop
fireplace

kit
11x12

ovs

rf

dw

h&
a/c   ref

mbr
16 x 16

living
18 x 17
open to 2nd floor ceiling

dining
11 x 16

foy

First Floor
1,531 sq. ft.

porch 34 x 9

Special features

2,194 total square feet of living area

- Energy efficient home with 2" x 6" exterior walls
- A convenient laundry drop on the second floor leads to the centrally located utility room
- Both second floor bedrooms have large closets and their own bath
- Bonus room on the second floor has an additional 352 square feet of living space
- 3 bedrooms, 3 1/2 baths, 2-car side entry garage
- Crawl space foundation, drawings also include slab and basement foundations

Special features

2,092 total square feet of living area

- Dining room can used as an office or den
- Living room can be converted to a guest room
- Expansion loft is ideal for a playroom or a fourth bedroom and includes an additional 300 square feet of living area
- 3 bedrooms, 2 1/2 baths, 2-car garage
- Basement, crawl space or slab foundation, please specify when ordering

Second Floor
940 sq. ft.

WIC

MASTER BATH

BATH

BEDRM 3
12'-0"x11'-4"

UNFINISHED
EXPANSION LOFT
PLAYRM/BR#4

LIN

LIN

CL

DN   RAILING   DN

MASTER
BEDRM
12'-0"x17'-0"
9'6 HIGH
STEPPED CEILING

BEDRM 2
12'-0"x15'-2"

CL

UPPER
FOYER

First Floor
1,152 sq. ft.

FR. SL. DR.

INFORMAL
DINING
10'-0"x17'-4"
9' CEILING

KIT

STORAGE

LOW WALL

FAMILY RM
15'-4"x15'-2"
9' CEILING

DESK OR
HUTCH

8'-0"x13'-4"

FP

TWO CAR GARAGE
20'-0"x24'-0"

STAIR TO
OPT. BSMT

UTIL

PANTRY

LAUN

D

© Jerold Axelrod, Architect

DN

LAV

LIVING RM
12'-0"x15'-2"
9' CEILING

CL

DINING/
OFFICE
12'-0"x13'-0"
9' CEILING

Width 54'-0"
Depth 43'-0"

UP

FOY

COVERED PORCH

br2
12'4x12'8

br3
10'x10'
OR OPTIONAL LOFT

3'6 RAILING

DN

OPEN TO BELOW

Second Floor
576 sq. ft.

PORCH

mbr
12'4x12'8

W | D

CABINETS

din
12'x10'

k
8'4x10'

DN

UP

BREAKFAST BAR

great rm
17'x13'6

PORCH

First Floor
1,012 sq. ft.

Width: 34'-0"
Depth: 38'-0"

Special features

1,588 total square feet of living area

- Energy efficient home with 2" x 6" exterior walls
- Master bedroom is located on the first floor for convenience
- Cozy great room has a fireplace
- Dining room has access to both the front and rear porches
- Two secondary bedrooms and a bath complete the second floor
- 3 bedrooms, 2 1/2 baths
- Basement or crawl space foundation, please specify when ordering

Special features

1,738 total square feet of living area

- Energy efficient home with 2" x 6" exterior walls
- A den in the front of the home can easily be converted to a third bedroom
- Kitchen includes an eating nook for family gatherings
- Master bedroom has an unforgettable bath with a super skylight
- Large sunken great room is centralized with a cozy fireplace
- 2 bedrooms, 2 baths, 3-car garage
- Basement, crawl space or slab foundation, please specify when ordering

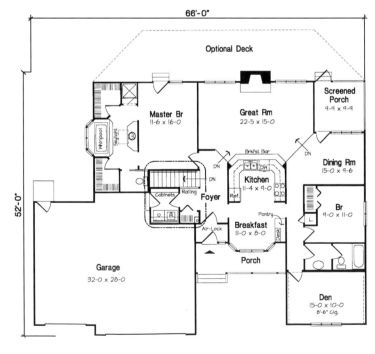

66'-0"

52'-0"

Optional Deck

Master Br
11-6 x 16-0

Whirlpool

Skylight

Great Rm
22-5 x 15-0

Screened Porch
9-9 x 9-9

Brkfst Bar

DN

DN

Dining Rm
15-0 x 9-6

Kitchen
11-4 x 9-0

Cabinets   Railing

Foyer

Ref.

Pantry

Br
9-0 x 11-0

Air-Lock

Breakfast
11-0 x 8-0

Desk

Garage
32-0 x 28-0

Porch

Den
15-0 x 10-0
8'-6" Clg.

Furn.

Crawl Space Access

Crawl / Slab Option

Special features

1,470 total square feet of living area

- Vaulted breakfast room is cheerful and sunny
- Private second floor master bedroom has a bath and walk-in closet
- Large utility room has access to the outdoors
- 3 bedrooms, 2 baths
- Basement, crawl space or slab foundation, please specify when ordering

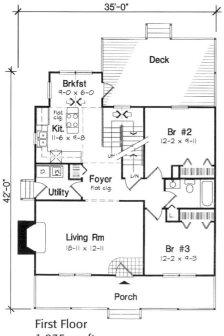

First Floor
1,035 sq. ft.

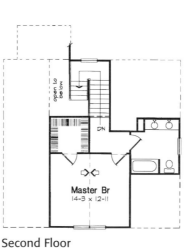

Second Floor
435 sq. ft.

Special features

2,059 total square feet of living area

- Large desk and pantry add to the breakfast room
- The laundry room is located on the second floor near the bedrooms
- Vaulted ceiling in the master bedroom
- Mud room is conveniently located near the garage
- 3 bedrooms, 2 1/2 baths, 2-car garage
- Basement foundation

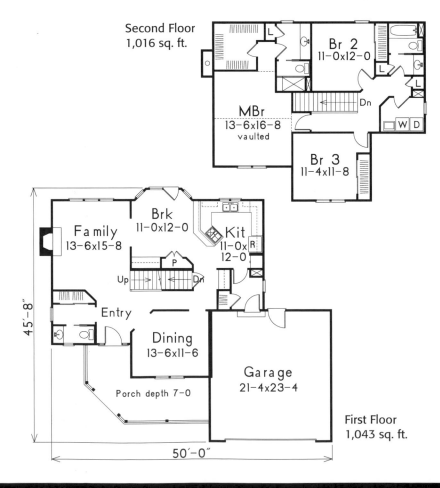

Second Floor
1,016 sq. ft.

Br 2
11-0x12-0

MBr
13-6x16-8
vaulted

Br 3
11-4x11-8

Family
13-6x15-8

Brk
11-0x12-0

Kit
11-0x
12-0

Up

Dn

P

Entry

Dining
13-6x11-6

Porch depth 7-0

Garage
21-4x23-4

45'-8"

50'-0"

First Floor
1,043 sq. ft.

Optional
Second Floor

GAME ROOM
37'-4" X 18'-8"

ATTIC
STORAGE

BATH

84'-0"

DECK

GRILLING
PORCH
18'-0" X 12'-0"

BEDROOM 2
12'-2" X 12'-2"

DINING /
HEARTH ROOM
13'-0" X 19'-6"

ATRIUM
DOORS

LAU.
12'-9" X 9'-9"

BATH

KITCHEN
14'-5" X 18'-6"

M. BATH
13'-8" X 7'-4"

GARAGE
23'-8" X 21'-4"

55'-6"

BEDROOM 3
12'-2" X 12'-2"

LIVING RM.
21'-0" X 18'-0"

MEDIA
CENTER

MASTER
SUITE
13'-8" X 13'-10"

8' COVERED PORCH

First Floor
1,921 sq. ft.

Special features

1,921 total square feet of living area

- The kitchen has a long, curved island with plenty of seating
- The charming front porch wraps around the house providing a relaxing outdoor retreat
- Fireplaces in the living and dining rooms warm the house
- The optional second floor has an additional 812 square feet of living space
- 3 bedrooms, 2 baths, 2-car side entry garage
- Slab, crawl space, basement or walk-out basement foundation, please specify when ordering

Special features

1,492 total square feet of living area

- High ceilings increase the spaciousness of this design
- The kitchen and dining area combine with a handy island snack bar and access to the rear porch
- A private master bedroom enjoys a deluxe bath with whirlpool tub and walk-in closet
- 3 bedrooms, 2 baths, 2-car side entry garage
- Crawl space, basement or slab foundation, please specify when ordering

Width
56-0

Porch
31-4x7-8
9' ceiling

Master
Bedroom
16-6x13-2
9' ceiling

Closet
6-6x8-0

Bedroom
11-4x11-4
9' ceiling

Kitchen/Dining
19-11x11-4
9' ceiling

Snack
Bar

Shlvs

M.Bath
12-4x11-0
9' ceiling

Laundry
6-7x5-10

Bath

Shlvs

Depth
45-8

Greatroom
16-11x19-0
11' ceiling

Garage
21-3x19-2
9' ceiling

Bedroom
11-4x11-4
9' Ceiling

Storage

©Larry James Designs

Porch
32-0x5-4
9' ceiling

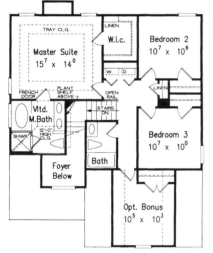

Second Floor
786 sq. ft.

LINEN

TRAY CLG.

W.i.c.

Master Suite
15⁷ x 14⁰

Bedroom 2
10⁷ x 10⁶

W.   D.

LINEN

FRENCH DOOR

PLANT SHELF ABOVE

OPEN RAIL

STAIRS DN.

Vtd. M.Bath

12'-0" HIGH CLG.

SHWR

Bath

Bedroom 3
10⁷ x 10⁰

Foyer Below

Opt. Bonus
10⁵ x 10³

Special features

1,482 total square feet of living area

- Family room includes 42" high built-in TV cabinet
- Spacious kitchen and dining room enjoys a built-in desk and a French door leading to the outdoors
- Optional bonus room on the second floor has an additional 141 square feet of living area
- 3 bedrooms, 2 1/2 baths, 2-car garage
- Walk-out basement, crawl space or slab foundation, please specify when ordering

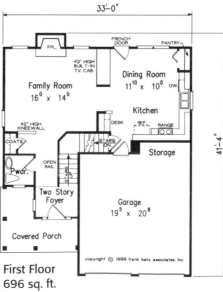

33'-0"

FPL.

FRENCH DOOR

PANTRY

42" HIGH BUILT-IN T.V. CAB.

Dining Room
11¹⁰ x 10⁰

DW.

Family Room
16⁰ x 14⁰

Kitchen

DESK   REF.   RANGE

42" HIGH KNEEWALL

COATS

STAIRS DN.

Storage

41'-4"

OPEN RAIL

STAIRS

Pwdr.

Two Story Foyer

Garage
19⁵ x 20⁸

Covered Porch

copyright © 1999 frank betz associates, inc.

First Floor
696 sq. ft.

Special features

1,458 total square feet of living area

- A convenient snack bar joins the kitchen with breakfast room
- Large living room has a fireplace, plenty of windows, vaulted ceiling and nearby plant shelf
- Master bedroom offers a private bath, walk-in closet, plant shelf and coffered ceiling
- Corner windows provide abundant light in the breakfast room
- 3 bedrooms, 2 baths, 2-car garage
- Crawl space foundation, drawings also include slab foundation

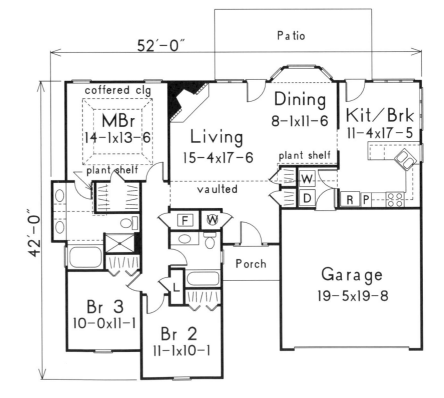

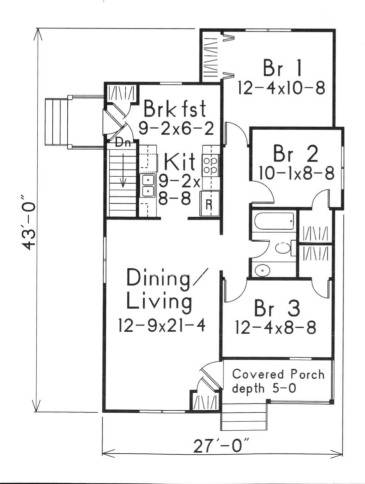

Special features

987 total square feet of living area

- Galley kitchen opens into the cozy breakfast room
- Convenient coat closets are located by both entrances
- Dining/living room offers an expansive open area
- Breakfast room has access to the outdoors
- Front porch is great for enjoying outdoor living
- 3 bedrooms, 1 bath
- Basement foundation

Special features

1,898 total square feet of living area

- The great room features a corner fireplace and French doors for outdoor access
- The island kitchen is open to the living areas and has a built-in eating bar and lots of cabinet and counter space
- A second floor loft area overlooks the great room and can serve as a play room
- 3 bedrooms, 2 1/2 baths
- Crawl space foundation

First Floor
1,200 sq. ft.

Second Floor
698 sq. ft.

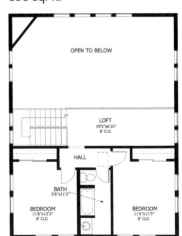

Width: 30'-0"
Depth: 40'-0'

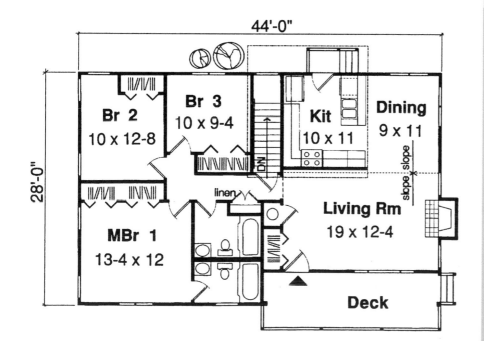

44'-0"

28'-0"

Br 2
10 x 12-8

Br 3
10 x 9-4

Kit
10 x 11

Dining
9 x 11

slope slope

linen

MBr 1
13-4 x 12

Living Rm
19 x 12-4

DN

Deck

Special features

1,146 total square feet of living area

- Master bedroom has a private bath
- Well-organized kitchen is loaded with cabinetry
- A sloped ceiling in the living and dining rooms creates a comfortable atmosphere
- 3 bedrooms, 2 baths
- Basement, slab or crawl space foundation, please specify when ordering

Special features

2,056 total square feet of living area

- Columned foyer projects past the living and dining rooms into the family room
- Kitchen conveniently accesses the dining room and breakfast area
- Master bedroom features double-door access to the patio and a pocket door to the private bath with walk-in closet, double-bowl vanity and tub
- 4 bedrooms, 2 baths, 2-car garage
- Slab foundation, drawings also include crawl space foundation

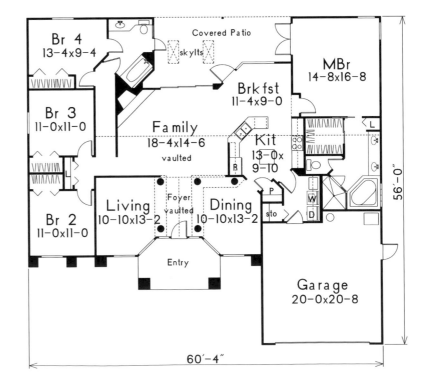

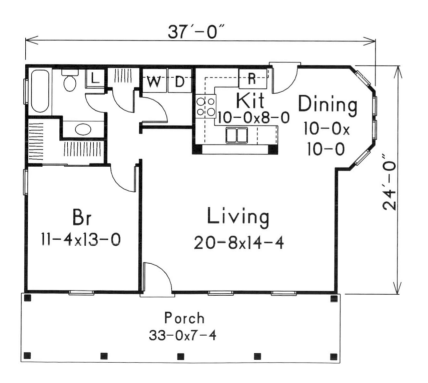

37'-0"

24'-0"

Kit
10-0x8-0

Dining
10-0x
10-0

Br
11-4x13-0

Living
20-8x14-4

Porch
33-0x7-4

Special features

829 total square feet of living area

- U-shaped kitchen opens into living area by a 42" high counter
- Oversized bay window and French door accent dining room
- Gathering space is created by the large living room
- Convenient utility room and linen closet
- 1 bedroom, 1 bath
- Slab foundation

QUICK FACT - Use newspapers to clean the windows of your house. It's a lot cheaper than paper towels, and the ink is a polishing agent that won't streak.

Special features

2,072 total square feet of living area

- Master suite has a large bay sitting area, private vaulted bath and an enormous walk-in closet
- Tray ceilings in the breakfast and dining rooms are charming touches
- Great room has a centered fireplace and a French door leading outdoors
- 3 bedrooms, 2 1/2 baths, 2-car side entry garage
- Walk-out basement, slab or crawl space foundation, please specify when ordering

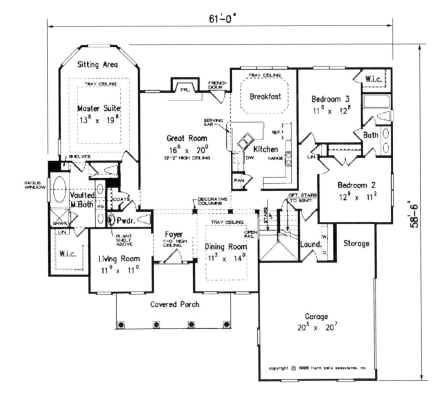

Second Floor 604 sq. ft.

First Floor 952 sq. ft.

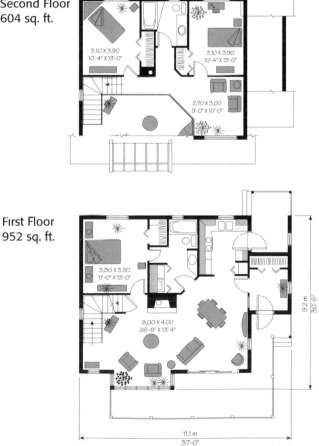

Special features

1,556 total square feet of living area

- Energy efficient home with 2" x 6" exterior walls
- Master bedroom has a walk-in closet
- Separate entry with closet is a unique feature
- 3 bedrooms, 2 baths
- Basement foundation

QUICK FACT - One of the top trends in home design currently is the use of "flexible" floor plans. Traditionally designed styles with separate living and dining rooms are being replaced by large family areas or great rooms which offer more flexibility for family living.

Special features

1,368 total square feet of living area

- Entry foyer steps down to an open living area which combines the great room and formal dining area
- Vaulted master bedroom includes a box-bay window and a bath with a large vanity, separate tub and shower
- Cozy breakfast area features direct access to the patio and pass-through kitchen
- Handy linen closet is located in the hall
- 3 bedrooms, 2 baths, 2-car garage
- Basement foundation

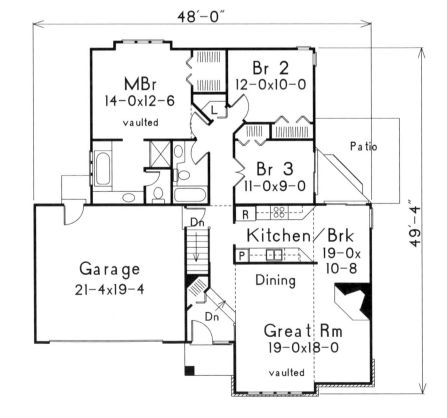

48'-0"

49'-4"

MBr
14-0x12-6
vaulted

Br 2
12-0x10-0

L

Br 3
11-0x9-0

Patio

R

Garage
21-4x19-4

Dn

Dn

Kitchen/Brk
19-0x10-8

P

Dining

Great Rm
19-0x18-0
vaulted

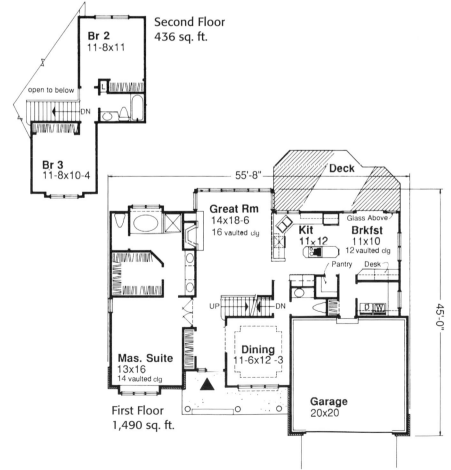

Br 2
11-8x11

Second Floor
436 sq. ft.

open to below

DN

L

Br 3
11-8x10-4

55'-8"

Deck

Great Rm
14x18-6
16 vaulted clg

Glass Above

Kit
11x12

Brkfst
11x10
12 vaulted clg

Pantry

Desk

UP   DN

D W

Mas. Suite
13x16
14 vaulted clg

Dining
11-6x12 -3

45'-0"

Garage
20x20

First Floor
1,490 sq. ft.

Special features

1,926 total square feet of living area

- A breathtaking wall of windows brightens the great room
- A double-door entry leads to the master suite which features a large bath and walk-in closet
- An island cooktop in the kitchen makes mealtime a breeze
- 3 bedrooms, 2 1/2 baths, 2-car garage
- Basement foundation

QUICK FACT - If you want to add an island to the kitchen, think thin. A narrow island will still provide a great work surface without compromising the overall space.

Special features

1,856 total square feet of living area

- The centrally located kitchen easily serves the formal dining room and informal breakfast area
- The grand master bedroom is the perfect place to relax with a corner whirlpool tub and large walk-in closet
- Home office/bedroom #4 enjoys a private bath
- The garage includes two large storage areas
- 4 bedrooms, 3 baths, 2-car side entry garage
- Slab or crawl space foundation, please specify when ordering

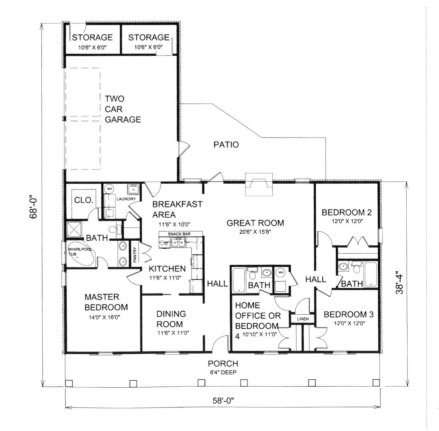

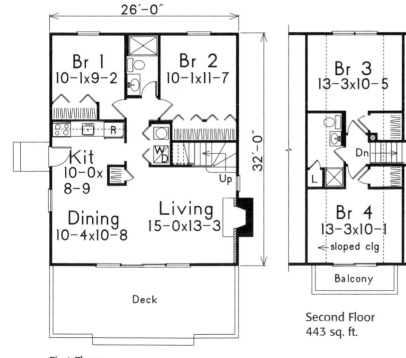

26'-0"

Br 1
10-1x9-2

Br 2
10-1x11-7

32'-0"

Kit
10-0x
8-9

W/D

Up

Dining
10-4x10-8

Living
15-0x13-3

R

Deck

First Floor
832 sq. ft.

Br 3
13-3x10-5

Dn

L

Br 4
13-3x10-1

← sloped clg

Balcony

Second Floor
443 sq. ft.

Special features

1,275 total square feet of living area

- Wall shingles and stone veneer fireplace all fashion an irresistible rustic appeal
- Living area features a fireplace and opens to an efficient kitchen
- Two bedrooms on the second floor
- 4 bedrooms, 2 baths
- Basement foundation, drawings also include crawl space and slab foundations

Special features

1,224 total square feet of living area

- Energy efficient home with 2" x 6" exterior walls
- Charming window seats are featured in bedrooms #2 and #3
- Optional lower level has an additional 682 square feet of living area
- 3 bedrooms, 2 baths
- Partial basement/slab foundation

QUICK FACT - Covering your gutters with either wire or plastic mesh drastically cuts down on drain clogging debris and also keeps your gutters from overflowing or damaging the exterior of your home.

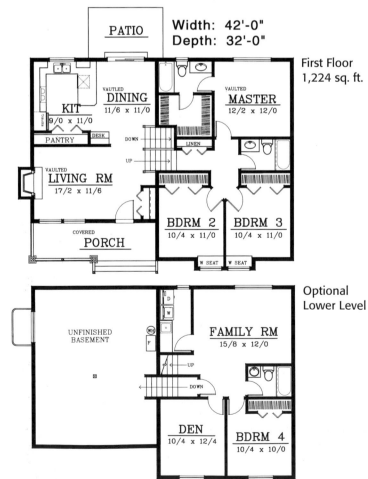

PATIO

Width: 42'-0"
Depth: 32'-0"

First Floor
1,224 sq. ft.

VAULTED
DINING
11/6 x 11/0

VAULTED
MASTER
12/2 x 12/0

KIT
9/0 x 11/0

PANTRY   DESK

DOWN

LINEN

UP

VAULTED
LIVING RM
17/2 x 11/6

BDRM 2
10/4 x 11/0

BDRM 3
10/4 x 11/0

COVERED
PORCH

W SEAT   W SEAT

Optional
Lower Level

UNFINISHED
BASEMENT

D

W

WH

F

FAMILY RM
15/8 x 12/0

UP

DOWN

DEN
10/4 x 12/4

BDRM 4
10/4 x 10/0

Special features

1,580 total square feet of living area

- Home offers great looks with an oversized front porch
- The large great room features a corner fireplace, vaulted ceiling, access to the patio and is open to the bayed dining area and kitchen breakfast bar
- The spacious kitchen enjoys an adjoining multi-purpose room ideal for a study or hobby room
- The master bedroom boasts a vaulted ceiling, two walk-in closets and a plush bath
- 3 bedrooms, 2 baths, 2-car garage
- Crawl space foundation, drawings also include slab and basement foundations

Special features

1,598 total square feet of living area

- Additional storage area in garage
- The master bedroom had a double-door entry and a luxurious master bath
- Entry opens into large family room with vaulted ceiling and open stairway to basement
- 3 bedrooms, 2 baths, 2-car garage
- Basement foundation

QUICK FACT - Some paint manufacturers offer kitchen and bathroom collections specially formulated for steamy rooms. Designed to resist moisture and inhibit mildew growth, they also give a wipe-clean finish.

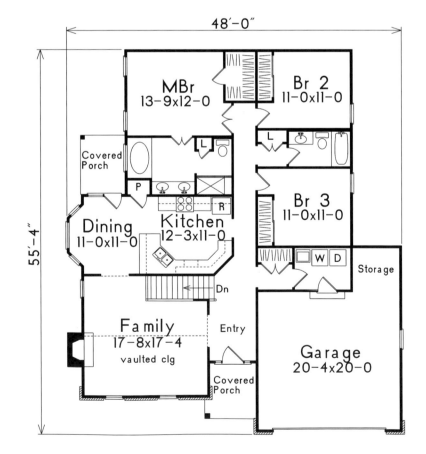

Special features

988 total square feet of living area

- Pleasant covered porch entry
- The kitchen, living and dining areas are combined to maximize space
- The entry has a convenient coat closet
- Laundry closet is located adjacent to bedrooms
- 3 bedrooms, 1 bath, 1-car garage
- Basement foundation, drawings also include crawl space foundation

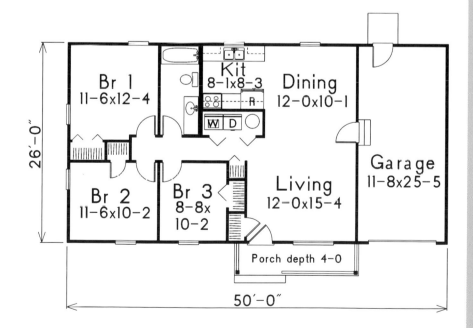

Special features

1,540 total square feet of living area

- Porch entrance into foyer leads to an impressive dining area with a full window and a half-circle window above
- Kitchen/breakfast room features a center island and cathedral ceiling
- Great room with cathedral ceiling and exposed beams is accessible from the foyer
- Master bedroom includes a full bath and walk-in closet
- Two additional bedrooms share a full bath
- 3 bedrooms, 2 baths, 2-car garage
- Basement foundation, drawings also include crawl space and slab foundations

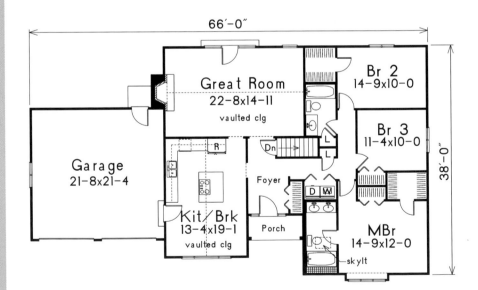

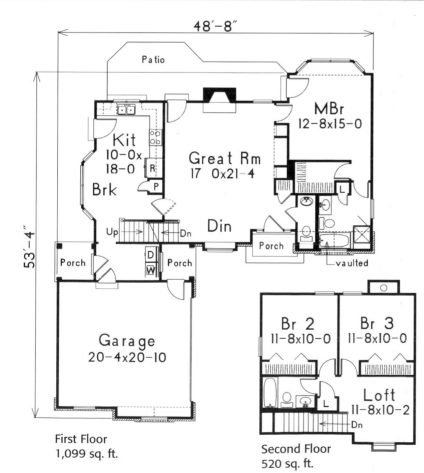

48'-8"

53'-4"

Patio

Kit
10-0x
18-0

Brk

Great Rm
17 0x21-4

MBr
12-8x15-0

R

P

Up

Dn

Din

Porch

vaulted

L

Porch

D
W

Porch

Garage
20-4x20-10

First Floor
1,099 sq. ft.

Br 2
11-8x10-0

Br 3
11-8x10-0

Loft
11-8x10-2

L

Dn

Second Floor
520 sq. ft.

Special features

1,619 total square feet of living area

- Elegant home features three quaint porches and a large rear patio
- Grand-scale great room offers a dining area, fireplace with a built-in alcove and shelves for an entertainment center
- First floor master bedroom has a walk-in closet, luxury bath, bay window and access to rear patio
- Breakfast room with bay window contains a staircase that leads to the second floor bedrooms and loft
- 3 bedrooms, 2 1/2 baths, 2-car side entry garage
- Basement foundation

Special features

1,670 total square feet of living area

- Energy efficient home with 2" x 6" exterior walls
- Living and dining areas combine making an ideal space for entertaining
- Master bedroom accesses rear verandah through sliding glass doors
- Second floor includes cozy family room with patio deck just outside of the secondary bedrooms
- 3 bedrooms, 2 baths
- Crawl space foundation

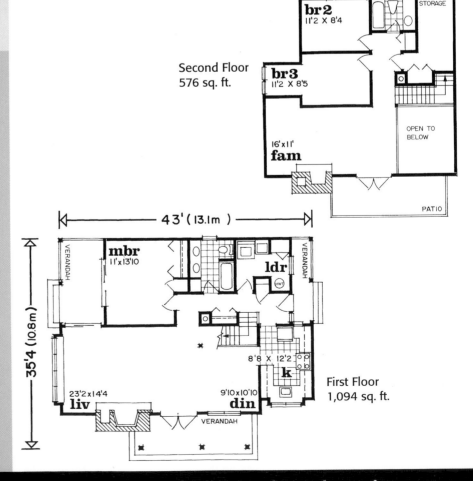

Second Floor
576 sq. ft.

br2
11'2 X 8'4

STORAGE

br3
11'2 X 8'5

OPEN TO BELOW

fam
16'x11'

PATIO

43' (13.1m)

35'4 (10.8m)

mbr
11'x13'10

VERANDAH

ldr

VERANDAH

k
8'8 X 12'2

liv
23'2 x14'4

din
9'10 x10'10

VERANDAH

First Floor
1,094 sq. ft.

Special features

1,176 total square feet of living area

- Efficient kitchen offers plenty of storage, a dining area and a stylish eating bar
- A gathering space is created by the large central living room
- Closet and storage space throughout helps keep sporting equipment organized and easily accessible
- Each end of the home is comprised of two bedrooms and a full bath
- 4 bedrooms, 2 baths
- Crawl space foundation, drawings also include slab foundation

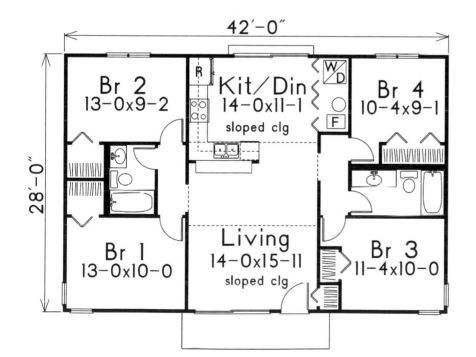

42'-0"

28'-0"

Br 2
13-0x9-2

Kit/Din
14-0x11-1
sloped clg

Br 4
10-4x9-1

Br 1
13-0x10-0

Living
14-0x15-11
sloped clg

Br 3
11-4x10-0

Special features

1,600 total square feet of living area

- Energy efficient home with 2" x 6" exterior walls
- First floor master bedroom is accessible from two points of entry
- Master bath dressing area includes separate vanities and a mirrored makeup counter
- Second floor bedrooms have generous storage space and share a full bath
- 3 bedrooms, 2 baths, 2-car side entry garage
- Crawl space foundation, drawings also include slab foundation

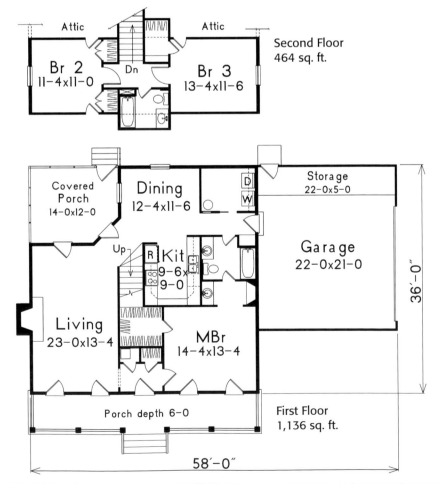

Attic

Second Floor
464 sq. ft.

Br 2
11-4x11-0

Dn

Br 3
13-4x11-6

Covered Porch
14-0x12-0

Dining
12-4x11-6

Storage
22-0x5-0

Up

R Kit
9-6x
9-0

Garage
22-0x21-0

Living
23-0x13-4

MBr
14-4x13-4

36'-0"

Porch depth 6-0

First Floor
1,136 sq. ft.

58'-0"

Special features

1,345 total square feet of living area

- Brick front details add a touch of elegance
- Master bedroom has a private full bath
- Great room combines with the dining area creating a sense of spaciousness
- Garage includes a handy storage area which could easily convert to a workshop space
- 3 bedrooms, 2 baths, 2-car side entry garage
- Basement foundation, drawings also include crawl space and slab foundations

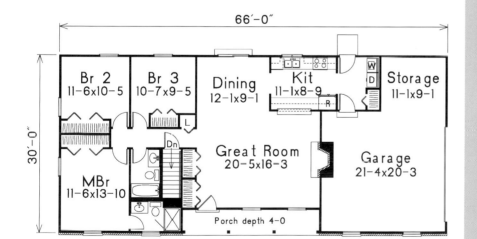

Special features

1,765 total square feet of living area

- A palladian window accenting the stone gable adds a new look to a popular cottage design
- Dormers above open the vaulted living room
- Kitchen extends to breakfast room with access to sundeck
- 3 bedrooms, 2 1/2 baths, 2-car drive under garage
- Basement foundation

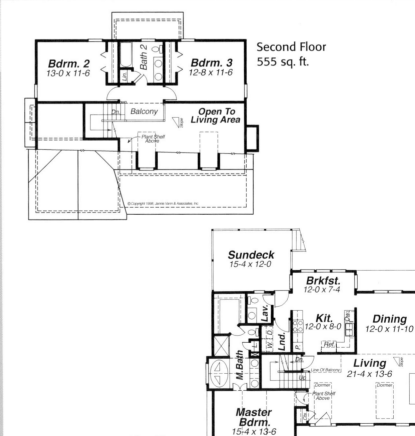

Bdrm. 2
13-0 x 11-6

Bath 2

Bdrm. 3
12-8 x 11-6

Second Floor
555 sq. ft.

Dn. Balcony

Open To
Living Area

Plant Shelf
Above

© Copyright 1998, Jannis Vann & Associates, Inc.

Sundeck
15-4 x 12-0

Brkfst.
12-0 x 7-4

Lav.

Kit.
12-0 x 8-0

Dining
12-0 x 11-10

Ref.

W.D. Lnd.

M. Bath

Dn. Up

Line Of Balcony

Living
21-4 x 13-6

Dormer

Plant Shelf
Above

Dormer

Master
Bdrm.
15-4 x 13-6

37-0

43-4

First Floor
1,210 sq. ft.

Special features

1,993 total square feet of living area

- Spacious country kitchen boasts a fireplace and plenty of natural light from windows
- Formal dining room features a large bay window and steps down to the sunken living room
- Master bedroom features corner windows, plant shelves and a deluxe private bath
- Entry opens into the vaulted living room with windows flanking the fireplace
- 3 bedrooms, 2 baths, 2-car garage
- Basement foundation

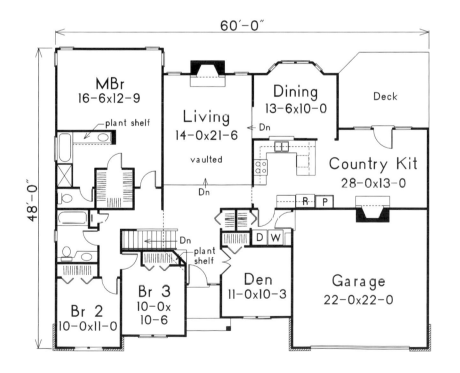

Special features

1,759 total square feet of living area

- The striking entry is created by a unique stair layout, an open high ceiling and a fireplace
- Bonus area over garage, which is included in the square footage, could easily convert to a fourth bedroom or activity center
- Second floor bedrooms share a private dressing area and bath
- 3 bedrooms, 2 1/2 baths, 2-car garage
- Basement foundation

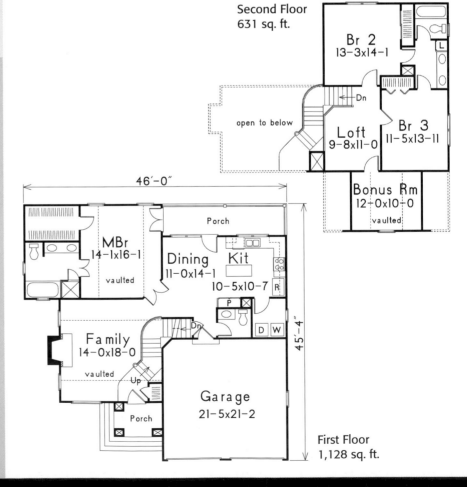

Second Floor 631 sq. ft.

Br 2 13-3x14-1

open to below

Loft 9-8x11-0

Dn

Br 3 11-5x13-11

Bonus Rm 12-0x10-0 vaulted

46'-0"

MBr 14-1x16-1 vaulted

Porch

Dining 11-0x14-1

Kit 10-5x10-7

Family 14-0x18-0 vaulted

Dn

Up

45'-4"

Garage 21-5x21-2

Porch

First Floor 1,128 sq. ft.

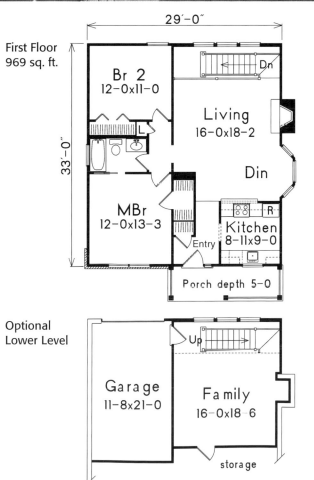

**First Floor
969 sq. ft.**

29'-0"

Br 2
12-0x11-0

Dn

Living
16-0x18-2

33'-0"

L

Din

MBr
12-0x13-3

Kitchen
8-11x9-0

R

Entry

Porch depth 5-0

**Optional
Lower Level**

Up

Garage
11-8x21-0

Family
16-0x18-6

storage

Special features

969 total square feet of living area

- Eye-pleasing facade enjoys stone accents with country porch for quiet evenings
- A bayed dining area, cozy fireplace and atrium with sunny two-story windows are the many features of the living room
- Step-saver kitchen includes a pass-through snack bar
- 325 square feet of optional living area on the lower level
- 2 bedrooms, 1 bath, 1-car rear entry garage
- Walk-out basement foundation

Special features

2,058 total square feet of living area

- Handsome two-story foyer with balcony creates a spacious entrance area
- Vaulted master bedroom has a private dressing area and large walk-in closet
- Skylights furnish natural lighting in the hall and master bath
- Laundry closet is conveniently located on the second floor near the bedrooms
- 3 bedrooms, 2 1/2 baths, 2-car garage
- Basement foundation, drawings also include slab and crawl space foundations

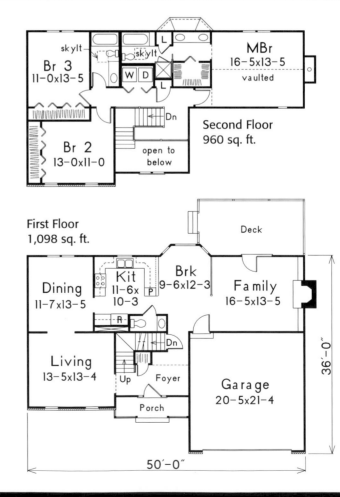

Br 3
11-0x13-5

skylt

skylt

MBr
16-5x13-5
vaulted

W D

Br 2
13-0x11-0

Dn

open to below

Second Floor
960 sq. ft.

First Floor
1,098 sq. ft.

Deck

Dining
11-7x13-5

Kit
11-6x
10-3

Brk
9-6x12-3

Family
16-5x13-5

R

Dn

Living
13-5x13-4

Up

Foyer

Garage
20-5x21-4

Porch

36'-0"

50'-0"

Special features

1,197 total square feet of living area

- U-shaped kitchen includes ample workspace, breakfast bar, laundry area and direct access to the outdoors
- Large living room has a convenient coat closet
- Bedroom #1 features a large walk-in closet
- 2" x 6" exterior walls available, please order plan #596-001D-0102
- 3 bedrooms, 1 bath
- Crawl space foundation, drawings also include basement and slab foundations

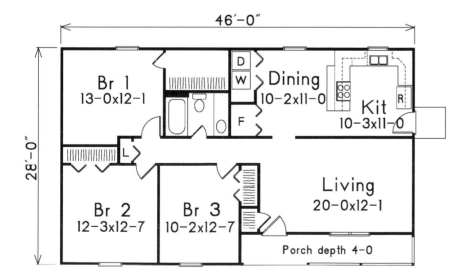

46'-0"

28'-0"

Br 1
13-0x12-1

Dining
10-2x11-0

Kit
10-3x11-0

D
W
F
L

Br 2
12-3x12-7

Br 3
10-2x12-7

Living
20-0x12-1

Porch depth 4-0

R

Special features

1,433 total square feet of living area

- Vaulted living room includes a cozy fireplace and an oversized entertainment center
- Bedrooms #2 and #3 share a full bath
- Master bedroom has a full bath and large walk-in closet
- 3 bedrooms, 2 baths, 2-car garage
- Basement foundation, drawings also include crawl space and slab foundations

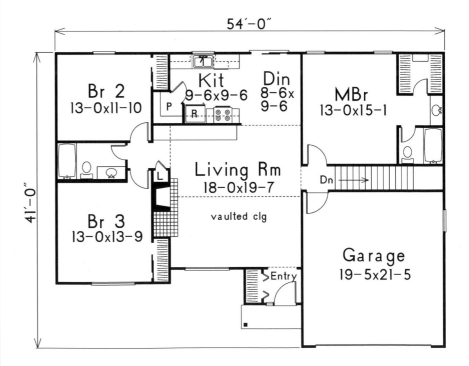

54'-0"

41'-0"

Br 2
13-0x11-10

Kit
9-6x9-6

Din
8-6x
9-6

MBr
13-0x15-1

Living Rm
18-0x19-7

vaulted clg

Dn

Br 3
13-0x13-9

Entry

Garage
19-5x21-5

Second Floor
710 sq. ft.

First Floor
1,080 sq. ft.

Special features

1,790 total square feet of living area

- A snack bar counter in the kitchen joins the spacious living and dining rooms to this family-friendly space
- The dining room enjoys corner windows and access to the expansive rear porch, perfect for extending meals to the outdoors
- The first floor bedroom with private bath access and full closet wall is the ideal master suite
- 3 bedrooms, 2 baths
- Slab foundation

Special features

1,712 total square feet of living area

- Stylish stucco exterior enhances curb appeal
- Sunken great room offers corner fireplace flanked by 9' wide patio doors
- Well-designed kitchen features ideal view of the great room and fireplace through breakfast bar opening
- 3 bedrooms, 2 1/2 baths, 2-car garage
- Crawl space foundation

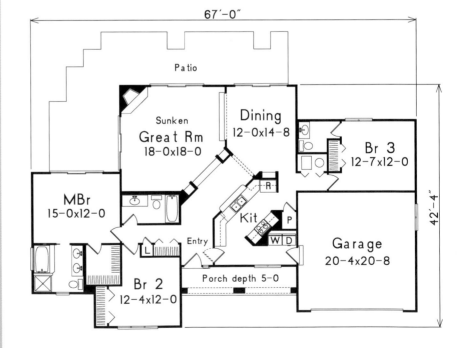

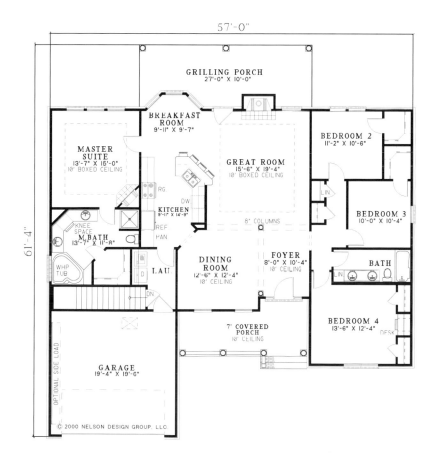

Special features

1,880 total square feet of living area

- Dining room conveniently accesses the kitchen
- Sunny breakfast room is brightened with a bay window
- Master suite has a cozy fireplace and luxurious private bath
- 4 bedrooms, 2 baths, 2-car garage
- Slab, crawl space or basement foundation, please specify when ordering

Special features

1,945 total square feet of living area

- Great room has a stepped ceiling and a fireplace
- Bayed dining area enjoys a stepped ceiling and French door leading to a covered porch
- Master bedroom has a tray ceiling, bay window and large walk-in closet
- 3 bedrooms, 2 1/2 baths, 2-car side entry garage
- Basement, crawl space or slab foundation, please specify when ordering

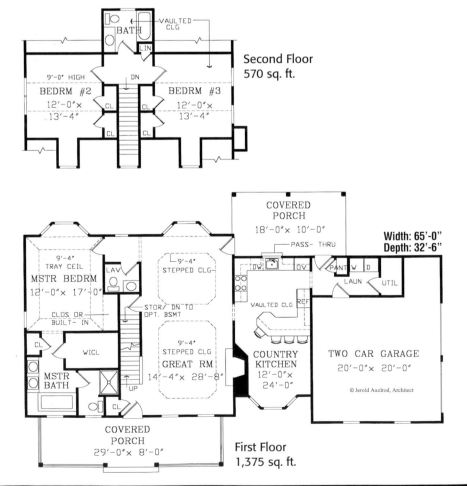

Second Floor
570 sq. ft.

BATH
VAULTED CLG
LIN
9'-0" HIGH
DN
BEDRM #2
12'-0" x
13'-4"
CL
CL
BEDRM #3
12'-0" x
13'-4"
CL
CL

Width: 65'-0"
Depth: 32'-6"

COVERED PORCH
18'-0" x 10'-0"
PASS-THRU

9'-4" TRAY CEIL
MSTR BEDRM
12'-0" x 17'-0"
LAV
9'-4" STEPPED CLG
DW
DV
PANT
W
D
LAUN
UTIL
CLOS OR BUILT-IN
STOR/ DN TO OPT. BSMT
VAULTED CLG
REF

CL
WICL
9'-4" STEPPED CLG
GREAT RM
14'-4" x 28'-8"
COUNTRY KITCHEN
12'-0" x 24'-0"
TWO CAR GARAGE
20'-0" x 20'-0"
© Jerold Axelrod, Architect

MSTR BATH
UP
CL

COVERED PORCH
29'-0" x 8'-0"

First Floor
1,375 sq. ft.

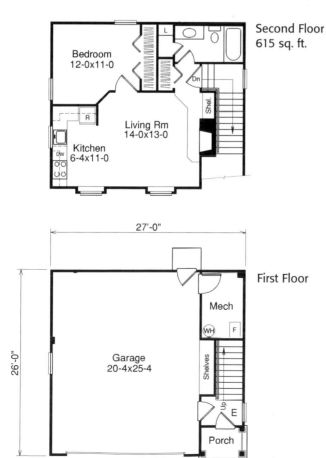

Second Floor
615 sq. ft.

Bedroom
12-0x11-0

Living Rm
14-0x13-0

Kitchen
6-4x11-0

Shel.

Dn

First Floor

27'-0"

26'-0"

Mech

WH   F

Garage
20-4x25-4

Shelves

Up

E

Porch

Special features

615 total square feet of living area

- The handsome exterior includes a front porch and upper gabled box windows
- The first floor features an oversized two-car garage with built-in storage shelves and a large mechanical room
- A large living room with fireplace, entertainment alcove and kitchen open to an eating area are just a few of the many features of the second floor
- 1 bedroom, 1 bath, 2-car garage
- Slab foundation

Special features

1,642 total square feet of living area

- Walk-through kitchen boasts a vaulted ceiling and corner sink overlooking the family room
- Vaulted family room features a cozy fireplace and access to the rear patio
- Master bedroom includes a sloped ceiling, walk-in closet and private bath
- 3 bedrooms, 2 baths, 2-car garage
- Basement foundation, drawings also include slab and crawl space foundations

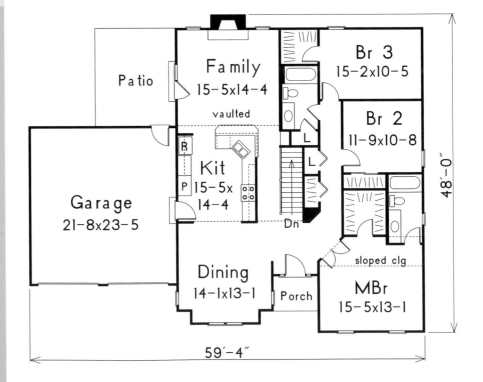

Width: 38'-0"
Depth: 32'-0"

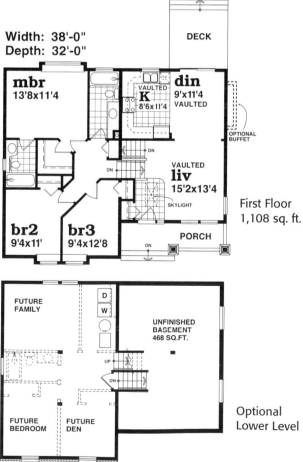

DECK

mbr
13'8x11'4

din
9'x11'4
VAULTED

VAULTED
K
8'6x11'4

OPTIONAL
BUFFET

DN

DN

VAULTED
liv
15'2x13'4

SKYLIGHT

First Floor
1,108 sq. ft.

br2
9'4x11'

br3
9'4x12'8

PORCH

DN

FUTURE
FAMILY

D
W

UNFINISHED
BASEMENT
468 SQ.FT.

UP

DN

FUTURE
BEDROOM

FUTURE
DEN

Optional
Lower Level

Special features

1,108 total square feet of living area

- Energy efficient home with 2" x 6" exterior walls
- Master bedroom offers a walk-in closet, a full bath and a box-bay window
- Vaulted ceilings in the kitchen, living and dining rooms make this home appear larger than its actual size
- Compact, but efficient kitchen is U-shaped so everything is within reach
- Optional lower level has an additional 1,108 square feet of living area
- 3 bedrooms, 2 baths
- Partial basement/crawl space or basement foundation, please specify when ordering

Special features

1,466 total square feet of living area

- The foyer flows into the great room which is warmed by a corner fireplace
- Sliding French doors open to the backyard from both the great room and adjoining formal dining room
- A turreted breakfast room overlooks the spacious front porch
- The master bedroom is separated for privacy and includes its own bath
- 3 bedrooms, 2 baths, 2-car side entry garage
- Basement, crawl space or slab foundation, please specify when ordering

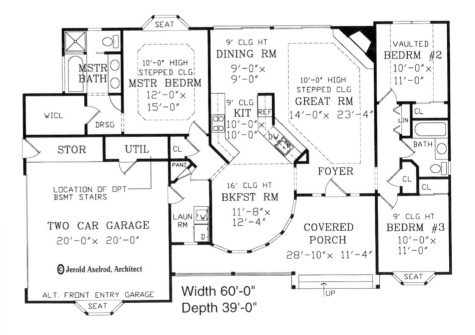

Second Floor
905 sq. ft.

Special features

1,998 total square feet of living area

- Lovely designed family room offers a double-door entrance into the living area
- Roomy kitchen with breakfast area is a natural gathering place
- 10' ceiling in the master bedroom
- 3 bedrooms, 2 1/2 baths, 2-car garage
- Basement foundation

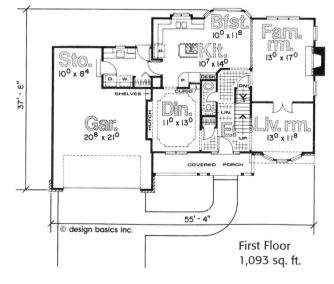

© design basics inc.

First Floor
1,093 sq. ft.

Special features

1,519 total square feet of living area

- The large living room boasts a vaulted ceiling with plant shelf, fireplace, and opens to the bayed dining area
- The kitchen has an adjoining laundry/mud room and features a vaulted ceiling, snack counter open to the living and dining areas and a built-in pantry
- Two walk-in closets, a stylish bath and small sitting area accompany the master bedroom
- 4 bedrooms, 2 baths, 2-car garage
- Crawl space foundation, drawings also include slab and basement foundations

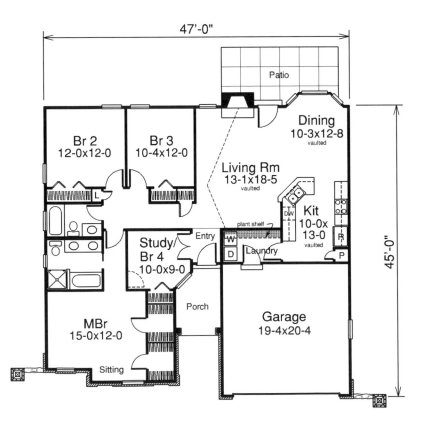

Special features

1,160 total square feet of living area

- U-shaped kitchen includes breakfast bar and convenient laundry area
- Master bedroom features private half bath and large closet
- Dining room has outdoor access
- Dining and great rooms combine to create an open living atmosphere
- 3 bedrooms, 1 1/2 baths
- Crawl space foundation, drawings also include basement and slab foundations

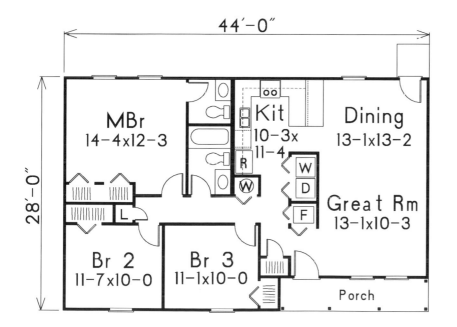

44'-0"

28'-0"

MBr
14-4x12-3

Kit
10-3x
11-4

Dining
13-1x13-2

Great Rm
13-1x10-3

Br 2
11-7x10-0

Br 3
11-1x10-0

Porch

Special features

1,772 total square feet of living area

- Extended porches in front and rear provide a charming touch
- Large bay windows lend distinction to the dining room and bedroom #3
- Efficient U-shaped kitchen
- Master bedroom includes two walk-in closets
- Full corner fireplace in family room
- 3 bedrooms, 2 baths, 2-car detached garage
- Slab foundation, drawings also include crawl space foundation

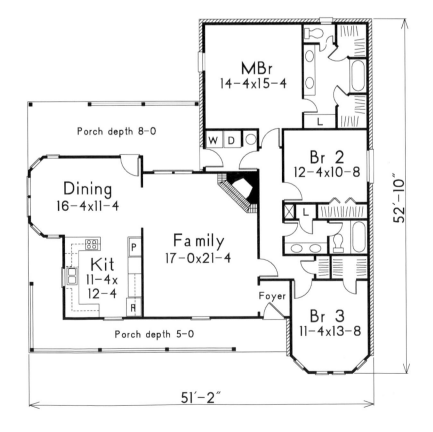

Second Floor
446 sq. ft.

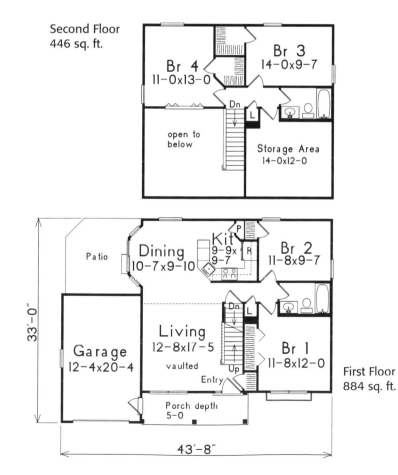

Br 4
11-0x13-0

Br 3
14-0x9-7

Dn
L

open to below

Storage Area
14-0x12-0

Patio

Dining
10-7x9-10

Kit
9-9x
9-7

P
R

Br 2
11-8x9-7

33'-0"

Dn
L

Garage
12-4x20-4

Living
12-8x17-5
vaulted

Up

Br 1
11-8x12-0

Entry

First Floor
884 sq. ft.

Porch depth
5-0

43'-8"

Special features

1,330 total square feet of living area

- Vaulted living room is open to the bayed dining room and kitchen creating an ideal space for entertaining
- Two bedrooms, a bath and linen closet complete the first floor and are easily accessible
- The second floor offers two bedrooms with walk-in closets, a very large storage room and an opening with louvered doors which overlooks the living room
- 4 bedrooms, 2 baths, 1-car garage
- Basement foundation

Special features

1,578 total square feet of living area

- Plenty of closet, linen and storage space
- Covered porches in the front and rear of home add charm to this design
- Open floor plan has a unique angled layout
- 3 bedrooms, 2 baths, 2-car garage
- Basement foundation

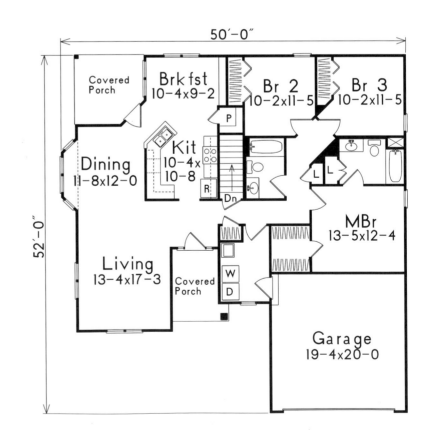

50'-0"

Covered Porch

Brk fst 10-4x9-2

Br 2 10-2x11-5

Br 3 10-2x11-5

Kit 10-4x 10-8

Dining 11-8x12-0

52'-0"

MBr 13-5x12-4

Living 13-4x17-3

Covered Porch

W D

Garage 19-4x20-0

QUICK FACT - Cold weather shouldn't be an issue anymore with exterior painting. Most conventional paints need to be applied during temperatures 55 degrees or warmer. But cold weather paints are designed to resist moisture, frost and blisters in temperatures as low as 35 degrees.

Second Floor
579 sq. ft.

STORAGE

BEDROOM 3
15X12

DN
OPEN TO BELOW

BEDROOM 2
15X12

DECK

SKYLIGHT

DINING
12x12

KITCHEN
10x12

VAULT

34

DN

VAULT

MASTER BEDRM
15x13

UP

FAMILY ROOM
18x15

First Floor
1,064 sq. ft.

38

Special features

1,643 total square feet of living area

- First floor master bedroom has a private bath, walk-in closet and easy access to the laundry closet
- Comfortable family room features a vaulted ceiling and a cozy fireplace
- Two bedrooms on the second floor share a bath
- 3 bedrooms, 2 1/2 baths, 2-car drive under garage
- Basement or crawl space foundation, please specify when ordering

Special features

1,388 total square feet of living area

- Handsome see-through fireplace offers a gathering point for the kitchen, family and breakfast rooms
- Vaulted ceiling and large bay window in the master bedroom add charm to this room
- A dramatic angular wall and large windows add brightness to the kitchen and breakfast room
- Kitchen, breakfast and family rooms have vaulted ceilings, adding to this central living area
- 3 bedrooms, 2 baths, 2-car garage
- Crawl space foundation, drawings also include slab foundation

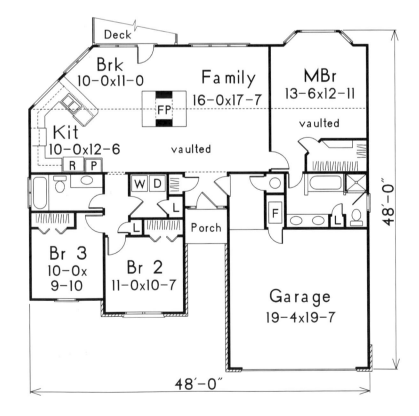

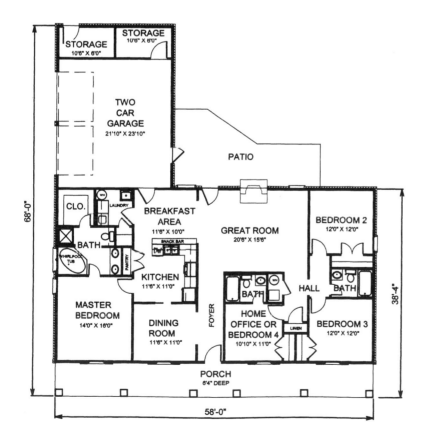

Special features

1,856 total square feet of living area

- Kitchen is well positioned between the formal dining room and the casual breakfast area
- Master bedroom has a luxurious bath with all the amenities
- Home office or bedroom #4 has its own private bath
- 4 bedrooms, 3 baths, 2-car side entry garage
- Crawl space or slab foundation, please specify when ordering

Special features

1,085 total square feet of living area

- Rear porch provides handy access through the kitchen
- Convenient hall linen closet is located on the second floor
- Breakfast bar in the kitchen offers additional counterspace
- Living and dining rooms combine for open living
- 3 bedrooms, 2 baths
- Basement foundation

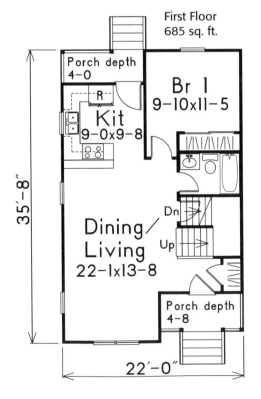

First Floor
685 sq. ft.

Porch depth
4-0

R

Kit
9-0x9-8

Br 1
9-10x11-5

Dining/
Living
22-1x13-8

Dn

Up

Porch depth
4-8

35'-8"

22'-0"

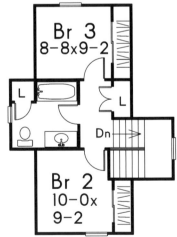

Second Floor
400 sq. ft.

Br 3
8-8x9-2

L

L

Dn

Br 2
10-0x
9-2

Special features

1,846 total square feet of living area

- Enormous living area combines with the dining and breakfast rooms that are both complemented by extensive windows and high ceilings
- Master bedroom has a walk-in closet, display niche and deluxe bath
- Secondary bedrooms share a bath and feature large closet space and a corner window
- Oversized two-car garage has plenty of storage and workspace with handy access to the kitchen through the utility area
- Breakfast nook has wrap-around windows adding to eating enjoyment
- 3 bedrooms, 2 baths, 2-car garage
- Slab foundation

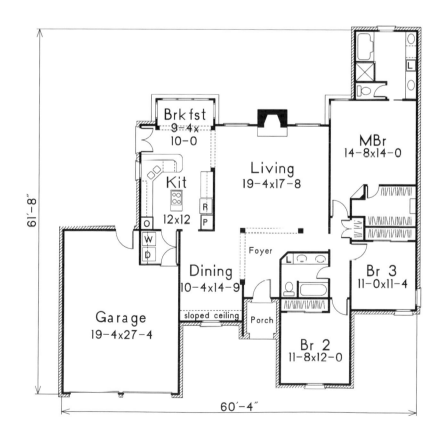

Special features

1,124 total square feet of living area

- Varied ceiling heights throughout this home
- Enormous bayed breakfast room overlooks the great room with fireplace
- The washer and dryer closet is conveniently located
- 3 bedrooms, 2 baths, 2-car drive under garage
- Walk-out basement foundation

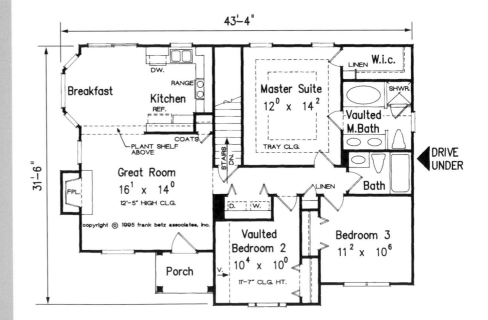

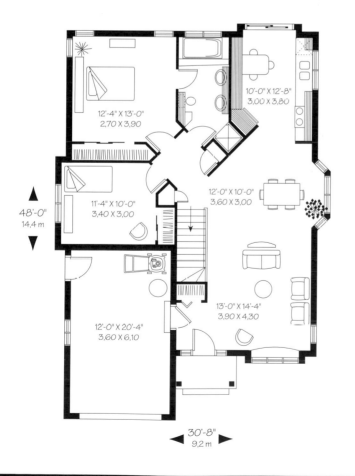

Special features

1,103 total square feet of living area

- Energy efficient home with 2" x 6" exterior walls
- All bedrooms are located in one area of the house for privacy
- Bay window enhances dining area
- Living and dining areas combine for a spacious feeling
- Lots of storage throughout
- 2 bedrooms, 1 bath, 1-car garage
- Basement foundation

Special features

1,672 total square feet of living area

- Energy efficient home with 2" x 6" exterior walls
- Vaulted master bedroom features a walk-in closet and adjoining bath with separate tub and shower
- Covered front and rear porches
- 12' ceilings in the living room, kitchen and bedroom #2
- Kitchen is complete with a pantry, angled bar and adjacent eating area
- Sloped ceiling in the dining room
- 3 bedrooms, 2 baths, 2-car side entry garage
- Crawl space foundation, drawings also include basement and slab foundations

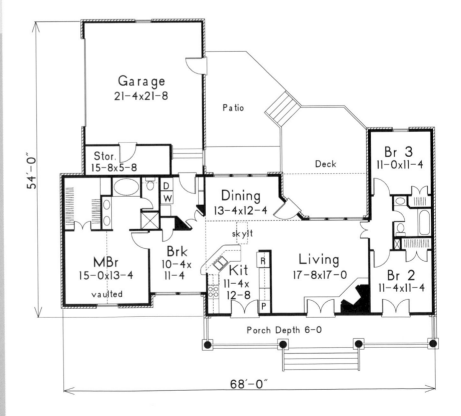

Special features

1,468 total square feet of living area

- Energy efficient home with 2" x 6" exterior walls
- Family room has a beautiful cathedral ceiling adding spaciousness and a fireplace creating a cozy feel
- Large kitchen has plenty of room for dining
- 3 bedrooms, 2 baths
- Basement foundation

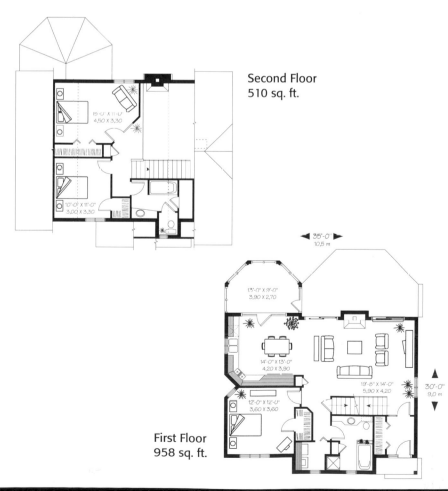

Second Floor
510 sq. ft.

15'-0" X 11'-0"
4,50 X 3,30

10'-0" X 11'-0"
3,00 X 3,30

◄ 35'-0" ►
10,5 m

13'-0" X 9'-0"
3,90 X 2,70

14'-0" X 13'-0"
4,20 X 3,90

19'-8" X 14'-0"
5,90 X 4,20

12'-0" X 12'-0"
3,60 X 3,60

30'-0"
9,0 m

First Floor
958 sq. ft.

Special features

2,084 total square feet of living area

- Charming bay window in the master suite allows sunlight in as well as style
- Great room accesses front covered porch extending the living area to the outdoors
- Large playroom on the second floor is ideal for family living
- 3 bedrooms, 2 1/2 baths, 2-car side entry garage
- Slab, crawl space or basement foundation, please specify when ordering

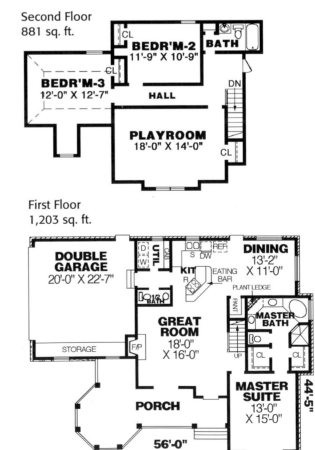

Second Floor
881 sq. ft.

CL

BEDR'M-2
11'-9" X 10'-9"

BATH

CL

BEDR'M-3
12'-0" X 12'-7"

HALL

DN

PLAYROOM
18'-0" X 14'-0"

CL

First Floor
1,203 sq. ft.

DOUBLE GARAGE
20'-0" X 22'-7"

UTIL

S DW

RER

DINING
13'-2" X 11'-0"

KIT

EATING BAR

PLANT LEDGE

BATH

PANT

MASTER BATH

GREAT ROOM
18'-0" X 16'-0"

STORAGE

F/P

UP

CL

CL

MASTER SUITE
13'-0" X 15'-0"

44'-5"

PORCH

56'-0"

Special features

1,364 total square feet of living area

- Master bedroom features a spacious walk-in closet and private bath
- Living room is highlighted with several windows
- Kitchen with snack bar is adjacent to the dining area
- Plenty of storage space throughout
- 3 bedrooms, 2 baths, optional 2-car garage
- Basement foundation, drawings also include crawl space foundation

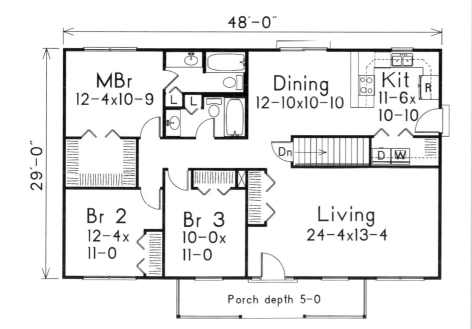

48'-0"

29'-0"

MBr
12-4x10-9

Dining
12-10x10-10

Kit
11-6x
10-10

R

Dn

D W

Br 2
12-4x
11-0

Br 3
10-0x
11-0

Living
24-4x13-4

Porch depth 5-0

Special features

1,588 total square feet of living area

- Energy efficient home with 2" x 6" exterior walls
- Workshop in garage is ideal for storage and projects
- 12' vaulted master suite has double closets as well as a lovely bath with bayed soaking tub and compartmentalized shower and toilet area
- Lovely arched entry to 14' vaulted great room flows into the dining room and sky-lit kitchen
- 3 bedrooms, 2 baths, 2-car garage
- Basement foundation

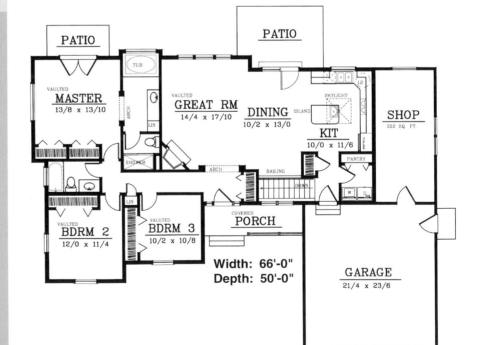

Width: 66'-0"
Depth: 50'-0"

Special features

1,929 total square feet of living area

- A classic traditional exterior for timeless elegance
- More than a great room for this size home, the grand room features a vaulted ceiling and a brick and wood mantle fireplace flanked by doors to the rear patio
- State-of-the-art U-shaped kitchen has a built-in pantry, computer desk, snack bar and breakfast room with bay window
- The master bedroom includes a vaulted ceiling, large walk-in closet, luxury bath and access to the rear patio
- 4 bedrooms, 3 baths, 3-car side entry garage
- Crawl space foundation, drawings also include slab and basement foundations

Special features

1,073 total square feet of living area

- Home includes a lovely covered front porch and a screened porch off the dining area
- Attractive box window brightens the kitchen
- Space for an efficiency washer and dryer is located conveniently between the bedrooms
- Family room is spotlighted by a fireplace with flanking bookshelves and spacious vaulted ceiling
- 2 bedrooms, 1 bath
- Crawl space foundation

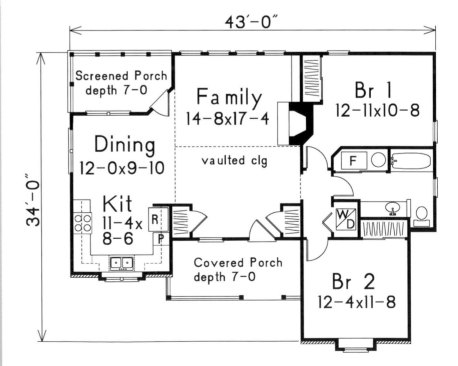

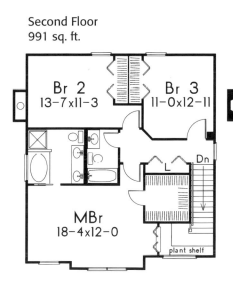

Second Floor
991 sq. ft.

Br 2
13-7x11-3

Br 3
11-0x12-11

Dn

L

MBr
18-4x12-0

plant shelf

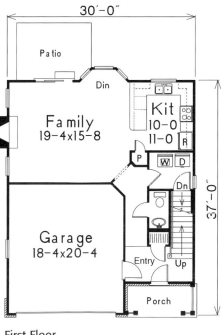

30'-0"

Patio

Din

Family
19-4x15-8

Kit
10-0
11-0

R

P

W   D

Dn

37'-0"

Garage
18-4x20-4

Up

Entry

Porch

First Floor
680 sq. ft.

Special features

1,671 total square feet of living area

- Triple gables and stone facade create great curb appeal
- Two-story entry with hallway leads to a spacious family room, dining area with bay window and U-shaped kitchen
- Second floor features a large master bedroom with luxury bath, huge walk-in closet, overlook to entry and two secondary bedrooms with hall bath
- 3 bedrooms, 2 1/2 baths, 2-car garage
- Basement foundation

Special features

1,643 total square feet of living area

- An attractive front entry porch gives this ranch a country accent
- Spacious family/dining room is the focal point of this design
- Kitchen and utility room are conveniently located near gathering areas
- Formal living room in the front of the home provides area for quiet and privacy
- Master bedroom has view to the rear of the home and a generous walk-in closet
- 3 bedrooms, 2 baths, 2-car garage
- Basement foundation, drawings also include crawl space and slab foundations

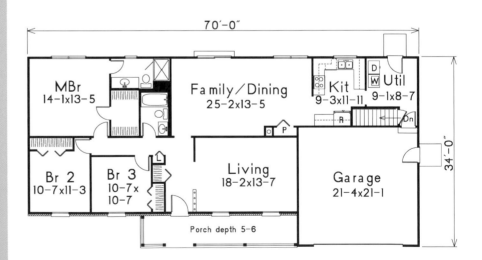

70'-0"

34'-0"

MBr 14-1x13-5

Family/Dining 25-2x13-5

Kit 9-3x11-11

Util 9-1x8-7

Br 2 10-7x11-3

Br 3 10-7x 10-7

Living 18-2x13-7

Garage 21-4x21-1

Porch depth 5-6

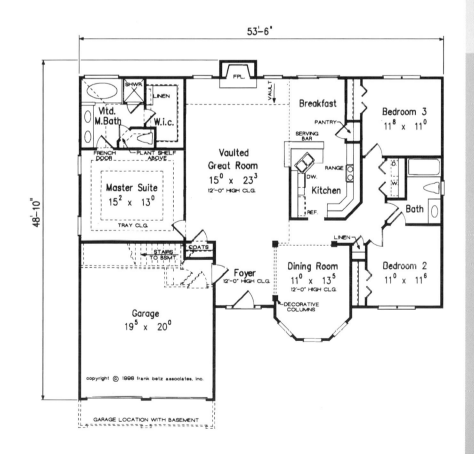

Special features

1,638 total square feet of living area

- Glass sliding doors bring the outdoors in to the breakfast room
- A laundry closet is conveniently located between the two secondary bedrooms
- 9' ceilings throughout home
- 3 bedrooms, 2 baths, 2-car garage
- Crawl space or walk-out basement foundation, please specify when ordering

Special features

1,400 total square feet of living area

- Front covered porch leads into the great room
- Great room features a vaulted ceiling and fireplace for warmth
- Rear grilling porch includes a practical and convenient supply room
- 2 bedrooms, 2 baths
- Crawl space or slab foundation, please specify when ordering

QUICK FACT - To avoid scuffing wood, vinyl or linoleum floors when rearranging furniture pieces, slide a folded towel under each side of the piece of furniture you wish to move. Not only does this avoid scratches and scrapes, but it tends to make moving the piece a lot easier.

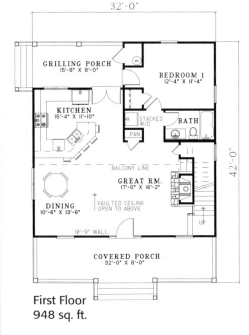

32'-0"

GRILLING PORCH
15'-8" X 8'-0"

BEDROOM 1
12'-4" X 11'-4"

KITCHEN
15'-4" X 11'-10"

STACKED
W/D

PAN

BATH

42'-0"

BALCONY LINE

GREAT RM.
17'-0" X 16'-2"

VAULTED CEILING
OPEN TO ABOVE

DINING
10'-6" X 13'-6"

UP

10'-9" WALL

COVERED PORCH
32'-0" X 8'-0"

First Floor
948 sq. ft.

BEDROOM 2
11'-4" X 11'-8"

STORAGE

SLEEPING LOFT
21'-0" X 8'-0"

BATH

DN

VAULTED
CEILING

Second Floor
452 sq. ft.

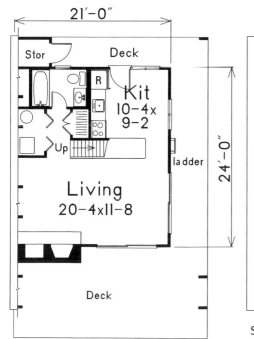

First Floor
495 sq. ft.

- 21'-0"
- Stor
- Deck
- Kit
  10-4x
  9-2
- R
- Up
- ladder
- Living
  20-4x11-8
- 24'-0"
- Deck

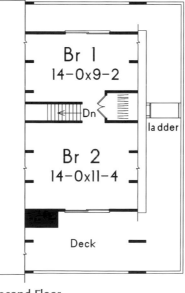

Second Floor
370 sq. ft.

- Br 1
  14-0x9-2
- Dn
- ladder
- Br 2
  14-0x11-4
- Deck

Special features

865 total square feet of living area

- Central living area provides an enormous amount of space for gathering around the fireplace
- The outdoor ladder on the wrap-around deck connects the top deck with the main deck
- Kitchen is bright and cheerful with lots of windows and access to the deck
- 2 bedrooms, 1 bath
- Pier foundation

Special features

1,856 total square feet of living area

- Energy efficient home with 2" x 6" exterior walls
- Living room features include fireplace, 12' ceiling and skylights
- Common vaulted ceiling creates an open atmosphere in the kitchen and breakfast room
- Garage with storage areas conveniently accesses home through handy utility room
- Private hall separates secondary bedrooms from living areas
- 3 bedrooms, 2 baths, 2-car side entry garage
- Slab foundation, drawings also include crawl space foundation

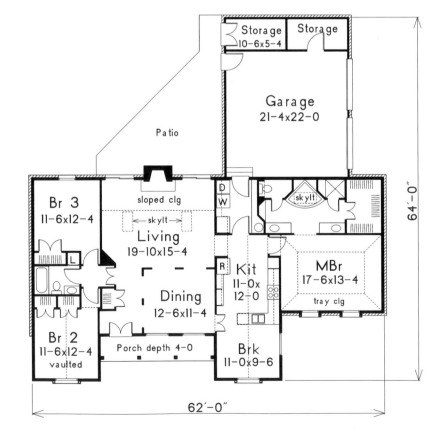

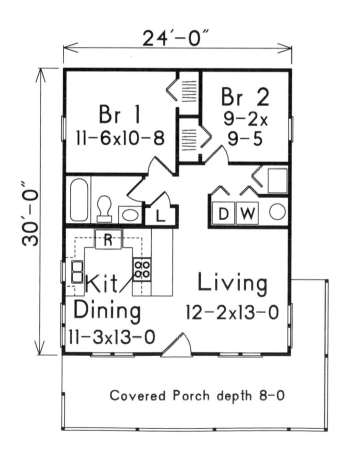

24'-0"

30'-0"

Br 1
11-6x10-8

Br 2
9-2x 9-5

L

D W

R

Kit
Dining
11-3x13-0

Living
12-2x13-0

Covered Porch depth 8-0

Special features

720 total square feet of living area

- Abundant windows in living and dining rooms provide generous sunlight
- Secluded laundry area has a handy storage closet
- U-shaped kitchen with large breakfast bar opens into living area
- Large covered deck offers plenty of outdoor living space
- 2 bedrooms, 1 bath
- Crawl space foundation, drawings also include slab foundation

Special features

1,556 total square feet of living area

- A compact home with all the amenities
- Country kitchen combines practicality with access to other areas for eating and entertaining
- Two-way fireplace joins the dining and living areas
- A plant shelf and vaulted ceiling highlight the master bedroom
- 3 bedrooms, 2 1/2 baths, 2-car garage
- Basement foundation

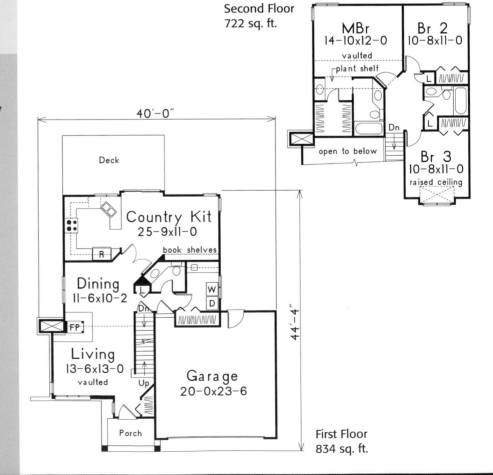

Second Floor
722 sq. ft.

MBr
14-10x12-0
vaulted
plant shelf

Br 2
10-8x11-0

open to below

Dn

Br 3
10-8x11-0
raised ceiling

40'-0"

Deck

Country Kit
25-9x11-0

book shelves

Dining
11-6x10-2

W
D

Dn

FP

Living
13-6x13-0
vaulted

Up

Garage
20-0x23-6

44'-4"

Porch

First Floor
834 sq. ft.

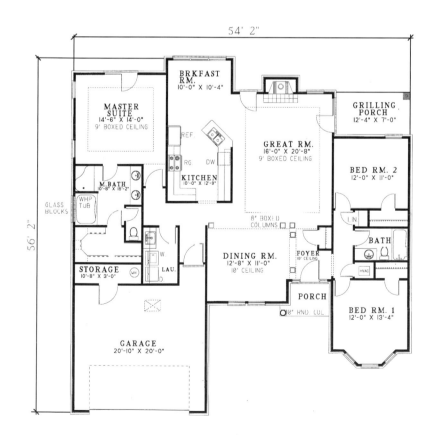

Special features

1,758 total square feet of living area

- Energy efficient home with 2" x 6" exterior walls
- The kitchen, breakfast, great and dining rooms combine for a spacious living area
- A wonderful grilling porch is perfect for entertaining
- 3 bedrooms, 2 baths, 2-car garage
- Walk-out basement, basement, crawl space or slab foundation, please specify when ordering

Special features

1,769 total square feet of living area

- Living room boasts an elegant cathedral ceiling and fireplace
- U-shaped kitchen and dining area combine for easy living
- Secondary bedrooms include double closets
- Secluded master bedroom features a sloped ceiling, large walk-in closet and private bath
- 2" x 6" exterior walls available, please order plan #596-001D-0124
- 3 bedrooms, 2 baths
- Basement foundation, drawings also include crawl space and slab foundations

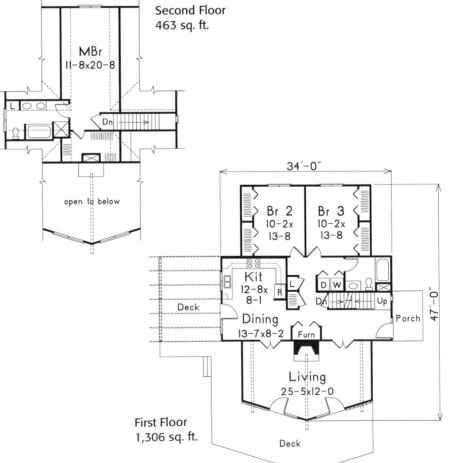

Second Floor
463 sq. ft.

MBr
11-8x20-8

Dn

open to below

First Floor
1,306 sq. ft.

34'-0"

47'-0"

Br 2
10-2x
13-8

Br 3
10-2x
13-8

Kit
12-8x
8-1

D W

Deck

Dining
13-7x8-2

Furn

Porch

Up

Living
25-5x12-0

Deck

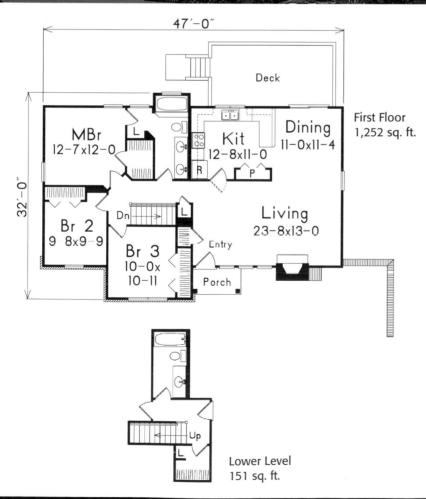

47′-0″

Deck

MBr
12-7x12-0

Kit
12-8x11-0

Dining
11-0x11-4

First Floor
1,252 sq. ft.

32′-0″

Br 2
9 8x9-9

Dn

Br 3
10-0x
10-11

Living
23-8x13-0

Entry

Porch

484

Lower Level
151 sq. ft.

Up

Special features

1,403 total square feet of living area

- Impressive living areas for a modest-sized home
- Special master/hall bath has linen storage, step-up tub and lots of window light
- Spacious closets everywhere you look
- 3 bedrooms, 2 baths, 2-car drive under garage
- Basement foundation

QUICK FACT - As building materials go, drywall is the same: one manufacturer's product will be the same as another; there are no hidden defects. This material is either smooth and solid or it isn't. If you see it on sale, buy it.

Special features

1,958 total square feet of living area

- Large wrap-around kitchen opens to a bright and cheerful breakfast area with access to a large covered deck and open stairway to basement
- Kitchen is nestled between the dining and breakfast rooms
- Master bedroom includes a large walk-in closet, double-bowl vanity, garden tub and separate shower
- Foyer features an attractive plant shelf and opens into the living room that includes a lovely central fireplace
- 3 bedrooms, 2 baths, 2-car garage
- Basement foundation

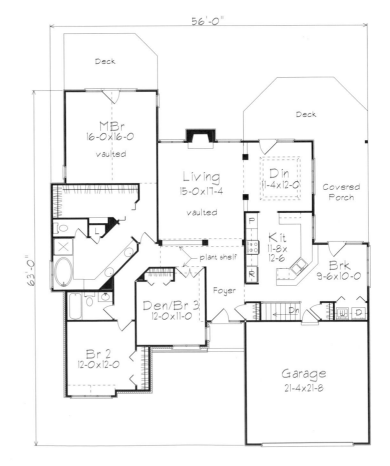

Special features

1,400 total square feet of living area

- Front porch offers warmth and welcome
- Large great room opens into the dining room creating an open living atmosphere
- Kitchen features convenient laundry area, pantry and breakfast bar
- 2" x 6" exterior walls available, please order plan #596-001D-0103
- 3 bedrooms, 2 baths, 2-car garage
- Crawl space foundation, drawings also include basement and slab foundations

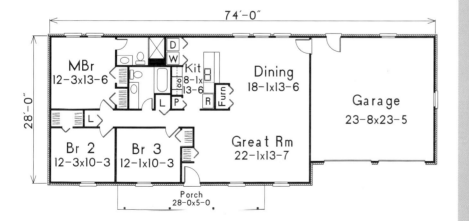

74'-0"

28'-0"

MBr
12-3x13-6

Kit
8-1x
13-6

Dining
18-1x13-6

Garage
23-8x23-5

Br 2
12-3x10-3

Br 3
12-1x10-3

Great Rm
22-1x13-7

Porch
28-0x5-0

Special features

1,277 total square feet of living area

- Expansive great room features an 11' vaulted ceiling, cozy fireplace and coat closet
- Utility room, kitchen and dining area combine for an open atmosphere
- Master bedroom is located away from the secondary bedrooms for privacy
- 3 bedrooms, 2 baths
- Slab or crawl space foundation, please specify when ordering

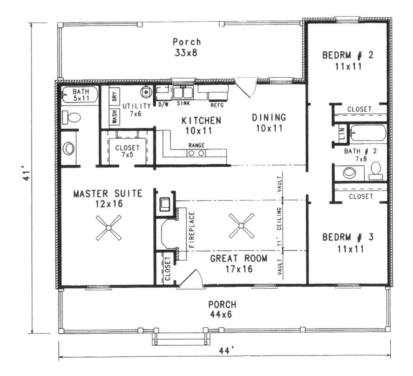

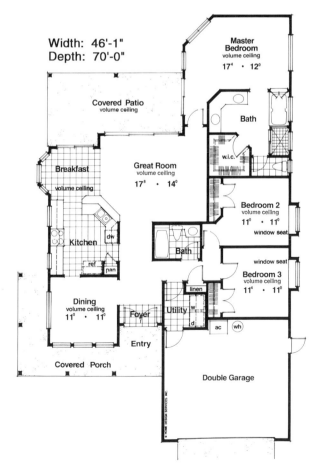

Width: 46'-1"
Depth: 70'-0"

Master Bedroom
volume ceiling
$17^4 \cdot 12^0$

Covered Patio
volume ceiling

Bath

w.i.c.

Breakfast
volume ceiling

Great Room
volume ceiling
$17^8 \cdot 14^0$

Bedroom 2
volume ceiling
$11^0 \cdot 11^0$
window seat

Kitchen

dw

ref

pan

Bath

window seat

Bedroom 3
volume ceiling
$11^4 \cdot 11^0$

linen

Dining
volume ceiling
$11^0 \cdot 11^0$

Foyer

Utility

w
d

ac

wh

Entry

Covered Porch

Double Garage

Special features

1,627 total square feet of living area

- Bay-shaped breakfast room is sunny and bright
- Angled window wall and volume ceiling in master bedroom add interest
- Box-bay windows are featured in secondary bedrooms
- 3 bedrooms, 2 baths, 2-car garage
- Slab foundation

Special features

1,742 total square feet of living area

- Efficient kitchen combines with the breakfast area and great room creating a spacious living area
- Master bedroom includes a private bath with huge walk-in closet, shower and corner tub
- Great room boasts a fireplace and access outdoors
- Laundry room is conveniently located near the kitchen and garage
- 3 bedrooms, 2 baths, 2-car garage
- Slab foundation, drawings also include crawl space foundation

Special features

1,210 total square feet of living area

- Inviting covered porch leads to a spacious great room
- Laundry room is centrally located for convenience
- Master suite has a private bath and a large walk-in closet
- 3 bedrooms, 2 baths, 2-car garage
- Crawl space or slab foundation, please specify when ordering

Special features

1,969 total square feet of living area

- Master bedroom boasts a luxurious bath with double sinks, two walk-in closets and an oversized tub
- Corner fireplace warms a conveniently located family area
- Formal living and dining areas in the front of the home lend a touch of privacy when entertaining
- Spacious utility room has counterspace and a sink
- 3 bedrooms, 2 baths, 2-car garage
- Crawl space foundation, drawings also include slab foundation

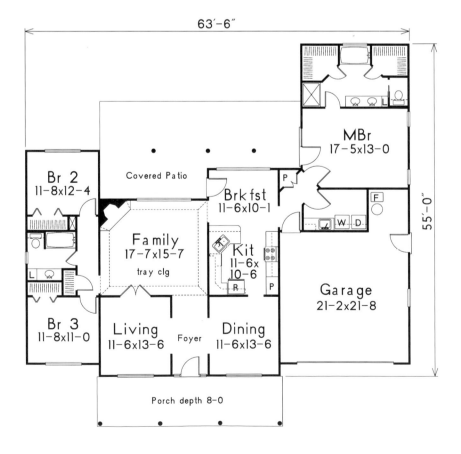

63'-6"

55'-0"

Br 2
11-8x12-4

Covered Patio

Brkfst
11-6x10-1

MBr
17-5x13-0

Family
17-7x15-7
tray clg

Kit
11-6x
10-6

Garage
21-2x21-8

Br 3
11-8x11-0

Living
11-6x13-6

Foyer

Dining
11-6x13-6

Porch depth 8-0

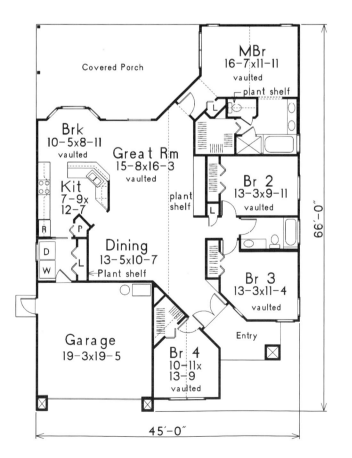

Special features

1,865 total square feet of living area

- The large foyer opens into an expansive dining area and great room
- Home features vaulted ceilings throughout
- Master bedroom features an angled entry, vaulted ceiling, plant shelf and bath with double vanity, tub and shower
- 4 bedrooms, 2 baths, 2-car garage
- Slab foundation, drawings also include crawl space foundation

Special features

1,294 total square feet of living area

- Great room features a fireplace and large bay with windows and patio doors
- Enjoy a laundry room immersed in light with large windows, an arched transom and attractive planter box
- Vaulted master bedroom features a bay window and two walk-in closets
- Bedroom #2 boasts a vaulted ceiling, plant shelf and half bath, perfect for a studio
- 2 bedrooms, 1 full bath, 2 half baths, 1-car rear entry garage
- Basement foundation

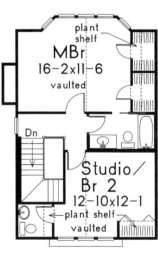

plant shelf

MBr
16-2x11-6
vaulted

Dn

Studio/
Br 2
12-10x12-1
← plant shelf
vaulted

Second Floor
576 sq. ft.

Great Rm
19-8x15-0

Dining

Dn

Kit
8-0x
9-6

Garage
12-4x20-4

35'-8"

Up

R   P

Entry

Porch depth 5-0

W
D

33'-0"

First Floor
718 sq. ft.

First Floor
1,157 sq. ft.

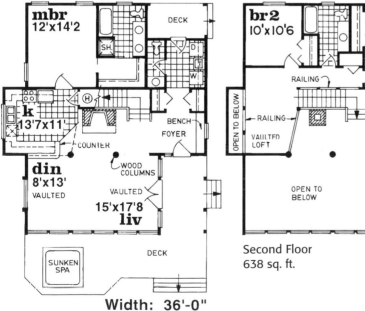

mbr
12'x14'2

DECK

br2
10'x10'6

br3
10'x14'
VAULTED

SH.

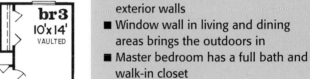

k
13'7x11'

H

RAILING

OPEN TO BELOW

RAILING

VAULTED LOFT

PLANT LEDGE

BENCH

FOYER

COUNTER

WOOD COLUMNS

OPEN TO BELOW

din
8'x13'
VAULTED

VAULTED

15'x17'8
liv

SUNKEN SPA

DECK

Second Floor
638 sq. ft.

Width: 36'-0"
Depth: 40'-0"

Special features

1,795 total square feet of living area

- Energy efficient home with 2" x 6" exterior walls
- Window wall in living and dining areas brings the outdoors in
- Master bedroom has a full bath and walk-in closet
- Vaulted loft on the second floor is a unique feature
- 3 bedrooms, 2 1/2 baths
- Basement or crawl space foundation, please specify when ordering

Special features

1,650 total square feet of living area

- Master bedroom is located on the second floor for privacy
- Open living area connects to the dining area
- Two-story living area features lots of windows for views to the outdoors and a large fireplace
- Efficiently designed kitchen
- 4 bedrooms, 2 baths
- Pier foundation

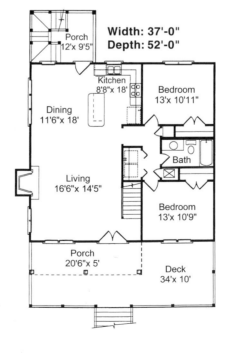

First Floor
1,122 sq. ft.

Porch
12'x 9'5"

Width: 37'-0"
Depth: 52'-0"

Kitchen
8'8"x 18'

Dining
11'6"x 18'

Bedroom
13'x 10'11"

Bath

Living
16'6"x 14'5"

Bedroom
13'x 10'9"

Porch
20'6"x 5'

Deck
34'x 10'

Second Floor
528 sq. ft.

Bedroom
14'x 11'2"

Ma. Ba.

Open to Below

Master Bedroom
13'x 13'6"

Special features

1,860 total square feet of living area

- Dining room has an 11' stepped ceiling with a bay window creating a pleasant dining experience
- Breakfast room has a 12' sloped ceiling with French doors leading to a covered porch
- Great room has a columned arched entrance, a built-in media center and a fireplace
- 3 bedrooms, 2 baths, 2-car side entry garage
- Basement, crawl space or slab foundation, please specify when ordering

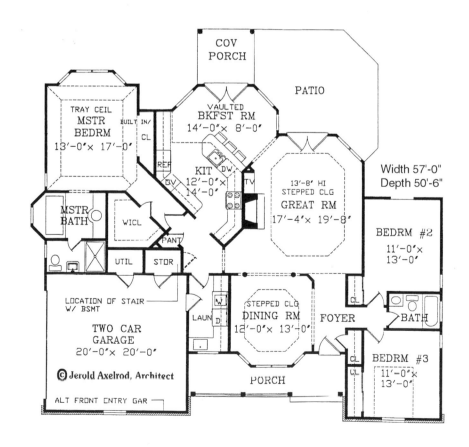

COV PORCH

PATIO

TRAY CEIL
MSTR BEDRM
13'-0" x 17'-0"

BUILT IN/
CL

VAULTED
BKFST RM
14'-0" x 8'-0"

REF

KIT
12'-0" x 14'-0"

DW

DV

TV

13'-8' HI
STEPPED CLG
GREAT RM
17'-4" x 19'-8"

Width 57'-0"
Depth 50'-6"

MSTR BATH

WICL

PANT

BEDRM #2
11'-0" x 13'-0"

UTIL

STOR

LOCATION OF STAIR
W/ BSMT

LAUN

STEPPED CLG
DINING RM
12'-0" x 13'-0"

FOYER

BATH

TWO CAR
GARAGE
20'-0" x 20'-0"

© Jerold Axelrod, Architect

BEDRM #3
11'-0" x 13'-0"

ALT FRONT ENTRY GAR

PORCH

Special features

1,314 total square feet of living area

- U-shaped kitchen joins the cozy dining area
- The family room has direct access into the garage
- Roomy closets serve the second floor bedrooms
- 3 bedrooms, 1 1/2 baths, 2-car garage
- Basement foundation, drawings also include crawl space foundation

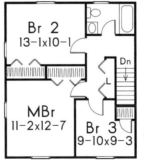

Br 2
13-1x10-1

Dn

MBr
11-2x12-7

Br 3
9-10x9-3

Second Floor
552 sq. ft.

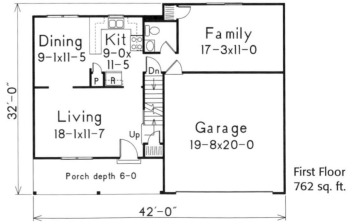

Dining
9-1x11-5

Kit
9-0x
11-5

Family
17-3x11-0

P R

Dn

Living
18-1x11-7

Up

Garage
19-8x20-0

32'-0"

Porch depth 6-0

First Floor
762 sq. ft.

42'-0"

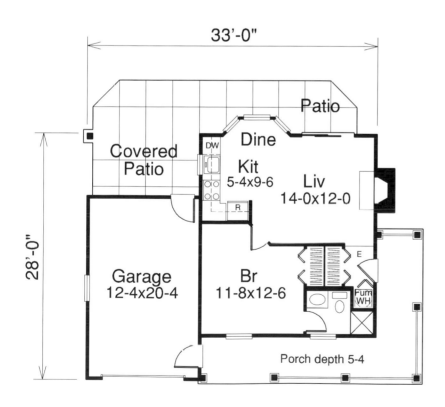

33'-0"

28'-0"

Covered Patio

Patio

Dine

Kit
5-4x9-6

DW

R

Liv
14-0x12-0

E

Garage
12-4x20-4

Br
11-8x12-6

Furn
WH

Porch depth 5-4

Special features

480 total square feet of living area

- Inviting wrap-around porch and rear covered patio are perfect for summer evenings
- Living room features a fireplace, separate entry foyer with coat closet and sliding doors to rear patio
- The compact but complete kitchen includes a dining area with bay window and window at sink for patio views
- 1 bedroom, 1 bath, 1-car garage
- Slab foundation

Special features

1,200 total square feet of living area

- Enjoy lazy summer evenings on this magnificent porch
- Activity area has a fireplace and ascending stair from the cozy loft
- Kitchen features a built-in pantry
- Master bedroom enjoys a large bath, walk-in closet and cozy loft overlooking the room below
- 2 bedrooms, 2 baths
- Crawl space foundation

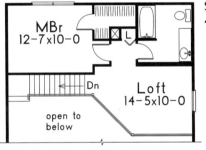

Second Floor
416 sq. ft.

MBr
12-7x10-0

Loft
14-5x10-0

Dn

open to below

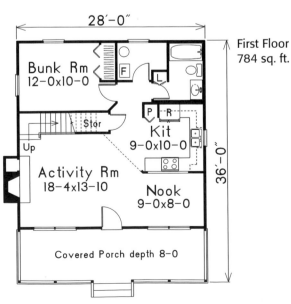

28'-0"

First Floor
784 sq. ft.

36'-0"

Bunk Rm
12-0x10-0

F

Stor

Up

P R

Kit
9-0x10-0

Activity Rm
18-4x13-10

Nook
9-0x8-0

Covered Porch depth 8-0

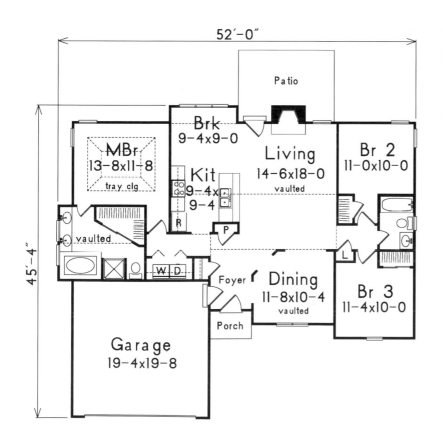

Special features

1,358 total square feet of living area

- Vaulted master bath has a walk-in closet, double bowl vanity, large tub, shower and toilet area
- Galley kitchen opens to both the living room and the breakfast area
- A vaulted ceiling joins the dining and living rooms
- Breakfast room has a full wall of windows
- 3 bedrooms, 2 baths, 2-car garage
- Slab foundation

Special features

2,066 total square feet of living area

- Large master bedroom includes a sitting area and private bath
- Open living room features a fireplace with built-in bookshelves
- Spacious kitchen accesses formal dining area and breakfast room
- 3 bedrooms, 2 1/2 baths, optional 2-car side entry garage
- Slab foundation

QUICK FACT - A compact kitchen can be efficient, but not when it lacks storage. One way to stretch the space without compromising design is to extend the cabinets to the ceiling. Although a harder reach, it is the perfect solution for items you rarely need.

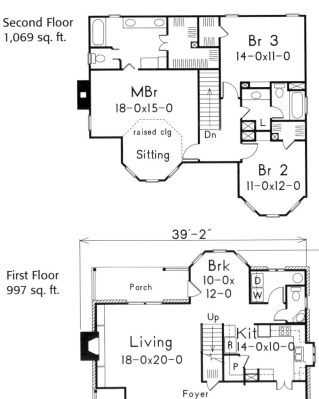

Second Floor
1,069 sq. ft.

MBr
18-0x15-0

raised clg

Sitting

Dn

Br 3
14-0x11-0

L

Br 2
11-0x12-0

First Floor
997 sq. ft.

39'-2"

Brk
10-0x 12-0

D

W

Porch

Up

Kit
14-0x10-0

R

P

37'-6"

Living
18-0x20-0

Foyer

Dining
10-0x 14-0

Porch depth 5-6

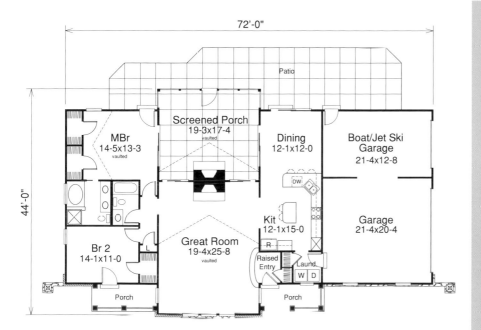

72'-0"

44'-0"

Patio

MBr
14-5x13-3
vaulted

Screened Porch
19-3x17-4
vaulted

Dining
12-1x12-0

Boat/Jet Ski
Garage
21-4x12-8

Kit
12-1x15-0

Garage
21-4x20-4

DW

R

Br 2
14-1x11-0

L

Great Room
19-4x25-8
vaulted

Raised
Entry

Laund.

W D

Porch

Porch

Special features

1,568 total square feet of living area

- Multiple entrances from three porches help to bring the outdoors in
- The lodge-like great room features a vaulted ceiling, stone fireplace, step-up entrance foyer and opens to a huge screened porch
- The kitchen has an island and peninsula, a convenient laundry room and adjoins a spacious dining area which leads to a screened porch and rear patio
- The master bedroom has two walk-in closets, a luxury bath and access to the screened porch and patio
- 2 bedrooms, 2 baths, 3-car side entry garage
- Crawl space foundation

Special features

1,379 total square feet of living area

- Living area has a spacious feel with an 11'-6" ceiling
- Kitchen has an eat-in breakfast bar open to the dining area
- Laundry area is located near the bedrooms
- Large cased opening with columns opens to the living and dining areas
- 3 bedrooms, 2 baths, 2-car drive under garage
- Basement foundation

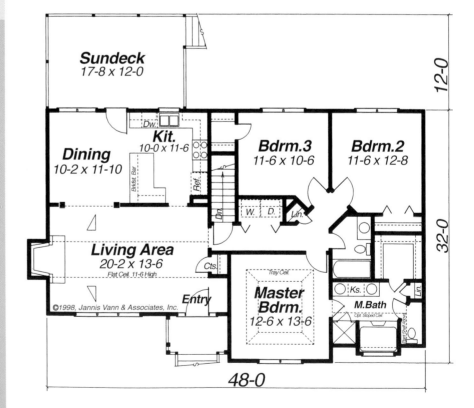

Sundeck 17-8 x 12-0

Kit. 10-0 x 11-6

Dining 10-2 x 11-10

Bdrm.3 11-6 x 10-6

Bdrm.2 11-6 x 12-8

Dw.

Brkfst. Bar

Ref.

Dn.

W. D. Lin.

Living Area 20-2 x 13-6
Flat Ceil. 11-6 High

Cts.

Entry

Master Bdrm. 12-6 x 13-6

Tray Ceil

M.Bath

Ks.

Lin.

©1998, Jannis Vann & Associates, Inc.

12-0

32-0

48-0

Special features

1,230 total square feet of living area

- Spacious living room accesses the huge deck
- Bedroom #3 features a balcony overlooking the deck
- Kitchen with dining area accesses the outdoors
- Washer and dryer are tucked under the stairs for space efficiency
- 3 bedrooms, 1 bath
- Crawl space foundation, drawings also include slab foundation

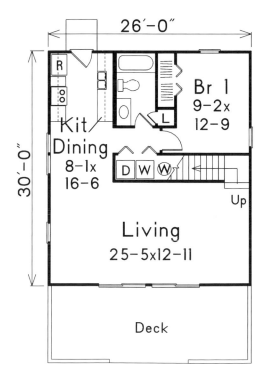

26'-0"

30'-0"

R

Kit
Dining
8-1x
16-6

Br 1
9-2x
12-9

L

D W W

Up

Living
25-5x12-11

Deck

First Floor
780 sq. ft.

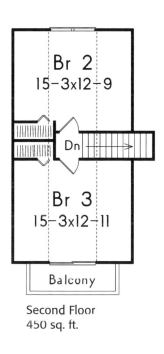

Br 2
15-3x12-9

Dn

Br 3
15-3x12-11

Balcony

Second Floor
450 sq. ft.

Special features

976 total square feet of living area

- Cozy front porch opens into the large living room
- Convenient half bath is located on the first floor
- All bedrooms are located on the second floor for privacy
- Dining room has access to the outdoors
- 3 bedrooms, 1 1/2 baths
- Basement foundation

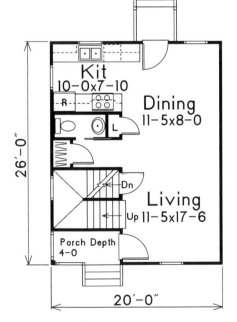

Kit
10-0x7-10

Dining
11-5x8-0

26'-0"

Living
Up 11-5x17-6

Porch Depth
4-0

20'-0"

First Floor
488 sq. ft.

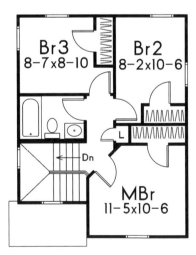

Br3
8-7x8-10

Br2
8-2x10-6

Dn

MBr
11-5x10-6

Second Floor
488 sq. ft.

Special features

1,991 total square feet of living area

- A large porch with roof dormers and flanking stonework creates a distinctive country appeal
- The highly functional U-shaped kitchen is open to the dining and living rooms defined by a colonnade
- Large bay windows are enjoyed by both the living room and master bedroom
- Every bedroom features spacious walk-in closets and their own private bath
- 3 bedrooms, 3 1/2 baths, 2-car side entry garage
- Basement foundation

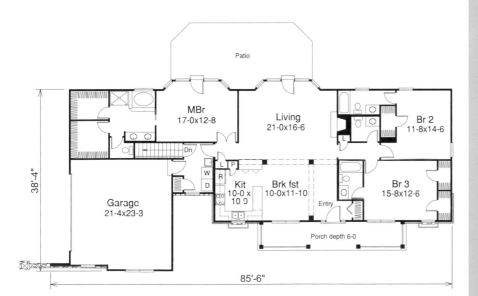

Patio

MBr
17-0x12-8

Living
21-0x16-6

Br 2
11-8x14-6

Dn

Garage
21-4x23-3

38'-4"

W
D

Kit
10-0 x
10 0

Brk fst
10-0x11-10

Br 3
15-8x12-6

Entry

Porch depth 6-0

85'-6"

Special features

1,373 total square feet of living area

- 9' ceilings throughout this home
- The sunny breakfast room is easily accessible to the kitchen
- Kitchen has a pass-through to the vaulted family room
- 3 bedrooms, 2 baths, 2-car garage
- Crawl space or walk-out basement foundation, please specify when ordering

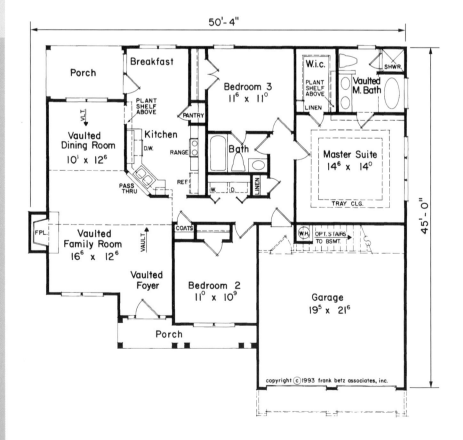

copyright (c)1993 frank betz associates, inc.

Special features

1,092 total square feet of living area

- Energy efficient home with 2" x 6" exterior walls
- Sunken family room adds interest
- Nice-sized bedrooms are convenient to the bath
- Handy work island in kitchen
- 3 bedrooms, 1 bath
- Basement foundation

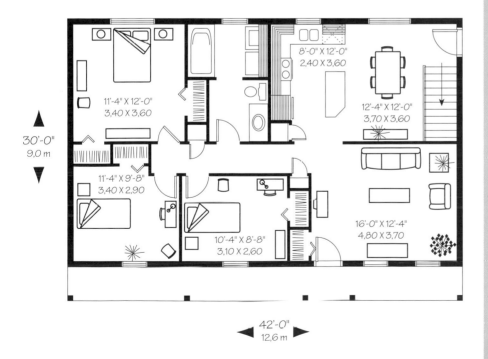

11'-4" X 12'-0"
3,40 X 3,60

8'-0" X 12'-0"
2,40 X 3,60

12'-4" X 12'-0"
3,70 X 3,60

11'-4" X 9'-8"
3,40 X 2,90

10'-4" X 8'-8"
3,10 X 2,60

16'-0" X 12'-4"
4,80 X 3,70

30'-0"
9,0 m

42'-0"
12,6 m

QUICK FACT - Any joints between building materials is a likely place to find heated air leaking out of the house. If two dissimilar materials meet, the chances of air leakage are even greater. When tightening up your house for the colder months, scrutinize these areas with particular care.

Special features

1,551 total square feet of living area

- A centrally located kitchen is able to effortlessly serve the formal dining room and casual breakfast area
- Four spacious bedrooms offer space for a large family
- The rear of the home includes an essential storage room accessed from the rear yard
- 4 bedrooms, 2 baths
- Slab foundation

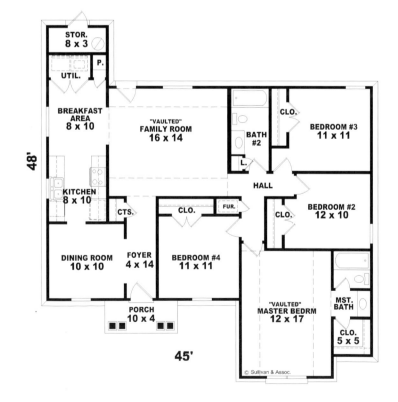

STOR.
8 x 3

P.

UTIL.

BREAKFAST AREA
8 x 10

"VAULTED" FAMILY ROOM
16 x 14

BATH #2

CLO.

BEDROOM #3
11 x 11

KITCHEN
8 x 10

CTS.

HALL

48'

CLO.

FUR.

CLO.

BEDROOM #2
12 x 10

DINING ROOM
10 x 10

FOYER
4 x 14

BEDROOM #4
11 x 11

"VAULTED" MASTER BEDRM
12 x 17

MST. BATH

CLO.
5 x 5

PORCH
10 x 4

45'

© Sullivan & Assoc.

Optional
Second Floor

Future
33-5x25-8

56-0

52-8

Porch
18-0x12-6

Owner's
Bedroom
16-6x14-0

Bath
8-6x14-0

Bedroom
12-0x10-4

Dining
10-0x15-4

Desk
Kitchen
11-0x15-4

Stor.
5-8x5-8

Bath

Garage
21-8x21-7

Bedroom
12-0x10-4

Greatroom
17-6x15-6

©Larry James Designs

Porch
21-0x6-6

First Floor
1,551 sq. ft.

Special features

1,551 total square feet of living area

- Enter the home and view the spacious great room with grand fireplace flanked by built-ins
- The kitchen boasts a large island with seating and a built-in desk
- The private owner's bedroom enjoys a deluxe bath, porch access and nearby laundry closet
- The optional second floor has an additional 684 square feet of living area
- 3 bedrooms, 2 baths, 2-car garage
- Basement, crawl space or slab foundation, please specify when ordering

Special features

2,074 total square feet of living area

- Unique sewing room is ideal for hobby enthusiasts and has counterspace for convenience
- Double walk-in closets are located in the luxurious master bath
- A built-in bookcase in the great room adds charm
- 3 bedrooms, 2 1/2 baths, 2-car side entry garage
- Slab foundation

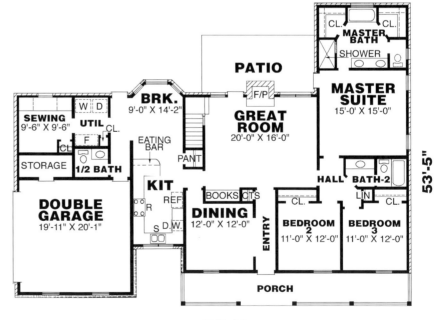

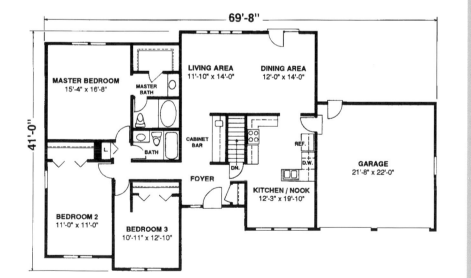

69'-8"

41'-0"

MASTER BEDROOM
15'-4" x 16'-8"

MASTER BATH

BATH

LIVING AREA
11'-10" x 14'-0"

DINING AREA
12'-0" x 14'-0"

CABINET BAR

DN.

REF.

D.W.

GARAGE
21'-8" x 22'-0"

FOYER

KITCHEN / NOOK
12'-3" x 19'-10"

BEDROOM 2
11'-0" x 11'-0"

BEDROOM 3
10'-11" x 12'-10"

L

Special features

1,704 total square feet of living area

- Open living and dining areas combine for added spaciousness
- Master bedroom features a private bath and walk-in closet
- Sunny kitchen/nook has space for dining
- Cabinet bar in hallway leading to the living area is designed for entertaining
- 3 bedrooms, 2 baths, 2-car garage
- Basement foundation

Special features

1,135 total square feet of living area

- Living and dining rooms feature vaulted ceilings and a corner fireplace
- Energy efficient home with 2" x 6" exterior walls
- Master bedroom offers a vaulted ceiling, private bath and generous closet space
- Compact but functional kitchen is complete with a pantry and adjacent utility room
- 3 bedrooms, 2 baths, 2-car garage
- Basement foundation, drawings also include crawl space foundation

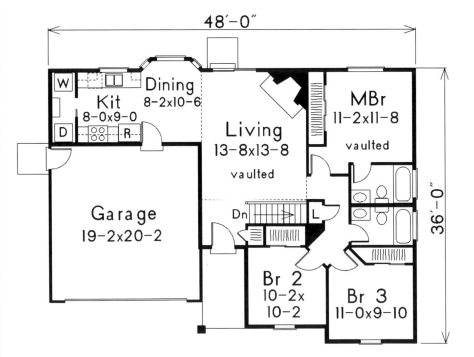

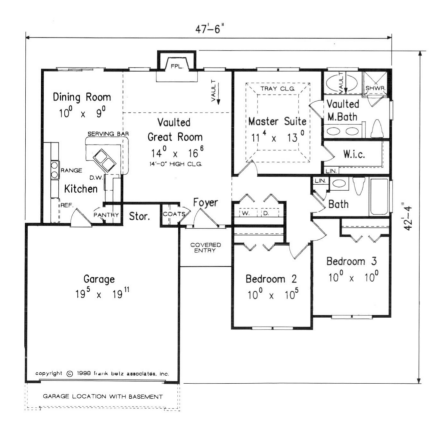

Special features

1,149 total square feet of living area

- Vaulted great room creates an open, airy feel
- Oversized serving bar in kitchen allows for extra seating in dining area
- 9' ceilings throughout home
- 3 bedrooms, 2 baths, 2-car garage
- Crawl space or walk-out basement foundation, please specify when ordering

Special features

1,013 total square feet of living area

- Vaulted ceilings in both the family room and kitchen with dining area just beyond the breakfast bar
- Plant shelf above kitchen is a special feature
- Oversized utility room has space for a full-size washer and dryer
- Hall bath is centrally located with easy access from both bedrooms
- 2" x 6" exterior walls available, please order plan #596-058D-0073
- 2 bedrooms, 1 bath
- Slab foundation

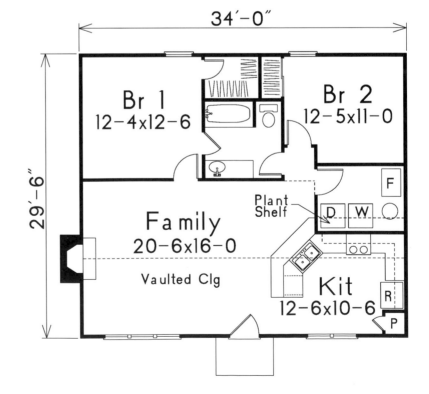

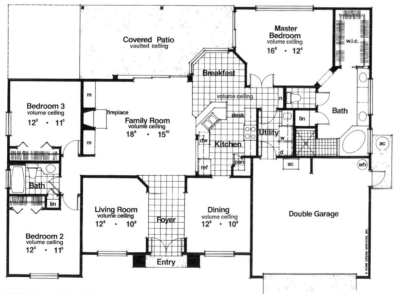

Width: 60'-0"
Depth: 45'-0"

Special features

1,783 total square feet of living area

- Grand foyer leads to the family room
- Walk-in pantry adds convenience to the kitchen
- Master bath has a step-down doorless shower, huge vanity and a large walk-in closet
- 3 bedrooms, 2 baths, 2-car garage
- Slab foundation

QUICK FACT - To add functional work space to a compact kitchen, think about purchasing a small rolling cart that can be moved around easily to free up space. Plus, when entertaining it can be moved out of sight.

Special features

1,741 total square feet of living area

- Handsome exterior has multiple gables and elegant brickwork
- The great room offers a fireplace, vaulted ceiling and is open to the bayed dining area and kitchen with breakfast bar
- The master bedroom boasts a vaulted ceiling, large walk-in closet, luxury bath and enjoys a nearby room perfect for a study, nursery or fifth bedroom
- 4 bedrooms, 2 baths, 2-car garage
- Crawl space foundation, drawings also inclue slab and basement foundations

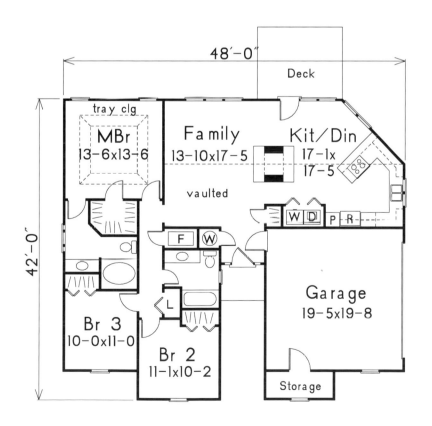

48'-0"

Deck

tray clg

MBr
13-6x13-6

Family
13-10x17-5

Kit/Din
17-1x
17-5

vaulted

42'-0"

F   W

W D   P R

Garage
19-5x19-8

Br 3
10-0x11-0

L

Br 2
11-1x10-2

Storage

Special features

1,340 total square feet of living area

- Master bedroom has a private bath and walk-in closet
- Recessed entry leads to the vaulted family room that shares a see-through fireplace with the kitchen/dining area
- Garage includes a handy storage area
- Convenient laundry closet is located in the kitchen
- 3 bedrooms, 2 baths, 2-car side entry garage
- Slab foundation, drawings also include crawl space foundation

Special features

1,472 total square feet of living area

- 8' wrap-around porch entry is inviting and creates an outdoor living area
- Great room has a rock hearth fireplace and is open to the second floor above
- Side grilling porch has a cleaning sink for fish or game
- Optional bonus room on the second floor has an additional 199 square feet of living area
- 3 bedrooms, 2 baths
- Crawl space or slab foundation, please specify when ordering

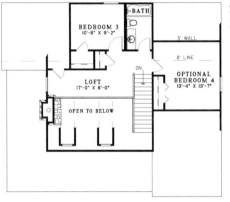

Second Floor
332 sq. ft.

BEDROOM 3
10'-8" X 9'-2"

BATH

5' WALL

8' LINE

LOFT
17'-0" X 6'-0"

DN

OPTIONAL
BEDROOM 4
13'-4" X 13'-7"

OPEN TO BELOW

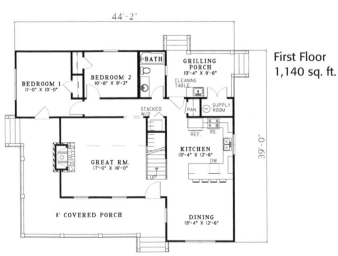

First Floor
1,140 sq. ft.

44'-2"

BEDROOM 1
11'-0" X 13'-0"

BEDROOM 2
10'-8" X 9'-2"

BATH

GRILLING
PORCH
13'-4" X 9'-6"

CLEANING
TABLE

SUPPLY
ROOM

STACKED
W/D

PAN.

39'-0"

GREAT RM.
17'-0" X 16'-0"

REF.

RG.

KITCHEN
13'-4" X 12'-6"

UP

DW

8' COVERED PORCH

DINING
13'-4" X 12'-6"

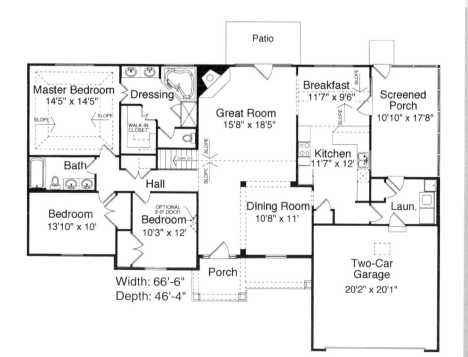

Patio

Master Bedroom
14'5" x 14'5"

Dressing

SLOPE   SLOPE

WALK-IN
CLOSET

Bath

Hall

DOWN 15 R.

SLOPE / SLOPE

SLOPE

Great Room
15'8" x 18'5"

Breakfast
11'7" x 9'6"

SLOPE

Screened
Porch
10'10" x 17'8"

Kitchen
11'7" x 12'

Laun.

Bedroom
13'10" x 10'

OPTIONAL
3'-0" DOOR

Bedroom
10'3" x 12'

Dining Room
10'8" x 11'

Width: 66'-6"
Depth: 46'-4"

Porch

Two-Car
Garage
20'2" x 20'1"

Special features

1,798 total square feet of living area

- The expansive great room enjoys a fireplace and has access onto the rear patio
- The centrally located kitchen is easily accessible to the dining room and breakfast area
- The master bedroom boasts a sloped ceiling and deluxe bath with a corner whirlpool tub and large walk-in closet
- A screened porch offers relaxing outdoor living
- 3 bedrooms, 2 baths, 2-car garage
- Basement foundation

Special features

1,868 total square feet of living area

- Energy efficient home with 2" x 6" exterior walls
- Luxurious master bath is impressive with an angled quarter-circle tub, separate vanities and large walk-in closet
- Dining room is surrounded by a series of arched openings which complement the open feeling of this design
- Living room has a 12' ceiling accented by skylights and a large fireplace flanked by sliding doors
- Large storage areas
- 3 bedrooms, 2 baths, 2-car side entry garage
- Slab foundation, drawings also include crawl space foundation

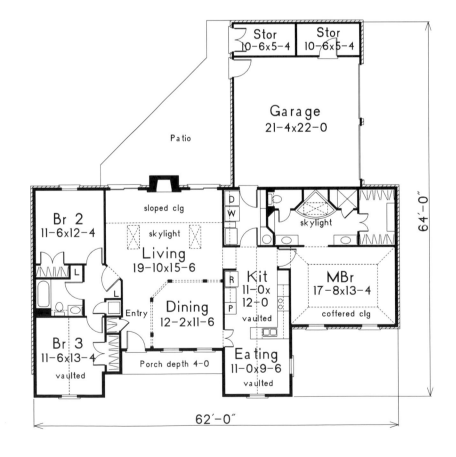

58'

GARAGE
19/4 X 21/8

©Alan Mascord Design Associates, Inc.

◀ 40' ▶

VAULTED
MASTER
13/8 X 11/8

PATIO

BR. 2
10/4 X 10/0
(9' CLG.)

DINING
10/0 X 13/6
(9' CLG.)

PAN. REF.

BR. 3
10/0 X 10/0
(9' CLG.)

C W L

VAULTED
LIVING
14/0 X 14/6

PORCH

Special features

1,275 total square feet of living area

- Energy efficient home with 2" x 6" exterior walls
- The kitchen expands into the dining area with the help of a center island
- Decorative columns keep the living area open to other areas
- Covered front porch adds charm to the entry
- 3 bedrooms, 2 baths, 2-car garage
- Crawl space foundation

Special features

2,050 total square feet of living area

- Large kitchen and dining area have access to garage and porch
- Master bedroom features a unique turret design, private bath and large walk-in closet
- Laundry facilities are conveniently located near the bedrooms
- 2" x 6" exterior walls available, please order plan #596-001D-0112
- 3 bedrooms, 2 1/2 baths, 2-car side entry garage
- Basement foundation, drawings also include crawl space and slab foundations

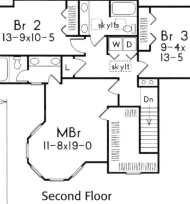

Br 2
13-9x10-5

Br 3
9-4x
13-5

skylts

W D

skylt

L

Dn

MBr
11-8x19-0

Second Floor
1,022 sq. ft.

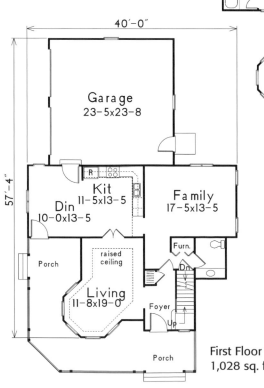

40'-0"

57'-4"

Garage
23-5x23-8

Kit
11-5x13-5

Din
10-0x13-5

Family
17-5x13-5

R

Furn.

Porch

raised ceiling

Dn

Living
11-8x19-0

Foyer

Up

Porch

First Floor
1,028 sq. ft.

Our Blueprint Packages Offer...

Quality plans for building your future, with extras that provide unsurpassed value, ensure good construction and long-term enjoyment.

A quality home - one that looks good, functions well, and provides years of enjoyment - is a product of many things - design, materials, craftsmanship.

But it's also the result of outstanding blueprints - the actual plans and specifications that tell the builder exactly how to build your home.

And with our **BLUEPRINT PACKAGES** you get the absolute best. A complete set of blueprints is available for every design in this book. These "working drawings" are highly detailed, resulting in two key benefits:

- Better understanding by the contractor of how to build your home and...

- More accurate construction estimates.

1. Cover Sheet is the artist's rendering of the exterior of the home
and is included with many of the plans. It will give you an idea of how your home will look when completed and landscaped.

2. Foundation plan shows the layout of the basement, crawl
space, slab or pier foundation. All necessary notations and dimensions are included. See the plan page for the foundation types included. If the home plan you choose does not have your desired foundation type, our Customer Service Representatives can advise you on how to customize your foundation to suit your specific needs or site conditions.

3. Floor Plans show the placement of walls, doors, closets, plumb-
ing fixtures, electrical outlets, columns, and beams for each level of the home.

4. Interior Elevations provide views of special interior
elements such as fireplaces, kitchen cabinets, built-in units and other features of the home.

5. Exterior Elevations illustrate the front, rear and both sides
of the house, with all details of exterior materials and the required dimensions.

6. Sections show detail views of the home or portions of the home
as if it were sliced from the roof to the foundation. This sheet shows important areas such as load-bearing walls, stairs, joists, trusses and other structural elements, which are critical for proper construction.

7. Details show how to construct certain components of your home,
such as the roof system, stairs, deck, etc.

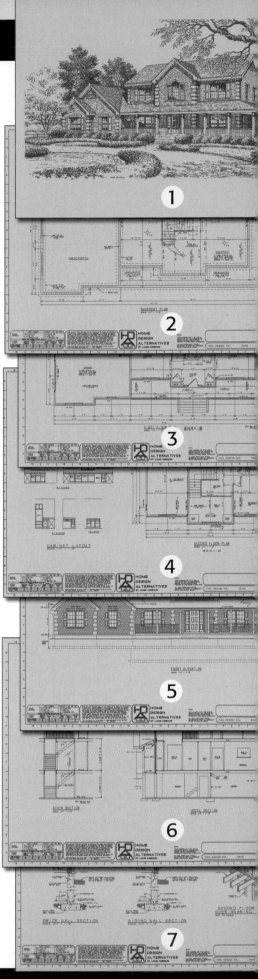

Home Plan Index

Plan Number	Square Feet	Price Code	Page	Material List	Right Read. Reverse	Can. Shipping
596-032D-0042	1,468	B	369	•	•	•
596-032D-0050	840	AAA	98	•	•	•
596-032D-0051	1,442	A	141	•	•	•
596-032D-0234	1,978	F	272	•	•	•
596-033D-0002	1,859	D	66	•		
596-033D-0012	1,546	C	16	•		
596-035D-0001	1,715	B	308	•		
596-035D-0004	1,425	A	197			
596-035D-0005	1,281	A	229	•		
596-035D-0006	1,671	B	251			
596-035D-0011	1,945	C	38	•		
596-035D-0013	1,497	A	259	•		
596-035D-0017	1,373	A	408	•		
596-035D-0021	1,978	C	96	•		
596-035D-0026	1,845	C	117	•		
596-035D-0027	1,544	B	247	•		
596-035D-0028	1,779	B	33	•		
596-035D-0030	1,124	AA	366	•		
596-035D-0031	2,052	C	295	•		
596-035D-0032	1,856	C	28	•		
596-035D-0038	1,862	C	297	•		
596-035D-0040	2,126	C	36	•		•
596-035D-0043	2,155	C	169	•		•
596-035D-0045	1,749	B	23	•		
596-035D-0046	1,080	AA	99	•		
596-035D-0047	1,818	C	45	•		
596-035D-0048	1,915	C	40	•		
596-035D-0049	1,638	B	377	•		
596-035D-0050	1,342	A	47	•		
596-035D-0051	1,491	A	82	•		
596-035D-0052	2,072	C	324	•		
596-035D-0053	1,467	A	137	•		
596-035D-0054	1,149	AA	415			
596-035D-0055	1,583	B	279	•		
596-035D-0057	1,324	A	199	•		
596-035D-0058	1,482	A	317	•		
596-035D-0060	1,290	A	230	•		
596-036D-0040	2,061	C	92	•		
596-036D-0048	1,830	C	100	•		
596-036D-0060	1,760	B	61	•		
596-037D-0002	1,816	C	225	•		
596-037D-0003	1,996	D	203	•		
596-037D-0006	1,772	C	358	•		
596-037D-0008	1,707	C	182	•		
596-037D-0009	2,059	C	277	•		
596-037D-0011	1,846	C	365	•		
596-037D-0016	2,066	C	402	•		
596-037D-0017	829	AAA	323	•		
596-037D-0019	581	AAA	282	•		
596-037D-0020	1,994	D	255	•		
596-037D-0026	1,824	C	233	•		
596-037D-0031	1,923	C	94	•		
596-038D-0008	1,738	B	312	•	•	
596-038D-0012	1,575	B	238	•		
596-038D-0018	1,792	B	209	•		
596-038D-0033	1,312	A	196	•		
596-038D-0034	1,625	B	187	•		
596-038D-0035	1,562	B	157	•		
596-038D-0036	1,470	A	313	•		
596-038D-0039	1,771	B	120	•		
596-038D-0040	1,642	B	74	•		
596-038D-0047	1,487	AA	298	•		
596-038D-0048	1,146	AA	321	•		
596-040D-0001	1,833	D	150	•		
596-040D-0003	1,475	B	12	•		
596-040D-0006	1,759	B	342	•		
596-040D-0007	2,073	D	52	•		
596-040D-0008	1,631	B	259	•		
596-040D-0019	1,854	D	253	•		
596-040D-0026	1,393	B	62	•		
596-040D-0027	1,597	C	58	•		
596-040D-0028	828	AAA	154	•		
596-040D-0029	1,028	AA	231	•		
596-041D-0004	1,195	AA	207	•		
596-041D-0006	1,189	AA	91	•		
596-045D-0003	1,958	C	386	•		
596-045D-0009	1,684	B	185	•		
596-045D-0012	976	AA	406	•		
596-045D-0013	1,085	AA	364	•		
596-045D-0014	987	AA	319	•		
596-045D-0017	954	AA	251	•		
596-047D-0012	1,627	B	389	•		
596-047D-0019	1,783	B	417	•		
596-047D-0020	1,783	B	201	•		
596-047D-0022	1,768	B	232	•		
596-047D-0032	1,963	C	261	•		
596-048D-0001	1,865	D	393	•		
596-048D-0008	2,089	C	128	•		
596-048D-0009	2,056	C	322	•		
596-048D-0011	1,550	B	37	•		
596-049D-0005	1,389	A	280	•		
596-049D-0006	1,771	B	101	•		
596-049D-0007	1,118	AA	183	•		
596-049D-0008	1,937	C	57	•		
596-049D-0009	1,673	B	105	•		
596-049D-0010	1,669	B	73	•		
596-049D-0012	1,295	A	236	•		
596-051D-0027	1,540	B	194	•		
596-051D-0033	2,196	C	205	•		
596-051D-0060	1,591	B	152	•		
596-052D-0013	1,379	A	404	•		
596-052D-0032	1,765	B	340			
596-052D-0048	1,870	C	138	•	•	
596-053D-0002	1,668	C	13	•		
596-053D-0003	1,992	C	135	•		
596-053D-0029	1,220	A	41	•		
596-053D-0030	1,657	B	22	•		
596-053D-0032	1,404	A	124	•		
596-053D-0037	1,388	A	362	•		
596-053D-0042	1,458	A	318	•		
596-053D-0044	1,340	A	419	•		
596-053D-0049	1,261	A	276	•		
596-053D-0053	1,609	B	203	•		
596-053D-0058	1,818	C	227	•		
596-055D-0012	1,381	A	249	•		•
596-055D-0013	930	AA	265	•		•
596-055D-0022	2,107	C	285	•		•
596-055D-0024	1,680	B	234	•		•
596-055D-0026	1,538	B	93	•		•
596-055D-0027	1,353	A	191	•		•
596-055D-0030	2,107	C	18	•		•
596-055D-0031	2,133	C	163	•		•
596-055D-0033	1,758	B	383	•		•
596-055D-0064	1,544	B	148	•		•
596-055D-0067	1,472	A	420	•		•
596-055D-0069	1,400	A	378	•		•
596-055D-0081	1,880	C	349	•		•
596 055D 0093	1,965	C	113	•		•
596-055D-0106	1,210	A	391	•		•
596-055D-0114	2,050	C	185	•		•
596-055D-0162	1,921	C	315	•		•
596-055D-0196	2,039	D	275	•		•
596-056D-0008	1,821	E	233	•		
596-056D-0009	1,606	B	132			
596-058D-0002	2,059	C	314	•		
596-058D-0004	962	AA	207	•		
596-058D-0006	1,339	A	20	•		•
596-058D-0007	1,013	AA	416	•		
596-058D-0008	1,285	A	229	•		•
596-058D-0010	676	AAA	83	•		
596-058D-0012	1,143	AA	88	•		•
596-058D-0013	1,073	AA	374	•		
596-058D-0014	416	AAA	223	•		•
596-058D-0016	1,558	B	25	•		•
596-058D-0020	1,428	A	48	•		•
596-058D-0021	1,477	A	112	•		•
596-058D-0022	1,578	B	360	•		
596-058D-0023	1,883	C	261	•		•
596-058D-0024	1,598	B	332	•		
596-058D-0025	2,164	C	305	•		
596-058D-0029	1,000	AA	290	•		•
596-058D-0030	990	AA	181	•		•
596-058D-0031	990	AA	250	•		
596-058D-0033	1,440	A	193	•		
596-058D-0038	1,680	B	155	•		
596-058D-0072	1,339	A	208	•		
596-058D-0075	1,143	AA	166	•		
596-060D-0006	1,945	C	291			
596-062D-0029	1,670	B	336			•
596-062D-0031	1,073	AA	179	•	•	•
596-062D-0048	1,543	B	81	•		•
596-062D-0050	1,408	A	34	•		•
596-062D-0052	1,795	B	395	•		•
596-062D-0053	1,405	A	263	•		•
596-062D-0058	1,108	AA	353	•	•	•
596-062D-0059	1,588	B	311	•	•	•
596-065D-0016	1,508	B	289	•		
596-065D-0017	1,856	C	133	•		
596-065D-0022	1,593	B	104	•		
596-065D-0028	1,611	B	144	•		
596-065D-0035	1,798	B	421	•		
596-065D-0040	1,874	C	293	•		
596-065D-0074	1,640	B	78	•		
596-067D-0004	1,698	B	281	•		
596-067D-0005	1,698	B	175	•		
596-067D-0007	1,840	C	254	•		
596-067D-0009	2,198	C	214	•		
596-068D-0003	1,784	B	111	•		
596-068D-0004	1,969	C	392	•		
596-068D-0005	1,433	A	346	•		
596-068D-0006	1,399	A	301	•		
596-068D-0009	2,128	C	256	•		
596-068D-0010	1,849	C	213	•		
596-069D-0005	1,267	A	173	•		
596-069D-0006	1,277	A	388	•		
596-069D-0012	1,594	B	171	•		
596-069D-0018	2,069	C	68	•		
596-070D-0001	1,300	A	205			
596-070D-0008	2,083	C	237			
596-070D-0009	2,153	C	240			
596-071D-0012	1,301	A	153			
596-071D-0246	755	AAA	306			
596-072D-0002	1,767	A	126			
596-072D-0004	1,926	C	327			
596-073D-0011	2,137	C	167			
596-073D-0024	1,591	B	131			
596-073D-0033	1,810	C	268			
596-076D-0005	1,322	B	224		•	•
596-076D-0009	1,251	B	183		•	•
596-076D-0013	1,177	B	142		•	•
596-076D-0017	1,123	B	241		•	•
596-077D-0001	1,638	C	265	•	•	
596-077D-0002	1,855	D	149	•		
596-077D-0004	2,024	D	181	•		
596-077D-0023	1,426	B	171	•		
596-077D-0030	1,600	C	253	•		
596-077D-0037	1,639	C	109	•		
596-077D-0045	1,799	C	190	•		
596-077D-0059	2,003	D	283	•		
596-077D-0079	2,005	D	211	•		
596-077D-0107	1,816	C	140	•		
596-077D-0109	2,000	D	243	•		
596-078D-0040	1,905	D	200	•		
596-078D-0047	2,000	D	161	•		
596-084D-0016	1,492	C	316	•		
596-084D-0026	1,551	D	411	•		
596-084D-0030	1,680	D	278	•		
596-084D-0046	1,698	D	198	•		
596-087D-0065	1,384	E	239	•		
596-087D-0071	1,437	E	249	•		
596-087D-0095	1,551	F	410	•		
596-087D-0262	1,812	H	114	•		
596-095D-0034	1,654	B	129	•		
596-095D-0035	1,790	AA	347	•		
596-099D-0019	2,094	C	188	•		
596-099D-0022	2,069	C	107	•		
596-099D-0024	1,898	C	320	•		
596-099D-0026	1,388	A	147	•		
596-101D-0002	1,612	C	284	•		
596-101D-0003	1,608	C	54	•		

What's the Right Plan For You?

Choosing a home plan is an exciting but difficult task. Many factors play a role in what home plan is best for you and your family. To help you get started, we have pinpointed some of the major factors to consider when searching for your dream home. Take the time to evaluate your family's needs and you will have an easier time sorting through all of the home plans offered in this book.

Budget: The first thing to consider is your budget. Many items take part in this budget, from ordering the blueprints to the last doorknob purchased. Once you have found your dream home plan, visit our website at www.houseplansandmore.com to get a cost-to-build estimate to ensure that the finished product is still within your cost range.

Family Lifestyle: After your budget is deciphered, you need to assess you and your family's lifestyle needs. Think about the stage of life you are at now, and what stages you will be going through in the future. Ask yourself questions to figure out how much room you need now and if you will need room for expansion. Are you married? Do you have children? How many children do you plan on having? Are you an empty-nester?

Incorporate in your planning any frequent guests you may have, including elderly parents, grandchildren or adult children who may live with you.

Does your family entertain a lot? If so, think about the rooms you will need to do so. Will you need both formal and informal spaces? Do you need a gourmet kitchen? Do you need a game room and/or a wet bar?

Experts in the field suggest that the best way to determine your needs is to begin by listing everything you like or dislike about your current home.

Floor Plan Layouts: When looking through our home plans, imagine yourself walking through the house. Consider the flow from the entry to the living, sleeping and gathering areas. Does the layout ensure privacy for the master bedroom? Does the garage enter near the kitchen for easy unloading? Does the placement of the windows provide enough privacy from any neighboring properties? Do you plan on using furniture you already have? Will this furniture fit in the appropriate rooms? When you find a plan you want to purchase, be sure to picture yourself actually living in it.

Exterior Spaces: There are many different home styles ranging from Traditional to Contemporary. Flip through and find which style most appeals to you and the neighborhood in which you plan to build. Also think of your site and how the entire house will fit on this site. Picture any landscaping you plan on incorporating into the design. Using your imagination is key when choosing a home plan.

Choosing a home plan can be an intimidating experience. Asking yourself these questions before you get started on the search will help you through the process. With our large selection of multiple styles we are certain you will find your dream home in the following pages.

What Kind of Plan Package Do You Need?

Once you find the home plan you've been looking for, here are some suggestions on how to make your Dream Home a reality. To get started, order the type of plans that fit your particular situation.

Your Choices:

The 1-Set Package - We offer a 1-set plan package so you can study your home in detail. This one set is considered a study set and is marked "not for construction." It is a copyright violation to reproduce blueprints.

The Minimum 5-Set Package - If you're ready to start the construction process, this 5-set package is the minimum number of blueprint sets you will need. It will require keeping close track of each set so they can be used by multiple subcontractors and tradespeople.

The Standard 8-Set Package - For best results in terms of cost, schedule and quality of construction, we recommend you order eight (or more) sets of blueprints. Besides one set for yourself, additional sets of blueprints will be required by your mortgage lender, local building department, general contractor and all subcontractors working on foundation, electrical, plumbing, heating/air conditioning, carpentry work, etc.

Reproducible Masters - If you wish to make some minor design changes, you'll want to order reproducible masters. These drawings contain the same information as the blueprints but are printed on reproducible paper that is easy to alter and clearly indicates your right to copy or reproduce. This will allow your builder or a local design professional to make the necessary drawing changes without the major expense of redrawing the plans. This package also allows you to print copies of the modified plans as needed. The right of building only one structure from these plans is licensed exclusively to the buyer. You may not use this design to build a second or multiple dwellings without purchasing another blueprint. Each violation of the Copyright Law is punishable in a fine.

Mirror Reverse Sets - Plans can be printed in mirror reverse. These plans are useful when the house would fit your site better if all the rooms were on the opposite side than shown. They are simply a mirror image of the original drawings causing the lettering and dimensions to read backwards. Therefore, when ordering mirror reverse drawings, you must purchase at least one set of right-reading plans. Some of our plans are offered mirror reverse right-reading. This means the plan, lettering and dimensions are flipped but read correctly. See the Home Plan Index on pages 426-427 for availability.

Other Great Products...

The Legal Kit - Avoid many legal pitfalls and build your home with confidence using the forms and contracts featured in this kit. Included are request for proposal documents, various fixed price and cost plus contracts, instructions on how and when to use each form, warranty statements and more. Save time and money before you break ground on your new home or start a remodeling project. All forms are reproducible. The kit is ideal for homebuilders and contractors. Cost: $35.00

Detail Plan Packages - Electrical, Plumbing and Framing Packages - Three separate packages offer homebuilders details for constructing various foundations; numerous floor, wall and roof framing techniques; simple to complex residential wiring; sump and water softener hookups; plumbing connection methods; installation of septic systems, and more. Each package includes three dimensional illustrations and a glossary of terms. Purchase one or all three. Note: These drawings do not pertain to a specific home plan. Cost: $20.00 each or all three for $40.00

More Helpful Building Aids

Your Blueprint Package contains the necessary construction information to build your home. We also offer the following products and services to save you time and money in the building process.

Express Delivery - Most orders are processed within 24 hours of receipt. Please allow 7-10 business days for delivery. If you need to place a rush order, please call us by 11:00 a.m. Monday-Friday CST and ask for express service (allow 1-2 business days).

Technical Assistance - If you have questions, please call our technical support line at 1-314-770-2228 between 8:00 a.m. and 5:00 p.m. Monday-Friday CST. Whether it involves design modifications or field assistance, our designers are extremely familiar with all of our designs and will be happy to help you. We want your home to be everything you expect it to be.

Material List - Material lists are available for many of the plans in this publication. Each list gives you the quantity, dimensions and description of the building materials necessary to construct your home. You'll get faster and more accurate bids from your contractor while saving money by paying for only the materials you need. See the Home Plan Index on pages 426-427 for availability. Note: Material lists are not refundable. Cost: $125.00

Making Changes To Your Plan

We understand that it is difficult to find blueprints for a home that will meet all your needs. That is why HDA, Inc. (Home Design Alternatives) is pleased to offer home plan modification services.

Typical home plan modifications include:
- Changing foundation type
- Adding square footage to a plan
- Changing the entry into a garage
- Changing a two-car garage to a three-car garage or making a garage larger
- Redesigning kitchen, baths, and bedrooms
- Changing exterior elevations
- Or most other home plan modifications you may desire!

Some home plan modifications we cannot make include:
- Reversing the plans
- Adapting/engineering plans to meet your local building codes
- Combining parts of two different plans (due to copyright laws)

Our plan modification service is easy to use. Simply:

1. Decide on the modifications you want. For the most accurate quote, be as detailed as possible and refer to rooms in the same manner as the floor plan (i.e. if the floor plan refers to a "den," use "den" in your description). Including a sketch of the modified floor plan is always helpful.

2. Complete and e-mail the modification request form that can be found online at www.houseplansandmore.com.

3. Within two business days, you will receive your quote. Quotes do not include the cost of the reproducible masters required for our designer to legally make changes.

4. Call to accept the quote and purchase the reproducible masters. For example, if your quote is $850 and the reproducible masters for your plan are $800, your order total will be $1650 plus two shipping and handling charges (one to ship the reproducible masters to our designer and one to ship the modified plans to you).

5. Our designer will send you up to three drafts to verify your initial changes. Extra costs apply after the third draft. If additional changes are made that alter the original request, extra charges may be incurred.

6. Once you approve a draft with the final changes, we then make the changes to the reproducible masters by adding additional sheets. The original reproducible masters (with no changes) plus your new changed sheets will be shipped to you.

Other Important Information:

- Plans cannot be redrawn in reverse format. All modifications will be made to match the reproducible master's original layout. Once you receive the plans, you can make reverse copies at your local blueprint shop.
- Our staff designer will provide the first draft for your review within 4 weeks (plus shipping time) of receiving your order.
- You will receive up to three drafts to review before your original changes are modified. The first draft will totally encompass all modifications based on your original request. Additional changes not included in your original request will be charged separately at an hourly rate of $75 or a flat quoted rate.
- Modifications will be drawn on a separate sheet with the changes shown and a note to see the main sheet for details. For example, a floor plan sheet from the original set (i.e. Sheet 3) would be followed by a new floor plan sheet with changes (i.e. Sheet A-3).
- Plans are drawn to meet national building codes. Modifications will not be drawn to any particular state or county codes, thus we cannot guarantee that the revisions will meet your local building codes. You may be required to have a local architect or designer review the plans in order to have them comply with your state or county building codes.
- Time and cost estimates are good for 90 calendar days.
- All modification requests need to be submitted in writing. Verbal requests will not be accepted.

2 Easy Steps for FAST service

1. Visit www.houseplansandmore.com to download the modification request form.

2. E-mail the completed form to customize@hdainc.com or fax to 913-856-7751.

   If you are not able to access the internet, please call 1-800-373-2646 (Monday-Friday, 8am-5pm CST).

Before You Order

Exchange Policies

Since blueprints are printed in response to your order, we cannot honor requests for refunds. However, if for some reason you find that the plan you have purchased does not meet your requirements, you may exchange that plan for another plan in our collection within 90 days of purchase. At the time of the exchange, you will be charged a processing fee of 25% of your original plan package price, plus the difference in price between the plan packages (if applicable) and the cost to ship the new plans to you. Please note: Reproducible drawings can only be exchanged if the package is unopened.

Building Codes & Requirements

At the time the construction drawings were prepared, every effort was made to ensure that these plans and specifications meet nationally recognized codes. Our plans conform to most national building codes. Because building codes vary from area to area, some drawing modifications and/or the assistance of a professional designer or architect may be necessary to comply with your local codes or to accommodate specific building site conditions. We advise you to consult with your local building official for information regarding codes governing your area.

Additional Sets†

Additional sets of the plan ordered are available for an additional cost of $45.00 each. Five-set, eight-set, and reproducible packages offer considerable savings.

Mirror Reverse Plans†

Available for an additional $15.00 per set, these plans are simply a mirror image of the original drawings causing the dimensions and lettering to read backwards. Therefore, when ordering mirror reverse plans, you must purchase at least one set of right-reading plans. Some of our plans are offered mirror reverse right-reading. This means the plan, lettering and dimensions are flipped but read correctly. To purchase a mirror reverse right-reading set, the cost is an additional $150.00. See the Home Plan Index on page 426-427 for availability.

One-Set Study Package

We offer a one-set plan package so you can study your home in detail. This one set is considered a study set and is marked "not for construction." It is a copyright violation to reproduce blueprints.

†Available only within 90 days after purchase of plan package or reproducible masters of same plan.

Blueprint Price Schedule

BEST VALUE

Price Code	1-Set	5-Sets (Save $110)	8-Sets (Save $200)	Reproducible Masters
AAA	$310	$380	$425	$525
AA	$410	$480	$525	$625
A	$470	$540	$585	$685
B	$530	$600	$645	$745
C	$585	$655	$700	$800
D	$635	$705	$750	$850
E	$695	$765	$810	$910
F	$750	$820	$865	$965
G	$850	$920	$965	$1065
H	$945	$1015	$1060	$1160

Plan prices are subject to change without notice.
Please note that plans and material lists are not refundable.

Shipping & Handling Charges

U.S. Shipping - (AK and HI express only)	1-4 Sets	5-7 Sets	8 Sets or Reproducibles
Regular (allow 7-10 business days)	$15.00	$17.50	$25.00
Priority (allow 3-5 business days)	$25.00	$30.00	$35.00
Express* (allow 1-2 business days)	$35.00	$40.00	$45.00

Canada Shipping (to/from)** - Plans with suffix 032D and 062D - see index

	1-4 Sets	5-7 Sets	8 Sets or Reproducibles
Standard (allow 8-12 business days)	$35.00	$40.00	$45.00
Express* (allow 3-5 business days)	$60.00	$70.00	$80.00

Overseas Shipping/International -
Call, fax, or e-mail (plans@hdainc.com) for shipping costs.
* For express delivery please call us by 11:00 a.m. Monday-Friday CST
** Orders may be subject to custom's fee and/or duties/taxes.

Questions? Call Our Customer Service Number
1-800-373-2646

Many of our plans are available in CAD. For availability, please call our Customer Service Number above.

How To Order

1.) **Call** toll-free 1-800-373-2646 for credit card orders.
Mastercard, Visa, Discover and American Express are accepted.

2.) **Fax** your order to 1-314-770-2226.

3.) **Mail** the Order Form to:

**HDA, Inc.
944 Anglum Road
St. Louis, MO 63042
ATTN: Customer Service Dept.**

4.) **Online** visit www.houseplansandmore.com

For fastest service, Call Toll-Free
1-800-DREAM HOME (1-800-373-2646) day or night

Order Form

Please send me -

PLAN NUMBER 596-_____

PRICE CODE _____   (see pages 426-427)

Specify Foundation Type (see plan page for availability)

☐ Slab   ☐ Crawl space   ☐ Pier

☐ Basement   ☐ Walk-out basement

☐ Reproducible Masters $_____

☐ Eight-Set Plan Package $_____

☐ Five-Set Plan Package $_____

☐ One-Set Study Package (no mirror reverse) $_____

Additional Plan Sets[†] (see page 431)

☐ ____ (Qty.) at $45.00 each $_____

Mirror Reverse[†] (see page 431)

☐ Right-reading $150 one-time charge
(see index on page 426-427 for availability) $_____

☐ Print in Mirror Reverse
(where right-reading is not available)

____ (Qty.) at $15.00 each $_____

☐ Material List[†] $125 (see page 426-427 for availability)
(see page 429 for more information)
$_____

☐ Legal Kit (002D-9991, see page 429) $_____

Detail Plan Packages: (see page 429)

☐ Framing   ☐ Electrical   ☐ Plumbing
(002D-9992)   (002D-9993)   (002D-9994)
$_____

SUBTOTAL $_____

Sales Tax (MO residents add 6%) $_____

☐ Shipping / Handling (see page 431) $_____

TOTAL (US funds only - sorry no CODs) $_____

432

[†]Available only within 90 days after purchase of plan package or reproducible masters of same plan.

I hereby authorize HDA, Inc. to charge this purchase to my credit card account (check one):

☐ MasterCard   ☐ VISA   ☐ DISCOVER   ☐ AMERICAN EXPRESS Cards

Plan prices are subject to change without notice. Please note that plans and material lists are not refundable.

Credit Card number _____

Expiration date _____

Signature _____

Name _____
(Please print or type)

Street Address _____
(Please do not use a P.O. Box)

_____

City _____

State _____

Zip _____

Daytime phone number   (____) - _____

E-mail address _____

I am a   ☐ Builder/Contractor
☐ Homeowner
☐ Renter

I ☐ have ☐ have not selected my general contractor.

Thank you for your order!